Helena Roerich
1879–1955

At the Threshold of the New World

Helena Roerich

White Mountain Education Association
Prescott, Arizona

At the Threshold of the New World

ISBN: 0-9624439-2-1

Library of Congress Catalog Card Number: 98-061285

Printed in the United States of America

Cover Design: *Lewis Agrell*
                Prescott, Arizona

Printed by: *Data Reproductions*
                Rochester Hills, MI 48307

Published by: **White Mountain Education Association**
                P. O. Box 11975
                Prescott, Arizona 86304
                United States of America

Acknowledgements

We would like to express our sincerest gratitude to the following people and organizations: Daniel Entin and Aida Tulskaya of the Agni Yoga Society in New York City, and Max Osinovsky and Raya Urmalsky for all their time and labor spent on the work of translating; to the staff of readers, editors, proofers, indexers and designers, including Joleen Dianne Du Bois, Shary Singer, Lewis Agrell, Kathryn Agrell, Cathy Ross, Gary Bettis, and Star Bettis; to the International Roerich Center in Moscow, Russia; and to those who through their generous financial contributions made the printing of this book possible.

Dedication

In Memory of a Beloved Teacher and Friend,

Torkom Saraydarian
(1915-1997)

Table of Contents

Fiery Creation of the Cosmic Evolution

by Ludmila Shaposhnikova

*B*ut, as was said, the Invisible will become visible and we shall be ready to apply the Fiery Baptism in life. Therefore, let us give due regard to the significance of the experiment performed by the Mother of Agni Yoga here, without abandoning life. From the first spatial sparks, through all fires up to Samadhi, she will leave writings which will become the threshold of the New World.

Heart, para. 210

Introduction

Sharp green-colored patches of clear space in a cloudy sky...
A foreboding straight line of the horizon soaring over barren flat
country... and, above all that, the bright flying ellipse of the Path
and a winged human figure that stretches out its thin arms in
desperation and anguish toward the fading brightness linking
Heaven and Earth ... The figure stands before a stepped altar, its
smooth flat surfaces mirroring the starry sky. Although the sky is
mirrored, it itself is not in sight. There are two streams of smoke,
a white one and a black one, the former streaming upwards to the
heavens and the latter falling to the ground in a heavy and inevitable movement. The black stream envelopes the snow-white
wings of the figure standing at the altar, evokes dark flowing
gleams in them, and precipitates black, implacable, earthly omens.
Here in the restricted space of the painting takes place some kind
of sacrament, which may be the most important event since the
emergence of man on Earth.

The Earth and the Heavens. An eternal attraction and an eternal repulsion, and fragile man between those, seemingly so unimportant and weak, but in fact strong, capable of linking to himself that Heaven and that Earth and establishing between them
the harmonious relationships so needed by them, by means of
first establishing harmony within himself.

The painting is titled "Sacrifice" and was created at the beginning of the twentieth century by M. K. Ciurlionius, a Lithuanian
painter. Ciurlionius was a strange person, and his canvases were
incomprehensible to many people. He was even considered mad.
Maybe it was because he was able to see what others could not
see. He lived a short life and suffered great hardship, but he left
his remarkable paintings to us. They reveal an unusual world,

with its unearthly colors and shapes, a world that is both like and unlike this world of ours, a world that is subtle and translucent. It is permeated with a strange music, holding in itself the mystery of the world, which sounds gently and invitingly like a chime of crystal bells.

The path of this extraordinary painter of Time and Space crossed that of another no less remarkable person. That it happened at all appears to be a significant and mysterious event. That person was a woman who was living at that time in St. Petersburg. An unearthly world, real and unreal at the same time, revealed itself to her, usually in her dreams; after that it was as if separated from the dreams and transformed into a vision-like reality. Already as a child, she realized that that strange world had a different kind of time—a time in which the past, the present, and the future seemed to coexist. She sometimes felt that it was she, and at the same time someone else, who long before had made a great journey through the ages and the countries, and that the memories of those were being revived by some mysterious and elusive entity.

A tall human figure in white appears in the morning in a garden with apple trees in full bloom in the background, then gradually dissolves into the air. This evokes from the very depth of her being a memory of a Teacher of Light living far off.

One day, when the girl was ill, she saw two tall, dark-skinned, turbaned men. They sat down on her bed, and one of them drew a silver thread out of her heart, while another one wound it into a ball.

Then the Teacher of Light came again, and they walked together in the garden. The Teacher told her about the suffering and misery of humanity, *podvig*, and compassion for the deprived.[1]

After she became the mother of two sons, a Luminous Boy appeared who reminded her of the Teacher of Light:

[T]he room began to fill with a bluish light reminiscent of bright moonlight. All objects behind the solid reflecting screen became visible, and the screen itself, while remaining solid, became transparent. A slim, luminous figure of a Beautiful Boy, around nine years old, in a white, softly glowing garment with blue shadows

in the folds, separated himself from a window rather distant from my bed. There was a large, wide area of most delicate opalescent Light glowing above His head. The Boy moved toward me as if floating in the air along the wall. ... His eyes were absolutely astonishing: huge, deep in their dark blueness, staring at me. ... [W]hen the Boy approached the head of my bed and bent forward slightly in order to better look into my eyes, my feeling of a growing intimacy and love changed into the ecstasy of an acute realization that my grief was His grief and my joy was His joy, and my entire being was flooded with a wave of all-embracing love for Him and for all that existed. The thought flashed into my mind that such a state is impossible on Earth, and therefore I was on some other plane of existence. ... It was impossible to judge how long that condition lasted. When it began to fade away, I opened my eyes and discovered that everything was gone, and the room was engulfed in almost absolute darkness, except for a narrow gap between the window curtains.

Sometimes she felt as if time had switched to some distant past, and the past in all its reality and tangibility entered into her ordinary daily life, as if coming from some unknown state of non-being hidden in millenia past and then retreating back into the same state. She floated into that life concealed in velvet folds of different times and spaces, acted in it, and experienced it. These "entries" echoed in her afterwards as a painful pulling feeling; a pressing, unquenchable yearning.

One scene follows another: *Now she is in Germany, walking in an old castle; in one room she sees a man at a table. Some drawings and instruments are spread over the table. The man has long, light-brown hair and wears a wide sleeveless jacket edged with fur. Then both the castle and the man fade away and disappear, and temples adorned with stone carvings, towers covered with ancient inscriptions, and a procession of Indians wearing white turbans appear.*

Stairs with wide landings emerge. "Everything is flooded with a golden light. I am standing on the top landing; I wear long clothes with tiny pleats and a high coiffure, and my silhouette stands out against the overall golden background. On the next landing below me there is a tripod supporting a shapely dark bronze bowl filled with burning incense."

Saddled Arabian horses impatiently beat the ground with their hoofs, white elephants whose backs are covered with gold-brocaded cloth wave their trunks in a state of reverie, while she is handing her little son to a slender, lithe ruler.

A huge hall with a table at the center covered with food and drink...She is right there pending execution. She will be decapitated. "Guests and the court in luxurious clothes crowd at the main inner entrance. The Owner of the castle, wearing a silver brocade caftan with blue velvet slits and a small beret decorated with an ostrich feather (in the time of Frances I), approaches the table at the center and sits down. My mother, a close relative of this Duke, sits beside him; my seat is supposed to be at the same table, but my chair has already been removed." *She is treated badly with hostility and ridicule. A servant carrying a dish spills sauce on her.*

One era and fashion followed another: castles were gone and nomadic tents appeared; snowy Russian fields were gone, and the Indian land scorched by the blazing sun emerged.

But one mysterious person emerged in those visions more often than anyone else. This happened for the first time in 1910.

...In a marble Italian palazzo she opens the door of her room, "where there is a tall pendulum clock in a case at the wall opposite the bed. She looks at the clock and notices that the case door opens, and the slightly luminous figure of a knight in silver armor appears from within. Looking at her, the knight utters in a distinct voice, 'Konrad Rudendorf.' And then he disappears."

This was her first encounter with someone who will follow her right up to the twentieth century and, in a Jesuit's robe, will try to take possession of the Stone given to her by the Great Teacher. Based on sparing hints contained in her records and the Teacher's talks, it is difficult to understand what kind of person that mysterious stranger from her dreams was, who afterwards acquired quite a real shape in her real life. The only thing one may tell is that he was an unusual person who was keenly interested in energies, most likely destructive ones, and who appeared at those moments when her historical life broke away from its smooth course and turned to Those Who guided her on the path of cosmic evolution. He started to obstruct her, letting her know that that path is not always smooth and that even a high-level hierarchical spirit when approaching Earth cannot avoid difficulties and confrontations. That knight in silver armor possessed a ray sufficiently strong to obstruct the Teacher's experimental work with her.

And, as if in an adventure novel, time calls out one more mysterious scene from a medieval Europe sunk into oblivion. The scene shows a galloping horseman in a flying cloak, who tries at any cost to intercept her, who is already approaching the monastery gates. There, behind strong walls, she was going to disappear, and together with her the Great Secret of a new energy whose time, as he knew, had not yet come. But the power of destruction can be unleashed at any time. He was already smiling complacently, fully confident that he would stand between her and the gates on the suspension bridge after a few more jumps of his horse. Then the longed-for formula would be in his hands. But at the last moment the suspension bridge unexpectedly began to raise, and his horse, after trying to leap over the growing gap in one jump, suddenly stood rigid as if stopped by an unknown force. The rider spurred it, but the spurs merely struck a stone mass. He could not believe his eyes: his horse had turned to stone. At the same time, at the other side of the monastery moat, heavy forged gates were, with finality, closing behind the fugitive. Shaken and hardly believing in what was happening, he slipped from the horse and collapsed on the grass. He had again lost a battle with she who was predestined by Fate to be his eternal opponent, an object of endless rivalry before the Highest Force.

Cosmos and the planet are founded on opposing principles, according to the Great Law. In the heavy and dark world of Earth the contraries enter into battle and thus generate the energies needed for ascent. On the Higher planes the contraries complement each other, and this complementariness generates harmonious synthesis; thus the Great Forces are set into motion.

She lived and acted on Earth, going through a long chain of earthly incarnations, and Konrad Rudendorf was destined for her as a manifestation of that Great Law down here, on Earth. For it is said, "As above, so below."

The universe is a vast animated energy system, and man constitutes in it merely one of many structures that is closely connected with other systems, and interacts with them. This is what the High Teachers spoke about in Their talks with her and in Their "transmissions." They created a new energy world view so needed to the crucial twentieth century. That world view, as well as any other, will be accepted with great difficulty and will be accompanied by misunderstanding and condemnation.

The books she composed as a result of those talks and transmissions are called Agni Yoga, or the Living Ethics. They provide an account of a Universal energy system living and evolving according to Great Cosmic Laws, such as the Law of Karma (or cause-effect relationships), the Law of Correspondence between form and energy, the Law of Cosmic Collaboration, the Law of Harmony of the two Principles, and many others. Vital activity in Cosmos is supported by the exchanges of energy between its various constituent structures. The cosmic evolution of humanity is essentially an energy process based on the same energy exchange. The latter is the main moving force of evolution. In our three-dimensional world the exchange goes in three directions: horizontally—an exchange among all and everything found on the face of the planet, and vertically—an exchange with celestial bodies, the sun, planets, zodiacal constellations, and so forth. Finally, there is a kind of exchange that may be called depth exchange, that is, exchange with worlds of other dimensions and other states of matter, elements of which are also present in the human being.

As a result of such energy exchanges, there are qualitative and quantitative accumulations of energy, which increase the energy potential of a human being, a nation, a country, or the planet, and create further possibilities for their evolutionary advancement. Man may move along this evolutionary path either as an object of that evolution or as its subject. The distance between these two notions is great. But it is within that distance of interaction between object and subject that very important energy processes take place, from the process of perfecting man to his shaping as an entity that affects the energies of his own evolution and seeks to achieve the status of a Cosmic Hierarch, or a God-man. The object of the evolution makes his way along the path automatically, as it were, using its energies, but, as a rule, not realizing that fact. On the other hand, the subject of the evolution behaves quite consciously and purposefully and acts in accordance with the evolutionary plan that is quite accessible to him. The level of consciousness involved is a key factor in the transformation of the object of the evolution into its subject. In the final analysis, consciousness is an energy phenomenon forming within man himself under the influence of cosmic processes.

While entering into interaction with various energy processes in the Cosmos, the subject of the evolution may either consciously further the evolution or obstruct it. This interaction, of control of the very evolution, is an intricately complicated process available to highly developed entities and always bearing, as it were, a scientific, experimental character. Man knows the unknown; the Cosmic Hierarch is doing the same, but on a different level.

It has turned out that at the end of the twentieth century our planet and humanity, inhabiting it, have come close to a new turn of the evolutionary spiral. The Living Ethics books indicate the principal characteristics of this turn: an approach of new energies to the planet, an enhanced interaction of worlds of other dimensions with our dense world, a skilled handling of psychic energy by man, an intense interaction with cosmic energy structures and expanded energy-information exchange with them, a rise in the level of synthesis of matter and spirit, and, finally, the formation of a new, higher and more refined type of humanity—humanity of the sixth type, or the sixth race, our race being the fifth one.

Writings by Helena Roerich presented in this volume, i.e., *Dreams and Visions, Fiery Experience,* and also her letters to Sina Fosdick, the Director of the Nicholas Roerich Museum in New York, are unique material that throw light on a creative evolutionary process in which Cosmic Hierarchs participated together with Helena Roerich. She played in that process a most important and decisive role, so that without her the creative process simply could not happen. Helena Roerich gives us an opportunity to witness a unique cosmic action; she herself went through that action in order to pave the way for humanity to the cosmic heights, to the heights of spirit, and to higher forms of matter. She gives us an opportunity to comprehend for ourselves the path she has traveled—a most complicated and difficult path followed by an earthly woman, a path full of sufferings, both physical and spiritual, but the one that is so necessary to us all. Always there is someone who brings Fire down to humanity....

The high and the low, Earth and Heaven, small and large dimensions, high vibrations of matter and spirit and low ones, subtle and dense worlds, evolution and involution—such is a far-from-complete list of what is confronted by someone who is taking part in the grandiose drama of cosmic creation. The difficulty lies, first of all, in the fact that in the entire complex and rich palette of the cosmic evolution, it is necessary to find that unique and inimitable point of energy which gives rise to evolutionary creation.

On October 31, 1913, in the early, dim light of dawn, Helena Roerich saw an unforgettable vision:

When I look to the right, the wall disappears, and a red-pink sphere opens up before my eyes. In the middle of it there is a broad, tall staircase, narrowing in perspective toward the top, which is lost from sight in the pink glow. On both sides of the stairway, on every step, people are standing in groups, wearing garments of the same style. Near the bottom of the staircase the groups are dressed in red, and ugly black spots cover their faces and garments. On the following steps upward, people have fewer and fewer spots, so that the higher toward the top they are, the lighter in color the people and their garments, and at the top all have merged into a pure pink glow.

On the very top of the staircase a beautiful giant figure in a red garment, with a dark coat over his shoulder, emerges. He has beautiful facial features and long, black hair that reaches down to his shoulders. This Being quickly descends the stairs, his dark coat flapping like wings behind him, but at the very bottom of the staircase he stops as if some obstacle has suddenly arisen in front of him. Exhausted, he leans against the barrier, his dark hair hanging down in unusually pretty waves, and his garment hangs in beautiful folds.

When I turn to the opposite wall, I see the same phenomenon— the wall disappears, and in its place there is a radiant rainbow sphere. There is the same kind of staircase in the middle, its top lost from sight in the sunlight. Similar groups of people are standing on both sides, on every step. At the bottom their garments are light blue, but up toward the top, both people and their garments gradually became lighter in color, more silvery, merging at the top into a radiant light. As with the first sphere, a Magnificent Image emerges at the very top, against a background of blinding sunlight. His face is impossible to discern due to the light, but the heart-consciousness suggests that it is the Christ Image.

Slowly, awfully slowly, He begins to descend, stretching in turn His right and left arm to touch groups of the standing people. Upon His touch, tongues of flame burst over people's heads, and each group has its specific color, all those flames forming a rainbow of the most delicate hues.

Full of admiration, I watch this beauty, when suddenly a whirlwind lifts me upwards, leaving my mourning dress (which I wore after my mother's death) behind on the floor, and I am being lifted up in a light-colored gown, carried toward the bottom of the staircase and placed among the lower group. I agonizingly wait to see whether Christ will approach me, whether His Hand will touch me, and what kind of light will be kindled over my head. ... He does approach and stretches out His right Hand, and I feel and know with a rapture that a flame is bursting out of the top of my head and is burning with silvery blue Fire.... that is, with the fire of a high entity.

That scene-vision carried in itself the most profound philosophical meaning. It showed that in every Cosmic phenomenon there are two principles, two opposites: Christ radiant with light and good, and another entity opposite to Christ. Each has its own path and its own ladder of ascent and descent. Those paths pass through the Cosmos, through worlds of various dimensions. The dense world is at the beginning of the path or at the foot of the ladder. That ladder, besides linking Heaven and Earth into a united energy system, contains in itself another important meaning. It may be used to either ascend or descend, for evolution and involution are also two opposite polarities that exist only in their mutual connection. The energy situation in the Cosmos is such that there is no evolution without involution. Evolution begins with involution in both general and particular senses. We speak a lot about evolution, while involution either goes unmentioned or is understood in a very narrow fashion: as a downfall, an inability to keep on a certain level of ascent, and thus a descent to a lower level. We fail to take into account the dialectics of interaction between evolution and involution in their broad cosmic meanings, and to take into consideration the energy aspect of that interaction. There is no evolution without involution—without appreciating this truth, it would be difficult or simply impossible to grasp the essence of the evolutionary energies.

In order for evolution to take place, the fiery spark of the spirit must enter the inert matter or descend into it. For spirit, it is an involution, while for matter, it marks the beginning of an evolution. There are many "beginnings" of this sort, for on every evolutionary stage there is its own type of matter and its own frequency of vibration of spirit. For every transition to a new turn of ascent there is an involutionary impulse, or, in other words, a new spark of spirit enters its corresponding matter. According to its energy and its frequency of vibration, the spark will create a difference in potentials of the two fundamental opposites, necessary for the energy of ascent to be set into action. It is the interaction between involution and evolution that generates the very conditions necessary for ascent. But what is the spark of the spirit? It is well-known that the spirit as such, i.e., in a pure state, is nonexistent in nature. Therefore, the role of that spark, as a rule, is played by a High Entity.

In order for matter of a lower world to acquire an ability for further evolution and further advancement, the High Entity, or the Cosmic Hierarch, has to descend, that is, to enter the involution. The vision that appeared before Helena Roerich's eyes reflected in accessible and vivid images that most important and complex moment of cosmic evolution. Recall that Christ slowly descends, going past those who have already achieved a certain degree of ascent. He proceeds to the foot of the ladder where those stand who did not ascend yet to a necessary level. Over their heads there were not yet those fires that were radiated by those who had ascended. Helena Roerich herself was found at the foot of the ladder. Christ stretched His hand, and a Fire burst out above her, the Fire so desperately needed by all those standing nearby. Thus a Great Mystery of the Cosmic Evolution was accomplished, and its creation, previously unheard of, began.

After completion of the cycle of his or her earthly incarnations, a subject of evolution, a High Entity, a Cosmic Hierarch, or a Mahatma, as they call such people in India, may keep ascending in Higher Worlds. But some of them voluntarily return to Earth. Having mastered evolutionary energy mechanisms, they, with the sparks of their spirits, initiate a new stage, or a new turn, of the cosmic evolution of humanity. By sacrificing themselves, deliberately embarking on involution, they lay the foundation for the evolution of humanity. At present it is difficult to tell how a High Entity makes this kind of willful decision. We do not know which objective and subjective factors are instrumental in making such a choice. This secret is not yet known to us. Upon His return to the heavy and disorganized world of Earth, the Great Soul brings in the energy rendered in the Latvian artist-seer Ciurlionius' painting so expressively and exactly. Christ, Who is also justly called the Savior, impregnated with His spiritual energy an entire era ranging over two thousands years. That period marked the flourishing and then decline of the fifth race. "When Christ was suffering on the Cross," Helena Roerich will write much later, "who understood that the old world came to an end, and a new day was breaking, and a new God has risen over the Earth?" Did she realize, when she was writing that, that it was she, a High Cosmic Hierarch, who was predestined to carry out such kind of mission? Did she remember, while being crucified on her cross between the two worlds, the dense one and the fiery one, about the blue-silvery Fire that Christ kindled over her head, and thus entrusted to this woman an evolutionary mission with all its heavy responsibility and dramatic quality?

The Teachers who dictated the Agni Yoga books to her spoke about the approaching time of the Mother of the World, a new evolutionary turn that will be nourished by female energy, when women will play the leading part in the building of the coming New World. That New World is one in which the sixth race of humanity will form, so unlike people of our fifth race as regards their abilities and energies. She has voluntarily returned to Earth in order to clear the way for the sixth race and help create a new energy passage for its evolution. She was standing at the threshold of that New World, having in herself both the new and the old energies, and creating in herself (a fifth race person) a new person of the sixth race. The sixth race could not form without that creative activity. Its feeble shoots, which began to appear on Earth in the 1940s, could perish without that support and nourishment.

But there was something in her path that made it different from the path of Christ. Christ remained to be a God-man while on Earth, and became a God after His death and resurrection. And even though His bare feet, the bare feet of a preacher and miracle worker, trod the sinful Earth, it seemed that its dense heaviness never touched Him. There was a Son of God invariably and irrevocably living in Him, and this always kept Him facing the heavens, where other, far-off worlds revealed themselves to Him. He always directed His disciples' attention to the heavens and spoke about the marvelous beauty of those unearthly worlds. He always remained to be a Son of Heaven, both in regard to the kind of unearthly beauty that filled Him and in regard to how He lived and spoke.

She, on the other hand, faced another, totally different task. An earthly woman, living an ordinary life, she had to bring through herself that Heaven down to Earth in order to make the latter better, subtler, and more energized. This is what the new stage of evolution required. This is how Earth could touch Heaven and make contact with other Worlds, the contact much needed for its further advancement. Helena Roerich was supposed to attract Higher Energies, Higher Forces, to an Earth weakened by consistent violation of all the Cosmic Laws. Only that could save the planet and divert the imminent catastrophe. We read in one of the Agni Yoga books:

"Creativeness is manifested in all that exists, and the awaiting energies find application in other cycles or in other worlds and forms.... Thus, the fire of the Agni Yogi creates its own forms, transmuting the forces around him. Thus, the Tara [Helena Roerich] propels the current, directing the creativeness of the New Step." [2]

And also:

"...the Agni Yoga is affirmed to be the direct link with the far-off worlds.... Thus, She Who carries the Chalice of the Sacred Fire will give to the planet a fiery purification. Thus the creativeness of psycho-spirituality is implanted into the new step. When the force of the Cosmic Magnet will assert the manifestation of the fires, then will it be possible to say that the New Time draws near." [3]

On Planet Earth in the twentieth century, on the eve of a new turn of its evolutionary spiral, an evolutionary experiment was beginning, which was scientifically described and interpreted for the first time in the history of humanity.

The experiment was conducted by Cosmic Hierarchs, i.e., those Subjects of evolution Who could change its course and guide it strictly in the framework of the Great Cosmic Laws. All of them were on different stages of cosmic evolution and were close to Earth in varying degrees. But down there, on Earth, by making her sacrifice, stood she, Helena Roerich, a Russian woman, a wife to her husband and a mother of two children, someone on whom the fate of Cosmic evolution on Earth now depended. But only her closest associates then knew about it. And only a few realized that the beginning of her painful experiment marked the dawn of a New World. But it was not a new god who was to preside over it. It was She, Cosmic Hierarch and Great Teacher.

Someone Who directed Cosmic creativeness wrote:

Urusvati will manifest the coming together of Earth and Heaven. Urusvati will manifest the measure of beauty by a symphony of the spheres. Urusvati will manifest a ray of Light penetrating the walls. Urusvati will manifest the Shield that shows the course of Celestial Bodies. Urusvati will manifest the flight of the arrows of spirit. Urusvati will manifest comprehension of the density of matter when her spirit wills it. Urusvati will expose the emptiness of thought not ignited by spirit, for Ours is the path of Earth to the Palace of transformation.

And also:

Now a new understanding of the earthly path to Heaven is growing. The Temple can be established only by way of Earth. We will all heave a deep sigh when the weight of the Temple stones have been passed from spirit to Earth. Urusvati feels. Urusvati knows. Urusvati will reveal. Urusvati appeared to kindle a miracle on Earth. Urusvati shall weave a pure cover for Our Shield; so I say, "Do not obstruct Our Urusvati!"

These two fragments from *Fiery Experience* include all the essential features: the specific character of the stage of cosmic evolution the planet is going through; the goals set before Helena Roerich, who consented to a painful and agonizing experiment; and, finally, the accomplishments to be brought to Earth by the labor of a Cosmic Hierarch Who placed Herself in difficult earthly conditions in order to change them.

She has consented to an ordinary earthly incarnation without making any allowance for or requiring relaxation of its peculiar conditions. This should be a "pure" experiment. Its "purity" determined the quality of that New World at the threshold of which the experiment was being performed. Hierarchs and Great Teachers watched her development in her childhood, and sent her dreams and visions, which she comprehended herself. She understood everything related to herself. They held Their Shield over her, seeking to safeguard her against unnecessary accidents and make her life easier. They could not save her from one thing only, namely, misunderstanding on the part of her relatives and associates, who did not believe in what she saw and heard. Her chief Teacher and Instructor, a high-level Hierarch, led her from her childhood to her last days. It was He Who many years ago stood under the tree one morning in the garden; it was He Who linked her heart with His, and later showed Himself to her as a Luminous Boy. And also it was He Who gave her an idea of that grandiose cosmic task that she fulfilled afterwards.

Helena Roerich wrote:[4]

After the age of forty, she established herself on a new level of approach to the Teacher and the Teaching of Light. The Teacher was perceived first as a Hindu, but after the consciousness of the disciple had expanded and was able to accommodate it, the Beautiful Image began to gradually change and eventually took the shape of a Majestic Image of Cosmic Significance, a Lord of Wisdom and Beauty, a Lord of the Sacred Shambhala.

The expansion of consciousness brought about a new possibility of approach to the Sacred Knowledge and of acceptance of the Fiery Experience, and finally of participation in the work of Cosmic Construction in collaboration with the Great Teacher, the Lord of Light.

Her unique records of "cosmic building," which she entitled *Fiery Experience*, go back to 1924 when the Roerichs were living in Darjeeling and were making preparations for their Central-Asian Expedition. The connection in space and time between the cosmic experiment and the planned expedition is another proof of evolutionary significance of the latter, the secret of which is not yet completely revealed.

Embarking directly on the evolutionary creation, the Great Teacher sought to explain to Helena Roerich its meaning and those difficulties that she had already encountered and that were still in store for her:

The construction of New World combinations does not flow easily. The discarded centers attempt to obstruct the efforts of the new ones. A new memory is formed. *We shall withstand the storm and downpour.*

He told that:

Our work is divided into three departments. First, search for ways to better the earthly plane. Second, search for ways to pass those results to people. Third, search for ways of communication with the far-off Worlds.

She participated in all three kinds of work, and in each of them she brought her energies, her pain and suffering. It was easy to speak or write about it. But to do it was "unearthly difficult," as she herself wrote in one of her letters. Perhaps it was she who, better than anyone else, realized the significance of Earth in the cosmic creation. After having passed through all that and comprehending the High Truth "by human feet and human hands," she was to write afterwards:

But on Earth it is like in a crucible—very different energies collide, are attracted to each other with refinement and transmutation as more perfected or subtle energies under the influence of the fire of the awakened spirit. From these collisions and unexpected connections of the different energies, new energies are born carrying new creativity and new possibilities. Earth is a place of testing, atonement and great creativity—the place of the last Judgment, because it is here that selection proceeds. Remember, dear one, that only on Earth can we accumulate and assimilate the new energies or renew the substance of our energies.

This was a new creative concept of Cosmic Hierarchs: first and foremost, gaining a foothold on Earth and bringing the Higher energies down. This was the only way to transform the dense matter of the earthly world, by refining it and raising its energy potential. The Teacher called this process "touching Heaven on Earth." It meant, not to escape life, not to escape Earth....

"The Supreme Instruction is to realize communion without changing the conditions of life," He said. This turn of cosmic creation was novel and unusual. It discarded the previous traditional, spiritual accumulations of humanity and called it to new heights. A stage of accelerated evolution dawned, and the evolutionary passage began to narrow. The acceleration demanded new conceptual approaches and methods. An unlimited and unrestricted science of the universe itself, of spirit and matter themselves, hidden from us by cosmic mysteries and our own ignorance, was being created and developed. It was an astounding and fantastic creation of animated matter, giving birth in its unceasing synthesis to energy flashes of evolutionary illuminations. A discovery of New Worlds for Earth and on Earth was going on. Earth was being equipped for a new journey toward a New World and a New Man. As a prayer, the words of the Cosmic Hierarchs sounded toward her who took upon herself all the earthly burden of the experiment: "Help Us, help Us, help Us in all ways. We create a new connection between Earth and Heaven." There is no need to describe here all of the course of the grandiose cosmic experiment. Rays of Cosmic Hierarchs, as delicate surgical instruments, shaped new energies, in which Earth was combined with Worlds of other states of matter and other dimensions. First of all it was the Fiery World, the world of spirit-creativity, without which neither renewal of Earth nor the new evolutionary turn sought by spirit-informed Cosmos would be possible. Every step of such creation was accompanied by its own difficulties and dangers. At a certain step the Creators realized that "rays can turn into waves of fire, burning out the coverings of the centers." That may present a mortal danger for Helena Roerich herself. It would be possible to choose another way: transmission by the way of accumulation without inflammation. But then the principle of Beauty created on a fiery basis would be excluded. The Hierarchs realized that "[n]ow it is impossible to advance without beauty. All may be tolerated, if only the foundation of beauty is preserved.... The manifestation of fire is to be guarded, otherwise the fire of spirit may burn away without [purpose]."

It is not given to us yet to know how They decided the problem of guarding the sheaths of Helena Roerich's centers and preserving the fiery manifestation of Beauty. She trod literally along a razor's edge. Only she herself knew its cost.

At times she experienced huge overloads of energy. Channels of communication opened one after another.

The channel of communication with the Teacher and the feeling of His Ray were long-standing and habitual. But cosmic creation and the preparation for a new evolutionary stage required that she communicate with all the Hierarchs in the energy Planetary Center called, variously, the Brotherhood, Shambhala, or the Sacred Land. The energies of Their Rays were intense and sometimes caused pains in her entire body.

It is then that she began to receive, via an opened communication channel, the information about the Inner life of the Brotherhood that was later used to compose a book entitled *Super-mundane*. In 1946, in one of her letters to America, she summed up what she had accomplished:

Indeed, the coming era will to some degree unveil the Supermundane World. Many things will become evident and accessible to earthly sensations, and this is exactly what is bringing me joy. The boundaries between the spiritual and the material, between the earthly and the Supermundane, will gradually disappear and people still in the earthly life will be consciously preparing themselves for usefulness in the Supermundane World. The earthly life itself won't be a senseless scrap, but will become a conscious, creative work through implementation and application of the accepted assignment in both worlds!

Earth was swiftly approaching a new evolutionary turn, and the Teacher's voice was heard as if from afar: *"My House is now in the Desert where We have come together for building the New Era."* The information about the Brotherhood found in the present volume is new and unexpected and reveals little-known aspects of its activities. Previously we learned about the life of the Brotherhood from myths and legends. The new channel provided the opportunity to receive information about its real life, so like and unlike our earthly life.

Besides short flowers, My Garden is full of long and stretching plants. If We are concerned about the weather, many plants are moved inside. Flowers are on balustrades of the stairs, and the old gardener takes away decaying plants. Truly, Urusvati grasps many details. The reddish-yellow Tower is connected by passages with the rest of the structure. From afar, the buildings may be taken for slightly sloping rocks weathered by time. Windows in the outer walls may be taken for birds' nests. The surrounding desert is intact. Often a traveler goes by without ever suspecting anything, but wondering at the behavior of his horse or camel. The animals turn their heads to the seemingly lifeless stones and even try to turn to what seems to be piled heaps of stones. Some people even saw inscriptions on the walls, but, of course, thought they were signs of deterioration. Of course, an unwelcome traveler will always be led away. Everyone feels something. But a desert dweller is accustomed to voices and fires of the desert.

Before she visited the Brotherhood, after having gone through necessary training, Helena Roerich was shown its Museum, a unique collection of exhibits illustrating the cosmic evolution of our planet. There also was, within the strong walls of the Tower of the Sacred Land, the Stone, one of the most mysterious phenomena on Earth:

Yes, the Stone rests on a cushion, which lies on a marble foundation and is separated from it by a disk of lithium. After establishing the rhythm, We silently saturate space. This Repository is located deep underground, and many people do not suspect that, during their sleep, the White Brotherhood descends through the galleries for a nightly vigil.

This "night vigil" was precisely and expressively shown by Nicholas Roerich in his painting *Treasure of the Mountain*. It shows a cave hidden deep underground, with enormous chunks of rock crystal, and a mysterious golden light flooding figures in long white robes, a flaming Chalice held by the Chief, and an indistinct object resting on "a marble foundation." The "night vigil" is a very important energy activity that puts the planetary rhythm into correspondence with the Cosmic Magnet. The energy rhythm of the Stone itself is the rhythm of the Cosmic Magnet or the Heart of our Universe, Whose Abode surrounds the constellation of Orion. Helena Roerich's energies were in tune with the rhythms of the Cosmic Magnet through the Stone. Otherwise the experiment could not be possible. "When the centers can flamingly reflect the will of the Cosmic Magnet, then the psycho dynamics of the spirit unite the higher planes with the planet." [5]

The Breath, or the rhythm of the Cosmic Magnet, determines the birth and death of universes. Therefore, any cosmic creation should keep pace with the Magnet, otherwise it will not bring the desired results. The Teacher said: The Stone *"contains a fragment of the Great Breath —a fragment of Orion's soul. I revealed the meaning of the Stone. I indicated the Treasure of the Great Spirit. Urusvati, it is necessary to link the Stone to your essence. The Stone, being near you, will assimilate your rhythm and, via the constellation of Orion, will reinforce the link in a way that is destined."*

This time evolution handed the Stone, the Treasure of the World, to a woman, for the blue star of the Mother of the World was rising over the new turn of cosmic evolution and the beginning of the New World was entrusted to a woman.

Despite all difficulties and dangers, the main phase of the cosmic experiment was completed successfully in the middle of 1924. On June 2, the Teacher's voice spoke with emotion: "Chr[ist] has kindled a blue Fire. Chr[ist] has sent a cross.... Lilies never before smelled so strong, and Buddha is clothed in a violet-colored garment.... Urusvati's celebration is Our Celebration...."

The planet did not hear the voice. But she, the only one, understood everything. A royal crown of the Brotherhood has touched her head. *"Urusvati, Our crown with the Stone is over you."*

Henceforth, Helena Roerich, a great entity and an earthly woman, felt and assimilated every new energy coming from the Cosmos. She brought it into correspondence with the evolutionary process and gave her energy impulse to that process on the Planet. She will exchange energies and information with the Brotherhood, Cosmic Hierarchs, other worlds, and finally with the Cosmic Magnet. Her earthly body, transformed and refined by the experiment, could no longer exist as other earthly bodies do. She now had a body of the sixth kind of energy and required new conditions; however, the old world, living out its last cosmic moments, was unable to provide those for her. In pain and suffering she paved for people the earthly way to the heights of the Cosmic evolution. People do not even suspect that without her assistance Earth cannot make its transition to a new evolutionary turn, and humanity will not have the energy necessary for further advancement. Such was the result of the most complex cosmic creation on Planet Earth in the twentieth century.

However, neither that creation nor new forces helped Helena Roerich get rid of conventional earthly concerns. Ordinary life with all its difficulties, troubles, and misfortunes remained with her as an inalienable part of her existence. She lost her husband, whom she deeply loved and respected. Nicholas Roerich, the great artist, thinker, and scholar, and her permanent companion, passed away in December 1947. She wrote in a letter: "Luminous spirits leave at the coming of darkness, and Their Images remain the only Beacons in the coming disasters." And then again in two months: "Really, who would be able to dedicate himself as much to that constant imminence, in front of the greatness and beauty of these summits, which embody and guard the greatest secret and Hope of the World—Sacred Shambhala?"

Long after his passing, acute anguish wrung her Cosmic heart. She, together with her son George, left the Himalayan valley of Kullu in the hope of returning to Russia and working for the welfare of the New Country (as she used to call Russia). They came to Bombay and waited for a ship from the Motherland. The ship was delayed, but when it emerged out of the fog of the Bombay harbor, it turned out that it brought no good news. Russia refused an entrance visa to its great daughter.

They did not go back to Kullu, but settled instead in the small resort town of Kalimpong in the Eastern Himalayas. She kept writing letters to her American friends about organizing the Banner of Peace activities, Nicholas Roerich's paintings, and publication and translation of the Agni Yoga books. She recalled Horch's monstrous betrayal, wrote about the difficult situation in India, the war in Kashmir, and many other subjects, for she was always keenly interested in current events and was able to judge them realistically and thoughtfully.[6] However, her old age made itself felt, and at times she was overwhelmed with inhuman tiredness.

"I am already seventy, and I have undergone the Yoga of Fire. And you know, my dearest ones, from the books of the Teaching, how unbearably difficult it is to accept in the physical body, amidst ordinary conditions, the fiery energy. The fiery transmutation refined my organism. I became extremely sensitive to all disharmony and all spatial currents. It is difficult for me to be among people, and now the monsoon, and the stuffy air it brings, fatigue me very much. My Heart often skips a beat, and I have to take strophanthus; this is my saver.

But also, I do not have enough time, because so much time is given receiving communications and recording them. My sight has weakened, and it is difficult to read my jottings, which are often written down with a light pencil. All these notes must be put in order, and the flow of new messages is unending."

Now she valued every minute and allowed herself to take walks only in the evening. She went down the wooden stairs from her attic to a parterre ornamented with flower beds. In Crookety, where she was living with her son, there was always an abundance of flowers. By evening the aroma of the flowers was strong. She descended the slope to a pine valley, where she could see the Kanchenjunga mountain range. The snow covering the sacred mountain shone in the evening with rosy, mysterious light.

Then she came back, and the window in her room lit up with a soft yellow glow. She wrote: "The cosmic step is approaching, and it needs to be met courageously."

This volume includes only a small fraction of the materials left by a Great Cosmic Entity with the only purpose in mind to make our paths easier, even if only a little bit, than her Path. And let our courage not fail us on our paths....

✐*Notes*

1. "The word *podvig* is untranslatable from the Russian. It means a great or heroic deed plus spiritual achievement." (This note is reprinted from *Letters of Helena Roerich, Vol. 2* (New York: Agni Yoga Society, 1967), p. 32.
2. *Infinity Vol. I*, para. 243 (New York: Agni Yoga Society, 1956).
3. Ibid., para. 237 (New York: Agni Yoga Society, 1956).
4. Helena Roerich is referring to herself in the third person.
5. *Infinity Vol. I*, para. 178 (New York: Agni Yoga Society, 1956).
6. Louis Horch was a member of the Board of the Nicholas Roerich Museum in New York. He was responsible for financial matters.

Dreams
and Visions

I have gathered up all my prophetic dreams and visions, and the ensuing picture is a grand, truly apocalyptic one.

February 7, 1949
Helena Roerich's letter to Sina Fosdick

*D*ifferent parts of the essay, *Dreams and Visions,* were written at various times over many years, and it was only in 1949 that Helena Roerich herself put them together. She wrote about it in her letter of February 7, 1949, to Sina Fosdick, the director of the Nicholas Roerich Museum in New York. In this section, descriptions of dreams are presented in italics.

Dreams
and Visions

On January 31 in St. Petersburg, in a house on Sergiyevsky Street, a daughter was born to the family of the architect-academician Ivan Ivanovich Shaposhnikov and his wife Ekaterina Vassilyevna, neé Golenishcheva-Kutuzova.[1-1] The daughter was named Elena.[1-2] The girl's birth was undesirable to the dark forces, and measures were taken by them to prevent her birth. During the pregnancy, her mother suffered from acute fits of nausea and vomiting. To alleviate them, she began taking all sorts of medicines, often without consulting her doctor, and became dangerously ill. Following the physician's advice, she was immediately taken to her parent's country estate in the province of Pskov, where she remained for a long time, so weak that she could not walk. For days she had to lie on a sofa in a big room. In this room was hung the painting called "The Prayer for the Chalice," which she grew to love very much. Later she often used to recall the painting and to express regret at not having taken it with her. She even claimed that, in profile, with her hair loose, her daughter resembled the image in the painting.

The girl's physical development was normal, or maybe even accelerated, for she learned to walk when she was only ten months old and also began to speak at an early age. She soon demonstrated a considerable grasp of and sensitivity to the subtlest nuances of speech and manifestations of harshness and injustice. When she was three, for no apparent reason, she began to have sudden fits of crying, which would end in frenzied shouts. Nothing and nobody could calm her down. Threats and intimidation had no effect. These attacks would stop as suddenly as they began. Gradually, they grew weaker, and by the age of five, they stopped altogether.

The girl was extremely sensitive to beauty in all its manifestations, especially to the beauty of nature, which had impressed itself strongly in her memory. Similarly engraved in her memory, from the age of three, were beautiful images of her mother and brother.

The girl's brother died of diphtheria when he was five-and-a-half years old. She was then in her fifth year. The mother began spending more time with the girl, and even started to teach her to read by way of playing with her. For example, in the morning, the girl used to bring a newspaper to her mother when she was still in bed. While the mother was having her tea, the girl would sit on the bed and ask about the meaning of big letters, primarily those in the obituaries. Gradually, using newspapers, toy blocks and picture books, the girl learned the alphabet and began to read fluently. With the same ease, she learned the French and German alphabets, and by the age of six, she was able to read and even write fluently in three languages.

In spite of having nannies and all kinds of governesses and private teachers, the girl grew quite independent; she mostly loved to play and read alone. Other girls of her age bored her or made no impression on her. Her independence also showed itself in her adamant refusal to repeat the words of a prayer that she and her brother were supposed to recite before going to bed. The girl prayed in her own words for what was dearest to her. There was a family story about one of her prayers that ran, "Dear God, please save and protect my Papa, Mama, my Granny, and my cow." (The cow was a toy, but it was so big that in a thick grass it often, much to the girl's great delight, was mistaken for a real calf.)

At a very early age she developed an interest in books. Books became her best tutors and friends. Her first and biggest joy was a two-volume Bible that had illustrations by Gustave Doré. These volumes were so big that the girl could not lift them. She could enjoy them only when an adult would hand them to her. But since the books were expensive, adults were reluctant to allow her to use them. For many years, these two volumes were a source of genuine joy. When she grew older, she would secretly carry a fat volume from her father's study, bending under its weight, and bring it to her room where she could again contemplate in awe and reverie a beloved Image of Christ and suffer His pains with Him.

Among her first books were two very old books on travels through Central Asia and the Far East. These enormously thick volumes were given to her to use instead of cushions on her chair at the family table. She liked to browse through the volumes, for they were richly illustrated. Thus, at an early age, the girl learned about nature, ethnography, and life in the Far East. This, of course, left its imprint in her imagination and upon her consciousness, which had not yet been spoiled by dull and deceitful children's books. The illustrated descriptions of all kinds of tortures and executions in China and Japan made an indelible impression on her. They evoked in her heart feelings of misgivings about and distrust of those two nations. It is quite possible that her strong disgust for any cruelty, reflecting painfully on the girl's sensitive nerves, could be traced back to the early impressions she received from these books.

Reading remained her favorite pastime even in the years that followed. She devoured books and was so emphatic about the joys and sorrows of the fictional characters that it almost made her sick. She cried bitterly over the fate of Mila and Nolya (in the tale of *Purry the Cat*) and remained in anguish for many days. Along with such books as [J. Mace's] *The Story of a Piece of Bread* and *Smile's Self-Help*, she loved all the books of Gustave Emard and Mark Twain, Alexandre Dumas' *The Count of Monte Cristo* and *The Three Musketeers,* Ponson du Terrail's *Rocambole,* [D. Brewster's] *The Martyrs of Science* and [Jules Verne's] *Captain Grant's Children.*

At a very early age, the girl began having remarkable dreams and visions. When she was only six, she had an unusual experience that was to remain forever fixed in her memory, without the loss of any of its original freshness and intensity of feeling. This happened in the late spring. Her parents moved to their summer house in the town of Pavlovsk, and the very first morning, the girl got up earlier than usual and ran to a small pond in the park to look at the goldfish. The morning was wonderful; the air seemed to be trembling and sparkling in the sun's rays. Nature itself seemed to have donned festive garments, and the blue of the sky was particularly deep. The girl stood on the pier, absorbing the beauty and joy of life with her entire being. While her eyes were fixed on a blossoming apple tree on the opposite shore, she suddenly saw, against the background of the tree, a tall male figure dressed in white. A recollection immediately surfaced in her consciousness that it was a Teacher of Light who lives somewhere far away. The girl's heart began to tremble, her joy turned into exaltation, and her entire being longed to be with that distant, beloved and Beautiful Being.

One of the first dreams that remained impressed in the girl's consciousness was a gloomy vision of heavy, thundering, black clouds, hanging low over a dark and raging sea, pierced through by lightning bolts. The waters were rising, and it seemed as if they were about to merge with the dark skies so that the wall of water would engulf all that existed. The girl, standing on the shore, feeling indescribable anguish and anxiety, peered into the gloomy picture that was unfolding before her eyes in the hope of seeing some spark of light, some kind of help. And lo, from afar, against a background of fiery-red clouds, a Starets appeared, surrounded by a soft glow, in a white monk's cassock with darkish crosses on it, Himself all luminous and with a white beard.[1-3] The Starets was tall and held a staff in His right hand. He walked calmly across the raging sea as if gliding over the waves. The girl roused herself. Her heart let her know that the Starets was coming to help her, and all her anguish and anxiety instantly vanished. In her childish mind she decided that it was God Himself who showed Himself to her in that wonderful Image; in fact, it was, as she later learned, St. Sergius of Radonezh.[1-4]

From early childhood, a foreboding that the Earth would face a catastrophe, a destruction, reigned over her mind. It might have been cast from biblical illustrations depicting formidable floods, or it might have been that those illustrations awakened her straight-knowledge. But the feeling was so strong that at times she was so completely overcome as to experience strong attacks of anguish. She even had dreams reflecting her premonitions.

Thus, she had the following dream that repeated itself with some variations:

Greyish-yellow and gloomy sea and sky; suddenly, a storm bursts and huge waves arise. One gigantic wave, carrying on its crest a lonely ship, collapses and engulfs everything on Earth, but the ship remains unharmed.

Another dream:

The girl stands at a window and in fear peers into the dark-yellow sky; the dusk is gathering fast. She notices some strange things: flocks of swallows anxiously chirping and flying low over the earth, worried people and animals rushing to hide in their homes. She clearly remembers a Tartar with a bag over his shoulder, who quickly ducked under gates. Then there is a deafening bang of either thunder or an explosion, and the earth begins to tremble. The terrified girl runs into the adjacent room where her parents are, and says, "Do you not see that the Earth is being destroyed and the end of the world has come?"

When she was six, while she was fully awake, she had an extremely vivid and colorful vision. It happened in the fall. One evening, the girl was sitting on the sill of a large window. In her lap she had a French anthology by Margot, which she had to read and, by tomorrow, memorize a piece of poetry called "A Cheerful Chaffinch." But the girl did not look at her book; her attention was drawn to the starry skies. In the same room, her mother was sitting at the table in anticipation of the evening tea. Suddenly the girl shouted, "Mama, Mama, look at the huge banner that just unfurled itself in the sky and formed a loop!" She had seen a Russian, tricolored banner spread broadly across the evening sky, like those title scrolls in old engravings, and all three colors were especially bright and beautiful: blue, silvery-white, and purple. The mother came to the window, but however hard she tried, much to the girl's great disappointment, she did not see a thing.

Yet that vision was so bright and powerful in its scope and vividness that even now it is still just as alive in her memory as then, in all its living power. Of course, all of this was ascribed to the onset of illness, and the girl was immediately sent to bed. It turned out afterwards that there was no sickness.

The girl often fell sick with something like a cold, which the doctors diagnosed as "false" croup. Whenever she was sick, she always had the same vision. *When she had a fever, she acquired a special ability to see through walls, and she saw the entrance door of their apartment open and two Giants enter. The one who was a little taller always walked in first, slightly obscuring the other one. The Giants walked along the long corridor and entered her room, then sat down at the foot of her bed and began to pull a silvery thread out of the left side of her body. The taller Giant would pass the thread to the other one, who sat behind him, winding it into a ball. In spite of the taller Giant's tender smile, the girl was a little afraid of them. It seemed to her that they wanted to pull her toward them by the thread, and if they succeeded, she would die. The taller Giant had blue eyes and brown hair, while the other's hair was darker, and he was more slender. They wore what she thought to be frock-coats, but as she learned later, they were actually Indian achkans.*[1-5] She had this vision repeatedly until the age of nine. Sometimes the girl saw at a close distance only the heads of these Giants, who would bend over her and gaze at her. She was afraid, but not too much, because these visions did not last long.

One more of her childhood dreams: *A Spacious Temple with numerous carved columns. The carved pattern is formed by small human and animal figures. Everything is lit up with an even, golden light. The girl is there with her cousin Stepan Mitusov, who is an inseparable companion of her childhood. They are riding around the columns on the backs of tiny horses, examining strange figures.* (Later, in India, I saw similar structures.)

A vision that took place when the girl was six:

It happened around three in the afternoon, after the girl's little sister was put to bed in the nursery. As usual, the wet nurse and the nanny went into the servants' room, and the girl studied in the room of her French governess. Realizing that she had left a needed book in the nursery, the girl ran back to fetch it. When she entered the room, the girl was fascinated by an unusually pleasant, dim bluish light created by the sun shining through the lowered curtains, and she felt a longing to stay there and lie down on the bed for awhile. It is hard to say how many minutes or maybe seconds she was lying there absorbing that quietude, when all of a sudden *she heard a thin, pure sound, like a small silver or crystal bell. The girl's attention was alerted, and she saw a slim, bluish, female figure, wrapped up in long luminous clothes, who separated from the window and glided in the air along the wall where the little sister's bed stood. The figure flew over the bed and then disappeared. Her movements were accompanied by the same soft ringing sound. It occurred to the girl that it was death that flew by, and that her little sister would not live long.* The sister died at the age of five.

A dream that occurred a little later: *A large figure of Christ against a pinkish-purple background, surrounded by three little angels. One angel was above Christ's head, and the girl recognized in him her late brother; the second one was her sister, near Christ's shoulder; and the third one was the girl herself, at the feet of Christ, holding His garment.* The girl realized that because her brother had died, he could fly, and her sister had ascended and, therefore, would fly away soon, while she herself would stay bound to the earth.

A dream she had a few days after her Grandmother died (in 1888):

The girl had turned nine. She saw her grandmother, who entered their drawing room, sit down on the chair, then call the girl over and take her onto her lap. The grandmother then produced a piece of a reeking rag, which had been impregnated with a substance that was usually put near the deceased, and tried to put it on the girl's naked leg. But the terrified girl jumped off the grandmother's lap, realizing that her real grandmother had died and that this was someone else in disguise, and that if the reeking rag touched her, she too would die. The girl ran to the nursery to tell about the visit of this strange "grandmother," when suddenly she stopped, having heard the grave chords of a funeral march coming from the drawing room. The girl said in impassioned excitement, "Nanny, listen, listen to what she is playing! Death has come to us!" This dream took place slightly earlier than one year before her sister died.

From her earliest childhood, the girl had premonitions of minor domestic happenings, in addition to those connected with significant events:

Two weeks before a fire in the building where they lived, the girl experienced anguish, knowing with certainty that a fire was imminent. On the day it happened, her mother had left for the theater and her father was napping after dinner; all the while the girl was restless due to an increasingly agonizing state of anxiety. She entered the nursery as her little sister was being put to bed. At that moment she heard shouts coming from the backyard. Their French governess (Mme. Lelong) ran to the window, opened the curtains, and a red glow lit up the entire room. It happened that in one of the quarters a servant had toppled a kerosene lamp. The girl's home was not affected, but seven apartments in their building were destroyed by the fire. There were also human casualties. Almost all night the girl sat on the windowsill watching the grim scenes.

About ten years prior to her father's death, the agonizing premonition that he would die came to the girl. It was corroborated by her dreams in which her father always died in a sudden way. This is why, whenever her father was delayed in the evening, she could not fall asleep until she heard the sound of the entrance door and her father's characteristic steps on the stairway. Her father died suddenly, of heart paralysis.

The last dream about her father's death took place about four months before he passed away. It was when the entire family, including Barbara Bradford, an orphaned niece, were planning their spring trip abroad. They talked all the time about the trip, contemplated interesting places to visit, and made their preparations. The girl had just turned nineteen when she had that dream: *She was on a train with her father. The train stopped at a station, seemingly in Tyrol. The girl got out of the train and called to her father, who had been delayed for some reason. Suddenly, the ground where the train had stopped was rent by a strong underground explosion; the earth under the train collapsed and the train was buried in the soil. The terrified girl ran to the station, imploring the station staff to quickly dig out the car where her father was buried. A few workers armed with crowbars and spades followed her and began gouging the rocky ground with crowbars. She heard the crowbars hitting the roof of the car where her father was buried alive, but all of a sudden the workers stopped their work and told her, "We are not going to dig any further. It is too dangerous. If we were to continue, the neighboring mountains would collapse and bury us."*

She awoke in terrible anguish, realizing that her father's death was approaching. Two months later her father had an attack of angina pectoris from which he recovered, and doctors reassured the family that his life was not in danger; but she knew with certainty that her father was living through the last days of his life. Two weeks later her father died in his sleep of heart paralysis, just as had been indicated in her first dreams about that sorrowful event.

When the girl was in her fourteenth year, she had a dream three days before her aunt died. Her aunt was her father's sister (a widow of General Bradford, who was an Englishman in Russian service), and she intensely hated the girl. In that dream *the girl saw her aunt dressed, as always, in long black garments that made her look like a stern nun. The aunt came to their house and threw a small but poisonous snake at the girl, which bit the girl's leg.*

Her aunt had left her orphaned granddaughter in the care of the girl's parents. She then lived in their family house, finishing her education, envying, and hating everybody.

Later she did "bite" the girl, but with no serious harm.

From her earliest childhood, the girl had foreknowledge of future events, some minor and some of importance. She knew the outcome of the Russo-Japanese War. She knew that the War of 1914 would end with the defeat of Germany.[1-6] She also knew that the horrors of the Revolution would not affect her immediate family.[1-7]

She knew when and where the circumstances would be favorable. She always knew what actions would be right. She came to understand people well.

When she was in her seventh year, she experienced, as if in a flash, an acute awareness that helped her to change her character, which leaned toward fits of anger and explosions of temper. This experience remained vividly impressed in her memory for many years:

The girl was reclining on a sofa and reading a book. A housemaid entered the room, carrying a bundle of wood for a stove, and began picking on and teasing the girl: "Is not the young lady ashamed to loll around in the middle of the day?" The girl did not like the housemaid, sensing her hypocritical nature, and was insulted by her unfair accusations. She yelled at the maid, calling her an idiot, a fox, Lizzy the Toady, and other names. Yet suddenly this outburst stoped, for she clearly realized the rudeness, indecency and absurdity of her bad language. This realization took hold of her with such an intensity that from then on all rude and bad expressions were abandoned.

Her reaction to even the smallest injustice was always particularly painful.

Part Two

Her attitude toward people varied greatly. Some people evoked in her a strong physical revulsion, which was often accompanied by a shudder or trembling in her entire organism. Her face would get covered with blotches and she would be filled with agonizing nausea. Those people who caused such a reaction might be considered by others as ordinary people, yet what they all had in common was impurity of expression. Early on the girl had learned to discern the quality of expression in people's eyes, and she could not stand those who had lewd expressions. She also suffered a painful disgust for obscenely suggestive words or jokes.

Notable was her oversensitivity to and extreme shame and revulsion for all bodily functions.

Thus for a long time, almost until she grew into an adult, the very thought that anyone could see or know that she had to withdraw because of a natural physiological need was so torturous that she learned to reduce her bodily functions to a bare minimum.

As a child, she intensely hated the darkness. Because of her fear, she never allowed the curtains in her room to be closed. It was not so much the darkness itself that frightened her as the feeling of blindness. From the age of nine, she slept alone in a large room, which was separated from other bedrooms by a long corridor. Often she could not fall asleep for a long time, wincing at the slightest rustle or tap. Gripping tightly her Christening cross, she firmly believed that all those frightening things she could see would not harm her as long as the cross was in her hand. Yet she was so ashamed of her fears that she never confessed them. Instead she learned to explain away all frightening, rustling, tapping, and cracking sounds as resulting from natural causes. She even came to enjoy this guesswork.

When she was about seven or eight, the girl began to see unusually beautiful and bright formations of light. These usually appeared in the evening, or in a darkened room, when the girl would close her eyes. Especially strong are her memories of one evening:

The girl was sitting in a deep chair with one of her favorite books that she had read many times, *The Story of a Piece of Bread*. The entire drawing room was in yellow and red, and a big lamp with a Japanese lampshade threw off red light. Lost in reverie, the girl stared at the opposite wall, which was covered with golden damask material and was lit up with red patches of light from the lamp. But soon she noticed that, against that background, bright luminous formations of a most unusual purity began to float— blue, lilac, purple, green, yellow, and silver ones. They suddenly appeared and, while floating, changed their shape, and then disappeared just as unexpectedly as they appeared. Sometimes, emerging out of space, it was as if they rushed toward her and, at a short distance from her, unfolded into the most intricate forms. Once the girl told her mother about that phenomenon, but it was attributed to an inflammation of her eyes.

She also liked to "watch Persian rugs," as she called it. She would close her eyes and then press slightly on her eyeballs. Immediately the most beautifully colored, luminous patterns of wonderful hues and designs would appear, ceaselessly changing their colors from deep saturations to the most subtle and radiant rainbow-like hues. She loved doing this while she lay in bed before falling asleep. But the same phenomenon was easily evoked in the daytime; and on sunny days, those formations were especially beautiful.

She felt a strong attraction to colorful images. Near her father's study, there was a small room where he kept huge folders with drawings, ornamental designs, and architectural plans. Because it was not encouraged, the girl used to sneak into the room. Sitting on the floor, she examined colorful details and decorations of palaces of Alhambra and Granada....[2-1] The folders were much bigger than she, and often those she wanted to see were blocked by other folders. This put her at risk of causing all the folders to collapse, or of not being able to put the folders back in their right place, thus provoking her father's [temper] and a cessation of her joyful pastime for a long time....

Studies came easily to her, so that by the age of seven she could already read and write in three languages. Her memory was always remarkable. When her teachers tested it, they were astonished, for the girl had only to read a short poem or a fragment of prose once, and she could repeat it word for word. French poems were the easiest to memorize, then German ones followed, while Russian ones were the most difficult.

All subjects were equally easy for her, but she was terribly bored by religion classes. She especially disliked memorizing church services, despite being rather religious by nature and having a great love for Christ's Image. It lived in her heart from the earliest childhood, and the cross that the girl wore in His Name was her best protection against her childhood fears.

After she turned nine, the girl enrolled in the first grade of the Mariinsky Women's Gymnasium, where for seven years she suffered the adoration of other girls. Both classmates and senior students would not leave her alone, kissing her until she began to cry. The teachers had to take measures for her protection, and those who had no chance to approach her waited for her outside the gymnasium entrance door in order to continue their torturous adoration. As the girl grew older, the habit of adoration was not extinguished, but, in fact, spread out over her junior grades as well. This adoration was manifested not only in poems dedicated to her or in gifts of flowers, but even extended to her personal belongings. Surreptitiously, students would cut pieces of ribbon from her school apron or her braid ribbons, or even cut locks of her hair. Given her acute squeamishness, it was very difficult for the girl to endure all those numerous touches. Often in tears, she begged others not to touch her.

When she was about twelve years old, an awareness arose in her of the existence of a Teacher of Light. This awareness remained with the girl for a long time and was especially strong during the period between her eleventh and thirteenth year. In her mind there was a vivid Image of a Teacher Who possessed unlimited knowledge. The girl clearly visualized herself as the Teacher's student, seeing herself living in His house and studying under His guidance. She definitely knew that the Teacher was engaged in speeding up some physiological process in her organism, and that this development was taking place under His direct supervision. This awareness would not leave the girl for long periods of time. In the evenings she hastened to retire to her room. There, in peace and solitude, she saw vivid pictures of her contacts with the Teacher. She saw herself strolling with Him in the garden, sitting on a low bench at His feet, and listening to His words about the sufferings of Earth and the miseries of mankind, about *podvig* and compassion for the deprived. In her mind, the Image of the Teacher merged with the Image of Christ, but the girl was afraid to admit it.

Around the age of nine, or perhaps even earlier, an acute pity for the unfortunate and deprived was awakened in her. Often in the evening, while lying in bed, the girl would imagine that she, carrying piles of warm clothes, would walk in the winter frost along the dark streets, and having found half-frozen children and old people, would wrap them up, bring them to her home, and serve them hot tea with rolls and jam. In her imagination the joy of those whom she saved was so vivid that she was enraptured and moved to tears.

Later, the girl tried, but could not understand how people could tolerate pauperism. Her mind could not embrace such a crying injustice as the existence of people who had no place to live and no bread to eat, while the nation was rich enough to provide everything in abundance. How was it possible that the government did not care that everyone should have food, footwear, and a job!

It was then that the girl got the first glimpse of an idea for an Order or a Community of Sisters that would bring to people from all walks of life the necessary knowledge and immediate help that they needed. She also contemplated establishing something akin to nurseries or kindergartens. She thought about the ways of improving the life of the families of factory workers. Of course, those thoughts were evoked by the stories told by her former wet nurse, who often visited the girl's parents on major holidays, and whose husband was employed as a worker at the Putilovsky factory. Being keenly interested in the workers' lives and listening to the nurse's stories, the girl was [appalled] by their accounts of drudgery and meager pay. All the piles of warm clothes that the girl in her imagination was giving away to the half-frozen children, she was actually handing to her former wet nurse for her big family.

From the ages of nine to twelve, the girl experienced the same dream three times, a dream that always left her with a feeling of great fear and anguish, even though there was nothing apparently frightening in it. It was its hidden meaning that was frightening, and that meaning revealed itself to her:

She saw herself standing in a room at a window that faced the backyard of a big house. *The girl looked at the lighted window at the opposite wall of the house and saw a male figure in an English-style shirt with rolled-up sleeves. He stooped down over some kind of machine or device resembling a modern switchboard at a power station. The man did not look vulgar. Rather, he seemed to be refined and intelligent. But looking at him and at the confident and quick movements of his hands, she felt pangs of anguish wringing her heart, and she realized that that man was engaged in some terrible work aimed at the destruction of the world.*

Later the girl thought that she was shown a symbol of workers who would launch a cruel revolution and thus destroy the entire world. But when she later understood the meaning of Armageddon, the dream took on an even more terrifying significance; for in the image revealed to her, the girl recognized the enemy of mankind. She was shown that in his work, he was seeking a horrible force that could explode the entire planet, and that even now the man was working on unleashing that truly hellish power through the medium of irresponsible people.

The girl had a dream in her fourteenth year on the eve of June 24, when Ivan Kupala's Day is celebrated in Russia.[2-2] In that dream she saw herself in a bridal gown and a veil, in a large empty church, kneeling before the big image of the Kazan Mother of God.[2-3] The entire church was dark except for the Image, which was lit by numerous candles. To the left of the Image, in a shadow, a tall male figure stood; she distinctly saw his refined profile and his black wavy hair thrown back from his forehead. There was a feeling of utter loneliness, of having abandoned everything in order to follow that man.

One of the girl's strongest and brightest traits was her impassioned love of nature and solitude, which manifested itself from very early childhood. She experienced her happiest moments precisely during her solitary hours, or when she was admiring the natural scenery by herself. The girl passionately loved early mornings out in nature, when she could run to her favorite places in the garden and enjoy its beauty and peace before the inevitable daily lessons at home with a variety of teachers would begin.

Even when she was seventeen and was permitted by her mother to ride a bicycle in the morning along certain alleys in the park, she was delighted to spend those solitary morning hours taking in the pure, morning solar prana and admiring the ever-fresh beauty of the natural scenery.

When she was in her seventeenth year, a sudden change in her attitude occurred. She became acutely aware of the banality and emptiness of the surrounding life. Her striving toward higher knowledge elicited no response from those around her. Her mother thought it was not at all necessary. Her father understood her better, but he would not permit her to enroll in the Higher Women's Courses, as he was afraid of the possibility that she might assimilate revolutionary ideas and be carried away by them.[2-4] She was permitted to continue her music lessons, but only at home, and to perfect her foreign languages—also at home, with poorly-educated French or English women teachers.

But for the rare exception, the so-called "gilded youth" that surrounded the girl did not offer her anything. The only bright spot in her life at that time was her cousin Stepan Mitusov, her companion from childhood. He would bring her books by popular poets and thinkers, and he introduced her to new trends in the arts, especially in music. But it could not quench her spiritual needs and did not help her uncover the meaning of life. Thus the girl nearly suffered a nervous collapse. She did not want to see anybody. She stopped going out and, in a state of complete apathy, lay for days on the couch, turning her face to the wall. At times she experienced such mortal anguish that she began to moan loudly. Due to her deep inhalations and exhalations, her body would tingle all over, as if pierced with sharp needles, and begin to stiffen. Her breath could come out only with difficulty between lips that were convulsively pressed together. It took great efforts to pour hot tea with brandy into her mouth in order to warm up limbs that were stiff with cold and to alleviate the spasms. Following the doctors' advice, she was taken abroad to Nice to undergo Charcot's shower treatment.[2-5] The change of climate and, for the most part, new impressions, plus a degree of freedom, restored the joy of life to her.

After she turned seventeen, a new series of dreams began in which there were clear predictions of certain events, but which seemed unimportant at the time. For example, the girl was taking music lessons with Professor S. Malozemova, and she went to those lessons accompanied by a maid. On the eve of one such lesson, the girl had a dream in which she arrived at Malozemova's, accompanied by the maid as always, and Malozemova herself came out and said, "Today we are going to have a lesson not in the reception room but in my studio." The girl told her dream to the maid, who had come in to wake her. What a surprise it was when Malozemova met them with exactly the same words as in the girl's dream.... The reason for the change was that workmen were polishing the floors in the reception room where the lessons were usually conducted.

A dream in 1898, a few months after her father died: *The girl, in a red dress, sees herself inside a small wooden house. The room is full of her relatives. In the middle of the house there is a wooden stairway leading to the next floor. The girl's father enters and takes the girl away from the crowded room. They go upstairs to a landing and then enter a room with an unusually large and wide window. With a broad gesture of his arm, the father points to the wide open spaces outside the window. She remembers a huge valley with mountains and hills in the background. Her attention is drawn to a solitary giant tree not far from the house; the tree looks like a cedar.*

She saw similar wide-open spaces much later while crossing Siberia.

A dream occurred on the eve of January 14, 1901, during a time of difficulties caused by a lack of clarity regarding her approaching marriage. She went to bed hoping that her father would come to her in her dream and tell her when and how everything would be resolved:

She sees the Pavlovsky railroad station, and herself standing there awaiting the arrival of her father. A telegrapher approaches and hands her a cable carrying the message, "I am arriving now. Father." She raises her head and sees her father approaching. Her father comes close, takes her hands and says, "By the Ascension Day everything will be settled. Everything will be fine." Having said that, her father leads her along an unfamiliar road toward a rather steep mountain. They begin to climb it, even though it is already dusk, and they are wading through thick mud. A crowd of relatives appears as if from nowhere and follows her as a dark mass. She remembers her cousin Sana Muromtseva, in a light dress, going up a side path to her right.

On the top of the hill, there is an iron pole that has been driven deeply into the ground. Having reached the top of the hill, she looks toward the opposite side and sees a vast panorama of floating and swirling light and dark clouds, cut through here and there by curly patches of open space. Her father touches the pole and disappears into the chaos of clouds. A thought flashes through her mind that if she follows him she will not return to earth, that it is not yet her time, and that someone else will do it. Glancing back, she sees the youngest of her uncles, who was standing right behind her, his face dark, and her mother behind him, dark, too. The uncle, as if following someone's order, jumps down into the abyss. .... Three months later this uncle died; the next death in the family happened a few years later, when her mother died.

Before she had that dream, she had another one involving the same uncle. She saw a small, grayish, almost empty room, with a coffin in the middle of it, and her Uncle R. in the coffin. His widow and his eldest daughter were standing by the coffin. His other children and all the numerous relatives were absent. Soon after this dream the uncle fell sick, and the doctors sent him to Capri, where he died. No relatives were present when that happened. His brother came later to bring the body back to the homeland for burial.

In the early spring of 1901, the girl and her mother went abroad. They stayed in Paris for ten days and then went to Nice, where the girl was supposed to undergo a three-week course of warm, salt bath treatments. After that they were planning to stay in Italy for two to three months. Before their departure, the mother decided to visit Monte Carlo. On the eve of the departure day, the girl saw in a dream an old man named Honoré, who used to always prepare salt baths for her, and whom she liked very much. The old man said to her, "Mademoiselle is going to go tomorrow to Monte Carlo, so let her try her luck and bet on the numbers 1, 3, and 4." He also gave her some other combinations, which she has since forgotten.

Upon awakening, the girl told the dream to her mother, and her mother decided to try the suggested numbers. They arrived in Monte Carlo, knowing nothing about the rules of gambling except that the minimum bet was five francs. They changed a 100 francs note (the amount allocated to the experiment) into coins. When they entered the gambling room, the girl sensed the disgusting atmosphere of a gambling house saturated with the most heavy emanations. She wanted to run away immediately, but her mother persuaded her to stay. They approached one of the longest gambling tables in the room. It was impossible to come close to the table, for not only were there no seats available, but there were three rows of people surrounding the table.

The girl again asked her Mother if they could leave, arguing that they could not see anything anyway and had no idea how to get started. A tall man who was standing right next to them turned out to be a Russian, and he suggested that they give him the sum they wanted to bet and the number to bet on, so that he could transfer their bet to the croupier. Mother was quick to give him five francs and the number "one." But the girl, feeling an attack of disgust, held back the elbow of the man. With a shrug of his shoulders, he returned the coin, and thus the chance was lost. The croupier announced, "Rien ne va plus."[2-6] The crowd froze, and only the light clicking of the ball impacting the walls of the revolving wheel was heard. The clicking slowed down, then stopped, and out of a dead silence a voice resounded, "Numéro Un en plein."[2-7]

Mother fell into an unspeakable agitation, and after shoving another five francs at the same young man, asked him to bet on the number "three", the next suggested number. This time the girl remained quiet. The game proceeded as before, until the voice of the croupier announced, "Numéro Trois en plein!"[2-8] This meant that, having bet five francs, they had won 180 francs, thirty-six times more money than they had bet. The next number, "four", and all other suggested combinations were successful as well. But when Mother, having used up all the indicated numbers, tried to bet again, she lost. The excitement caused by what had happened was so great, and the surrounding public became so interested in them, that neither the mother nor the girl wanted to stay in Monte Carlo any longer. Without any sightseeing, they rushed to the railroad station. Sitting in the car, with their knees trembling, they could only repeat, "What was that? How could it have happened?"

Of course, they did not fully use the chance given to them, for had they bet the entire allocated amount and transferred the money from one suggested number to the next, they would have won a seven-digit sum.

In one of her dreams she was instructed by her father to marry N. K. [2-9] This dream was repeated three times, the last time with minor variations. The first two were virtually identical:

She finds herself in a room. The door opens and her father enters the room. Gazing at her, he says, "Lyalya, marry N.K." [2-10] Then she wakes up. In the third dream, there was a large dining room, a huge table piled with platters of food, and she and her relatives are sitting around the table. Through an open, large window facing the garden, a big, light-colored swan with a circle of black around its neck flies into the room, lands on her chest, and curls around her neck. At the same time, the door opens, the tall figure of her father emerges, and he says, "Lyalya, marry N. K."

Another dream: *Her father brings her a son.* (She saw this

dream before her son was born.) *She sees her father walking toward her carrying a young boy of about two, who is wearing a white sailor's suit. Upon approaching her, her father hands the child to her and leads her up a mountain. During their ascent, silver ruble coins come rolling out of her eyes, ears, and mouth, dropping to the ground and covering their path.*[2-11] The boy in the dream looks exactly like her first-born son did at that age. She saw the same boy, but much younger, in the hands of a wet nurse, in one of her dreams a few months before her wedding.

Since 1910 a series of dreams began that apparently were related to her past lives. Unfortunately, her notes were lost and some of the dreams were forgotten.

A dream: *The setting is some place in Italy. She and her mother are riding in a big heavy carriage down a broad alley, which then turns in to a wide square and comes to a white marble palace with a big, flat cupola. The front staircase is decorated with sleeping marble lions. She notices silhouettes of cypresses and triangles of trimmed trees in the square. At the entrance they are met by a crowd of servants carrying torches. Both she and her mother pass through the vestibule and enter a large, brightly lit hall that is quickly being filled with servants and other household staff. After taking off her heavy warm clothes with help from the servants, the girl goes to her quarters, entering a long room with one very large window, tapestried walls, and a canopy bed covered with multicolored silk fabric. She suddenly feels very tired and throws herself onto the bed. At the opposite wall, there is a tall pendulum floor clock in a case. She looks at the clock and sees the case door open, and out of the case a slightly luminous figure of a knight in silver armor appears. The knight looks at her and says in a distinct voice, "Konrad Rudendorf." And then he disappears.*

About the same time, she sees herself as a young girl, again in a palace, but this time in Germany: *Feeling sad, she walks through halls with huge multi-section windows and enters a small room whose walls are painted in some kind of warm color with black and gold ornamentation. At a table, covered with some drawings and instruments or devices, there is a beautiful tall man with long blond hair, in a loose, black velvet, sleeveless jacket lined with fur. She knows the man is either an astrologer or the court physician. Without paying any attention to him, she keeps walking and enters the lavishly furnished bedroom of her mother. In the middle of the room, some distance away from the walls, there is a wide canopied bed on an elevated platform. There are huge windows with heavy damask curtains; tapestries and rugs on the floor make a colorful pattern. Mother, a tall, beautiful, and apparently very authoritative woman, stands at a dressing table covered with fancy bottles that make rainbow refractions of the sun's rays. She looks sternly at the girl. A frightening feeling of utter loneliness grips the girl, and she acutely realizes the hostile attitudes toward her on the part of her mother and her sister who is also in the room. The girl knows that she was called by her mother, who wants her to give up, or relinquish, something in favor of her sister; it seems that the issue in question is inheritance.* Her mother in the dream is her current mother, and her sister in the dream is V. Bradford.

...A palace in Germany. She is a hostess. Down a large, long hall, there are a lot of guests—officials, foreign representatives and courtiers—sitting around a large table. A large dinner party...

...Departure of guests in a large vestibule of Roman-Gothic style. German speech is distinctly heard....

Such fragmentary scenes followed one another, sometimes two or three in a row, with little connection between them. These dreams-visions were always accompanied by feelings of loneliness and anguish.

Part Three

A dream in 1911: *A vision of a Giant Fiery Fish cast down from the Heavens. N. K. and I are riding in a tarantass in the evening twilight, across a broad valley on a road lined with trees.*[3-1] *Suddenly, a strong hurricane begins and the sky turns a velvet black. The trees, whistling in the wind, bend down to the earth. Our tarantass turns upside down. We fall into a ditch, but remain unharmed. With a deafening explosion of thunder, the dark vault of Heaven opens; and from a Crucible of Fire, like a lightning bolt, a Giant, Fiery, scaly Fish falls head first upon the Earth. Its forked tail curls up forming a caryatid propped against the dark sky. The gigantic pillar of fire thus connects Heaven and Earth.*[3-2]

Later I learned that in the East the Fish is the symbol of an Avatar, or Messiah, and, of course, when He appears, the Avatar cannot help but shake the heavenly and earthly spheres.

The next night's dream:[3-3] *My husband and I are riding in the same tarantass across a dismal countryside, which is utterly devoid of any sign of either vegetation or dwellings. Everything around us is scorched. The sky and the ground are of the same gray or grayish-yellow color. For a long time we ride across this horrible wasteland, seeing neither birds nor animals. At last we see a distant hill. Rejoicing, we approach the hill, intending to climb to its top in the hope of seeing something on the horizon. But to our horror, after drawing close to the hill, we see that it is not a hill at all, but a huge, coiled, sleeping serpent of the same color as the land around it. It crosses my mind that this reptile has devoured everything and then has fallen asleep.*

About the same time, I often saw in my dreams a blackboard and a male hand writing some numbers on it in chalk. Those numbers were encountered in real life and served as guiding signs.

A dream in 1911 foretelling the death of my mother: *Accompanied by my mother, I enter the apartment of my aunt, Princess Evdokiya Vassilyevna Putyatina, where she and my mother live.*

At the living room door we are met by a nun who, with one hand, is holding a tray with candles, and in the other hand, a burning candle that she gives to us. Puzzled, we take the candles and proceed to the next room. It is the dining room, which looks completely different: all the usual items have been moved out, and in the middle of the room there is only a round black table with heavy dark armchairs around it. In all of the chairs, except for two that remain vacant, ugly, hunched, old women sit wrapped up in long black veils covering their faces. My mother and I approach the table, knowing that we must sit down on the two vacant, black chairs. But as soon as my mother enters the circle and sits down on one chair, the other chair disappears and the circle closes. Mother is left alone in that dreary circle. It vividly occurs to me that all those black figures are symbols of calamities that will befall my mother, and that it will end with her death. In fear and anguish, and not wanting to leave my mother alone, I begin looking around trying to find a chair where I can sit near my mother, even if it is outside the circle.

All of a sudden, the room, which has been empty until this time, is filled with people, and above all their heads, the head of my long absent cousin is moving around in the air. At the same time, the door opens and my father enters, as always with his face slightly darkened. He carries an all-white chair by its legs, and holding it high above all others' heads, brings it toward my mother, and without a word, puts it down behind her, outside the circle. ...

Soon after I had this dream, a string of calamities befell my mother: she was diagnosed with diabetes; had an attack of appendicitis; lost some of her money; and broke her arm, of which the torn ligaments did not heal properly and her entire arm ceased to function. Then there was a second attack of appendicitis, followed by peritonitis, a surgery, and horrible sufferings caused by inflammation of the major nerves in her legs. This was accompanied by a clouded consciousness and tormenting hallucinations. On October 24, 1913, after nine months of suffering, death occurred from heart paralysis.

The first of these calamities coincided with the reappearance of a long-absent cousin. One of the hallucinations recurring during her illness was the one in which my mother saw herself sentenced to death at the stake for allegedly murdering her own child. The other hallucination was a vision of a *skhimnik* looking sternly at her.[3-4] (She often saw herself being thrown into a pit full of snakes and all kinds of reptiles).

In 1911, we were spending the summer in the province of Smolensk at the estate of Princess M[ariya] Kl[avdievna] Tenisheva, where N. K. and his assistants and students were creating church paintings. At the beginning of August, N. K. had to go to Petrograd on business.[3-5] The day before his departure he told me, "I would really like to know what we should do about this large quantity of securities. Try to get advice in your dream." The next morning he asked me if I had seen anything and I said, "No, but I heard a voice telling me to sell all the securities." N. K. left with the firm intention to sell the securities. Yet, when he arrived in the capital and told his friends and his acquaintances among the bankers of his intentions, all of them were decisively against it and told him, "One should buy rather than sell, since prices on all the securities are rapidly going up." As a result, N. K., following their insistent advice, bought more securities. A few weeks later the incident took place that caused the Balkan war, and the prices on all securities went down.

In 1913, sometime around July, at dawn, I distinctly heard a Voice telling me, "All the securities have to be sold." (This advice was not followed.) This was the year when the Balkan war began.[3-6]

A dream in March 1914: *A large dining room in the residence of my uncle V. Golenishchev-Kutuzov, my mother's brother. The uncle's entire family and many relatives are sitting around the table. She sits next to her aunt, the uncle's wife, who is glowing but at the same time is covered with dark spots.[3-7] The aunt turns to her and says, "I am not afraid of death, but I am sorry to leave them (her family)."* Upon awakening, I understood that the aunt was sick and would die soon. The same morning, my uncle told me over the phone that the aunt had another attack of the illness with which she had been sick for quite a long time, but was feeling better now. Three weeks later she died.

In the Nobility House at the Hofman's concert, we saw Tsionglinsky, an artist; I had an acute feeling that his life was leaving him.[3-8] The very next day he was taken to the hospital where he had liver surgery and died one week after that.

While in America, I visited a family of our friends. When I saw their unusually lively daughter, I clearly felt that the girl would not live long. I also felt a strong antipathy toward the girl's nanny, for it seemed as if she was draining the girl's vitality. (The girl died a few months later.)

A dream-vision that I had toward morning on October 31, 1913, which was accompanied by an unusually strong feeling of spiritual exaltation:

I am walking along a lighted corridor and come to a door, open it, and enter a large light-filled room with no windows. Then I look around for the next door so that I can proceed further. When I look to the right, the wall disappears, and a red-pink sphere opens up before my eyes. In the middle of it there is a broad, tall staircase, narrowing in perspective toward the top, which is lost from sight in the pink glow. On both sides of the stairway, on every step, people are standing in groups, wearing garments of the same style. Near the bottom of the ladder the groups are dressed in red, and ugly black spots cover their faces and garments. On the following steps upward, people have fewer and fewer spots, so that the higher toward the top they are, the lighter in color the people and their garments, and at the top all have merged into a pure pink glow.

On the very top of the staircase a beautiful giant figure emerges in a red garment, with a dark coat over his shoulder. He has beautiful facial features and long, black hair that reaches down to his shoulders. This Being quickly descends the stairs, his dark coat flapping like wings behind him, but at the very bottom of the staircase he stops as if some obstacle has suddenly risen up in front of him. Exhausted, he leans against the barrier, his dark hair hanging down in unusually pretty waves, and his garment hangs in beautiful folds.

When I turn to the opposite wall, I see the same phenomenon—

the wall disappears, and in its place there is a radiant rainbow sphere. There is the same kind of staircase in the middle, its top lost from sight in the sunlight. Similar groups of people are standing on both sides, on every step. At the bottom their garments are light blue, but up toward the top, both people and their garments gradually became lighter in color, more silvery, merging at the top into a radiant light. As with the first sphere, a Magnificent Image emerges at the very top, against a background of blinding sunlight. His face is impossible to discern due to the light, but the heart-consciousness suggests that it is the Christ Image.

Slowly, awfully slowly, He begins to descend, stretching in turn His right and left arm to touch groups of the standing people. Upon His touch, tongues of flame burst over people's heads, and each group has its specific color, all those flames forming a rainbow of the most delicate hues.

Full of admiration, I watch this beauty, when suddenly a whirlwind lifts me upwards, leaving my mourning dress (which I wore after my mother's death) behind on the floor; and I am being lifted up in a light-colored gown, carried toward the bottom of the staircase and placed among the lower group. I agonizingly wait to see whether Christ will approach me, whether His Hand will touch me, and what kind of light will be kindled over my head. ... He does approach and stretches out His right Hand, and I feel and know with a rapture that a flame is bursting out of the top of my head and is burning with silvery blue Fire.

During Easter week, the night before March 24, 1914, I had a vision of a Luminous Boy. The eve of this remarkable and joyful event was quiet, with no visitors. I remember that throughout the day I was in an unusually peaceful mood, full of joy. I do not remember any other event like this. As always, I went to bed very late. I turned off the electric bedside lamp and waited for a few moments for the impression of light in my eyes to disappear. Then I raised myself up on my elbows and glanced at the space between the wall and a screen that separated the alcove from the rest of the room, in order to make sure that I did not forget to leave a gap between the heavy curtains at the window. (I hated complete darkness.) To my astonishment, the room began to fill with a bluish light reminiscent of bright moonlight. All objects behind the solid reflecting screen became visible, and the screen itself, while remaining solid, became transparent. A slim, luminous figure of a Beautiful Boy, around nine years old, in a white, softly glowing garment with blue shadows in the folds, separated from the window rather far from my bed. There was a large, wide sector of a circle of the most delicate opalescent Light glowing above His head.

The Boy moved toward me along the wall as if gliding in the air. His folded arms were hidden by long, wide sleeves. My attention was focused on the extraordinary beauty of His perfectly proportioned face. The thick, dark, and wavy crown of His hair, slightly parted to one side, shone slightly with a reflected golden light coming from the glow above His head. The reality of His hair was extraordinary. How I wanted to touch it! But it was His eyes that were absolutely astonishing: huge, deep in their dark blueness, staring at me. When I saw Him approaching, my first thought was that it was the soul of someone close to me who had come to visit. However, that thought was immediately rejected, because as He was coming nearer a feeling of unspeakable intimacy began to grow inside me with such a strength that, when the Boy approached the head of my bed and bent slightly forward in order to better look into my eyes, my feeling of growing closeness and love changed into the ecstasy of an acute realization that my grief was His grief and my joy was His joy, and my entire being was flooded with a wave of all-embracing love for Him and for all that existed. The thought flashed in my mind that such a state is impossible on earth, and therefore I was on some other plane of existence. I saw the images of my children and my husband, whom I was leaving without saying a single word, and my mind was filled with confusion. My eyes involuntarily rolled up and closed, and my entire body was filled with an indescribable trembling. I felt that my heart—indeed, my entire being—was about to explode, and I made enormous efforts, pressing on my chest, in order to cope with this state. It was impossible to judge how long this condition lasted. When it began to fade away, I opened my eyes and discovered that everything was gone, and the room was engulfed in an almost absolute darkness, except for the narrow gap between the window curtains.

In approximately 1915 I had a dream—a vision of some scenes from one of my previous lives: *A sunny, bright winter day. The road is covered with a layer of dense virgin snow with a thin crust of ice over it. Muffled up in furs and covered by a warm bearskin lap robe, I am riding in a wide sleigh. Magnificent horses are galloping, and after making a wide dashing turn into a round court, we come to a white house. Several servants run out to help me get out of the tightly tucked lap robe. I enter a rotunda, which has large windows that reach down almost to the floor. Against the walls between the windows, there are chairs and benches upholstered in bright-red damask or rep; there is a strong aroma of apples and sunniness, and my mood is unusually bright and cheerful.*[3-9]

Another picture: *The same house; it is evening. I am standing at a window in a long dark bedroom. I can see below a frozen, snow-covered, winding river enclosed between steep banks and lit by the bright moonlight. A crowd of peasants with lanterns carries a litter with a large ornamented mica lamp on it; they go down toward the river, cross it, and climb the pine-covered hill on the opposite bank, where there is a lighted church that is partially obscured by the trees. Apparently, some kind of Holiday service is taking place. I am enveloped by a feeling of acutely painful anguish and loneliness.*

I am in the family of someone who is close to me, someone who is my friend. His mother and sister are very unfriendly, for they are afraid of our friendship.

A winter evening. I and an officer in the uniform of Tsar Alexander's or Tsar Nicholas' times are riding in a large-pair horse sleigh across the countryside, when we come to a high stone wall with cast-iron gates and cast-iron lanterns hanging from stone posts. The gates are open, and our sleigh passes through them into an alley lined with snow-clad trees. Suddenly a dark figure runs out from a snowdrift, jumps onto the step at the back of the sleigh (the seat for a footman), and grabs at the back of our seat. It seems to me that it was my cousin who was waiting

*for us and was intent on playing a prank to scare us; so I turn
slightly toward him and whisper, "Étienne, Étienne, is it you?"
Bursting into spiteful laughter, the dark figure jumps off the sleigh
and disappears into the shadows of the bushes. Saddened, I realize that the relatives of the man who sits next to me had sent
someone to spy on us. We come to a white house where a meeting
is to be held, perhaps a gathering of Decembrists or Masons.*[3-10]

In 1916, a few months before the February Revolution, I had a
dream in which all the Tsar's palaces in different locations were
joined, became empty, and their dwellers had left:[3-11] *Puzzled, I
walk from one empty room to another seeing no one, not even
servants. Finally I enter a large lighted hall where all sorts of
objects are piled in disarray. A rather large group of people are
gathered in the room, among them some members of the World
of Art, as well as some other artists.*[3-12] *It seems that all of them
are busy making a palace inventory because they are moving
around, examining objects, and attaching labels to them. Count
Dm[itry] Iv[anovich] Tolstoy, the Director of the Hermitage, is
sitting at a long table and entering items into a huge, open, inventory book.*[3-13] *None of them notice me. A wide door behind
Count Tolstoy opens and my father appears. He stares at me,
and his look conveys to me the urgency of departing, of leaving.
I also understand that a time of blasphemies and crimes has come,
and following the direction, I run away. I run through a park,
then to a forest, then across green hillocks and hills until I reach
a small fenced house with a garden, and from there I cannot find
a way out. I know that I am caged in there, but I feel no fear
because there is a blue sky above and the fence is covered with
blossoming dogroses. ...*[3-14] In the spring, we left for Finland where
we lived in a small fenced house with a garden, and dogroses
grew there.

A dream in 1917: *An almost empty room with a high ceiling,
and I am standing at a long table on which a map of the Earth is
being put together. A big male Hand from above, as if from the
ceiling, throws down cut-out pieces of the map and fits them together. When the map of Europe, Siberia, and the Urals is assembled, the pieces corresponding to Manchuria, Korea, and*

China are thrown around but not put in their proper place. With a red pencil, the Hand draws a straight line from the north to the south, separating the Baltic region—Poland, Lithuania, and Bessarabia—from the rest of Russia.[3-15] *Then in the same Hand, a little yellow dog, like a ratcatcher, appears and the Hand places the dog on the disorderly pile of pieces of China. The dog begins to snap at one piece after another, in no apparent order, immediately releasing them, apparently trying to get to Siberia. The Voice from above declares, "Russia is an inland State, but nevertheless it will be strong."*

After the war ended with the Peace Treaty of Versailles, all lands that were separated by the red pencil were taken away from Russia.

A dream I had in the spring of 1919 before we left for London: *There is a very tall ladder with horizontal rungs. The ladder stands on Russian land, near its northern part, in an open valley; it stands almost vertically and does not lean against anything. It is so tall that it is possible to view every country from its top. I stand on the top rung, viewing the wide-open spaces all around. The sky over my head is dark, and it is even darker toward the south and north. Staring toward England, I can barely discern the outline of the dome of St. Paul's Cathedral. Behind it, against the background of a velvety-black sky, almost on the horizon, I see with terrifying clarity some kind of bloody omen: two red triangles, whereas over all the other countries there is only a grave darkness. I turn my head toward the north to see what is going on there and see that the darkness is rushing from that direction, and the dark clouds over there are not so dense and some gray gaps appear amidst the darkness. I know that I have to go down the ladder, and that I have to be very careful because someone else is below, and my first careless step may cause us to be crushed. The ladder is narrow, unsteady, and very steep, and I have to go down with my back toward the rungs. I am looking for something to hold onto, when, on both sides of the stairs, as if out of nowhere, long sticks reach toward me so that I can grab at them. But the sticks are so shaky and hang in the air so precariously that I do not dare to grab at either of them. Then, from above my head and along my body, a firm, thick, steady stick, showing no sign of swaying, slides down; I grab at it with both hands and, holding onto it, calmly go down the ladder....*

A dream in November 1919: *I am helping my cousin and her children to cross a London street in a dangerous place and then help them board the omnibus.* (As far as I knew, my cousin was then in Constantinople. But just a few days after that dream she and her children moved to London.)

A dream in November 1919: *A Red Messenger standing on pillars of light. I am on the balcony of our rented house in London, and from there I can see a distant square and adjacent streets. The sky is leaden-colored and gloomy, and the entire atmosphere is unusually heavy and ominous. People, who appear dark and gray, are hustling and bustling on the streets, hastening to find shelter from the coming thunderstorm. The sky is quickly growing darker and darker, and in the west it has become completely black. Against a background of this horrible darkness, all of a sudden there appears a gigantic, fiery-red figure of an Archangel radiating rose-colored light that takes up almost half the sky. He is standing on pillars of light, holding a scroll that curls in His hand, and he has a large golden key fastened to His girdle.*

I understood it to mean that the time of retribution was approaching. I turned my head toward the East and saw in the evening twilight, near the horizon, the rising crescent of a new moon and a beautiful Child resting on it, with one of his little legs hanging down. I interpreted this as an oriental symbol of the birth of a New Era and a New Race.

Part Four

During our stay in London, after our meeting with the Great Teachers and Their close approach, a series of remarkable phenomena commenced. I began noticing flashes of yellow flame in the mediastinum.[4-1] Every evening two slender, luminous figures appeared at my bed; their heads were obscured by a silvery mist, and only their hands, which offered me books, were seen clearly. This vision, with slight variations, occurred repeatedly for a rather long time. At times, I was shown a few books in red covers; at other times, a huge open book. Often a hand appeared in the air holding a small oriental vessel, from which it poured something around me. Sometimes two luminous, silvery figures appeared at my bed, with certain dates in glowing digits written on their foreheads.

One night, the Luminous Boy appeared at the head of my bed holding a tray of brushes. I understood that I was supposed to give Him my hands for anointing, so I stretched out my arms one at a time with the palms open, and the Boy touched them with a brush. After that I lay down on my back and saw a hand in front of me, reaching toward me to give me a burning candle. I took the candle, of course, but without feeling it. Also, more than once I saw many eyes around me, looking at me; they were unusually alive, and many of them were narrow, oriental eyes.

Often I would wake up, as if being awakened by a push or by the spark of an electric discharge, and begin to have visions. Thus, I saw two bluish-silvery rays, one filled with innumerable human blue and dark eyes; the other, which flashed right after the first one, full of small silvery fish of various shapes.

There were moving visions that were difficult for me to capture. Thus, in a whirlwind of red light, a female figure flew by. But that vision was not a clear one. More than once I had a vision of a silvery dove, sometimes with an olive branch in its beak.

There were visions of a very vivid rainbow; the yellow and red colors were especially intense.

About that time, I had two remarkable visions inside myself in the area of the solar plexus. The first one happened late in the evening when I was already in bed. Against a bluish-green background, vibrating with a silvery glow, a male head appeared, which had fine features and closed eyes and no hair at all, as if he was carved of ivory. The facial type was that of a refined, handsome Chinese man. This vision was accompanied by a strong trembling in my entire body, which, however, lasted less time and was weaker than when I was visited by the Luminous Boy.

Another vision happened toward evening, when I was alone sitting in a chair and concentrating on the Image of the Great Teacher. In the area of my solar plexus, an image of a nun appeared in brown clothes edged with red; she was kneeling with her arms stretched upward in the ecstasy of prayer. I was looking at her as if from above, and I could clearly see above her the lower segment of a large fiery circle. This vision did not cause the slightest shock.

The second vision of the nun happened a little while later. I saw her outside of me, at a considerable distance, and all the proportions were smaller. It was the same nun, again kneeling, with her head bent backward and her tense arms spread out and slightly lowered. Above her head there was a silvery, scaly dove, and a long bluish-silvery spark in the form of a vibrating thread, which issued from the dove and entered the top of the nun's head. I was completely calm while watching this.

Another vision, a very important one. I saw it not within myself, but very close to the head of my bed. It was the torso of a man in lightly colored clothes, with a rather heavy head of an oriental type and fine curly hair, which below formed a very short, curly beard. He had narrow eyes, slightly slanted up toward a wide forehead, a short neck, and well-developed shoulders and chest. On his chest there was a chalice with a serpent coiled in a circle inside of it. There was an impression of an unusual power, of a leonine quality. I felt no shock.

Early one morning I was awakened by the loud whistle of a steamboat, and I instantly had a vision that seemed strikingly real. Against the background of a dark blue sky, there was a sunlit, ancient, yellow sandstone tower on a rock at the edge of a precipice. It appeared as if it was worm-eaten throughout or all covered with ancient inscriptions.

During the same time, or maybe before, I had a recurrent vision, mostly with my eyes closed, of the refined head of a man of a clearly pronounced oriental type. He had long, dark, slightly wavy hair; fine facial features; a short and slightly forked beard; a matte, dark complexion; and huge eyes that were mostly closed, but which sometimes would open widely, which gave the impression of silvery rays bursting out of them. This head was turning around in all directions so that I could better examine it. It always appeared against a rosy-lilac background and was smaller than life-size.

Another vision: A rather crowded procession of turbaned Hindus in white garments, some of whose heads were surrounded by a golden radiance. They proceeded toward the gates within the walls of an oriental city. Behind the walls one could see towers of pagodas and minarets. One of those with the radiance turned and looked at me, smiling.

Another vision against a purple background: A silhouette of a dark-complexioned, crowned Hindu with thick curly hair and a beard.

A vision of two turbaned Hindus, against the background of a red polished board, with Their eyes moving. The vision lasted several seconds, and it was also seen by both of my sons. This vision was reminiscent of television.

In America at the beginning of 1921, there was a vision of a materialization of an extraordinary power and vividness. I was awakened by a strong push at my side. A kind of blue light emerged over the bedside table. Between the beds, against a background of velvety darkness, a slim male hand appeared illumined by a golden-green aura; the hand was writing with a pencil on a sheet of white paper. The sheet was lying on something black, as if on a table. The vision was so materialized that I could hear the squeak of the pencil writing on the paper. It was this reality that caused some fear in me and doubt about the genuine quality of the vision.

A vision in 1921, before we left for New Mexico: A tall and very wide staircase with low steps and the flights separated by landings. A flat roof above is supported by many wooden columns with capitals shaped as twisting serpents.[4-2] Everything is lit with a golden light. I stand on the topmost landing, with a high coiffure, dressed in a long gown with numerous tiny folds. My silhouette is clearly seen against the general golden background. On the next landing below and before me there is a tripod with a decorated, dark bronze bowl with incense burning in it.

1921. A dream: *St. Sergius on a mountain. In search of the Teacher, I pass through many rooms and finally reach a long hall in which, on a dais along the walls, there are high chairs, and in them sit tall men in long garments. All the men are beautiful, with long hair, and all resemble the Teacher, whose Image is permanently before my eyes. Yet I am struck by their red cheeks, their complacent look, and something repulsive in the expression of their eyes. So I decide to keep going. I exit to some empty lot, behind which there is a mountain or a hill with winding paths leading toward its top. Along these paths the strangest animals and calves are climbing: in addition to their four legs, they have a fifth one protruding upward from the middle of their backs.*

Intrigued by such a sight, I follow those paths, reach the top of the mountain, and there I see St. Sergius in sacerdotal robes. He takes my hands, sits me down on the bench next to him, and says with reproach, "At last, Elena! I kept calling and calling you!"

A dream-vision in March 1922: *Accompanied by the Teacher, I enter an unusually high room and notice there are no windows. Already there are two or three people standing, dressed as I am, in rosy-lilac garments; I join them. In front of us, there is a podium with a four-sided stone throne on it. The Teacher, in a lilac garment and a white turban, ascends to the podium and, standing with His face turned to us, stretches out His arm toward the throne. Instantly below and above the throne, silvery, rosy-lilac, and blue rays appear. They make a geometric figure of a huge double triangle forming a kind of six-pointed star pierced by the rays.* I woke up feeling extraordinary joy, and during the next few days, a solemn hymn sounded inside me all the time.

1922: *A lavishly appointed room in Oriental-Arabic style. I am surrounded by a crowd of my relatives who are wearing rich, red silk caftans embroidered with gold. They are inspecting my wedding presents, which fill almost the entire room. The relatives have been invited to my wedding to an Arab Sheik.*

The second scene: *A large inner courtyard surrounded by covered galleries with thin columns. I am standing there together with relatives and the Sheik. One by one they lead beautifully adorned Arabian horses before us, accompanied by numerous servants whose black faces and multicolored silk clothes make a striking sight.*

The third scene: *In the same room I am sitting on multicolored silk cushions holding my little son. I am already accustomed to my new life and am receiving my brother who has come to visit me. For some reason my brother does not like my husband, who at that moment is entering the room, and I think sadly, How could it be that my brother does not see the beauty of the Sheik's Image?*

The fourth scene: *The same Sheik is ready for travel. I see horses and richly adorned elephants. Holding my little son, I approach the white elephant on which the Sheik sits, raise the boy up, and hand him to the Sheik. I am parting with my son, but I know that it is necessary because he is the heir.*

The fifth scene: *The Sheik, now an elderly man, sits on silk cushions. On both sides of him, but a little lower, are seated young girls on cushions. I stand at a distance in front of the Sheik, and I feel the Sheik's loving eyes riveted on me. I know that the young bodies surrounding the Sheik emanate fluids of health and thus replenish his waning vitality.*

1922: *An opulent palace chamber, possibly a reception hall. My mother, in a rich, heavy garment, sits in a gilded armchair. In front of her there are strange figures in some kind of pointed hats sitting on low benches. I know that these are envoys who have come to take part in a celebration. The preparations for a betrothal are underway, but I decide to avoid the ceremony. I retreat into an attic and pass through to the upper gallery. I hide in a dark corner from where I can see the large, brightly lit hall full of dressed-up guests. Notable among them is a certain man, perfectly dressed, beautiful, slender; all the guests, seeing him, whisper, "What refinement!" I, on the contrary, experience a definitely hostile feeling toward this man.*

1922: *I am wandering through some long galleries with large multi-sectioned windows, peeking into the inner yards of a huge palace structure. I know that I have been sentenced to death by beheading. The execution had been scheduled for that morning, but I did not notice any sign of preparation for it. It is about noon. I enter a spacious hall with long dinner tables all set for a meal. At the main inner entrance, there is a crowd of lavishly dressed guests and courtiers. The owner of the castle, in a silver brocade caftan with blue velvet slits and a small beret decorated with an ostrich feather (as in the times of Francis I), approaches the table at the center and sits down. My mother, a close relative of this Duke, sits beside him. My seat is supposed to be at the same table, but my chair has been removed. I come to the table. I know that for these people I no longer exist, and they pretend not to see me.*

The owner of the castle looks at me derisively, and my mother, indifferently, though she obviously is not pleased that I am there. ... Having stood at the table for a few seconds and seen their complete lack of attention or desire to exchange even a word with me, I go out. I enter a corridor, along which numerous servants are hastily carrying huge, fancifully adorned dishes. One of the servants accidentally hits me with the edge of a dish and spills pasta with a fatty sauce on my shoulder; disgusted, I throw it off and go on. ... While awakening, I still felt an acute disgust for the pasta; it seemed to me that it was still on my shoulder.

On the night of June 23, 1924, there were two unusual experiences. I saw myself in a loose white garment, standing in a bright and very large room at a long table, on which was lying open a book of records. My attention was attracted to a line in parentheses that included the name of some Nephrit[e] of Ala [ ] clan. I could not read further, for I felt that my entire being was being pulled out of my body, then drawn back. It was a very painful sensation and it caused me fear. But I soon recovered, having realized that it was a test of projection of one of my subtle bodies.

Sometime later when I was lying down, but fully conscious, the same kind of pulling out happened again, and I found myself in an unfamiliar room. From what I was able to gather, there were simple, office-style furniture; light-colored walls; a dark sofa along one wall; a simple electric lamp on the wall; and a desk to my side at the window. I felt a strong desire to leave some evidence of my presence there, and feeling that I must rush, and not seeing anything to write with, I pulled out a hairpin from my coiffure and decided to write with it on the black folders lying on the desk. I scratched, "Roerich is a great man." After that I was lifted up with terrifying speed, with my knees bent, and was drawn out through the door. I had a vague glimpse of a staircase and of the main entrance. Right after that, with a wearisome feeling, I saw myself lying in bed, and luminous hands were holding onto a metal dish or plate, a piece of stone or metal, and some kind of tool or electric discharge device. At the same time I heard a sound as if someone had dropped a coin on a metal tray. This sound then echoed in the top of my head. Then everything disappeared.

On the night of July 18, 1924, a vision of the Mother of the World. Toward the morning, my dream transformed into a vision that I was seeing outside the dream: *It is a bright morning. I am standing amidst abandoned palaces built in a Roman-Gothic style. My entire being seems to split in two. One self remains standing amidst the ruins; another self, wrapped in a thin, white garment, begins to move away, walking in the air as if going into the depths of the blue. Then, in the clear, cloudless, turquoise sky, a small, bright white cloud appears at a distance. It is quickly approaching and assumes the shape of a female figure in radiant white garments. These garments, shimmering with dazzling light and shining silvery-blue in the folds, begin to unfold and assume various shapes, as if each is transforming into the other. Suddenly the silver of the garment breaks apart into multicolored sparks, which then quickly gather together again into the silver, and the harmony of magnetic movements into a rainbow spiral star, a dodecahedron of extraordinary beauty, which then forms an almost perfect circle against the background of the dazzling silvery glow. This star sparkles, vibrates, and seems alive. Against its background, from a coil of the spiral, there emerges a white turban, a miter, and an icon-like face of a Starets with a white beard, His shoulder and arm wrapped in a white garb. In front of Him, in the foreground on His right and half-turned, there is a seated female figure in bluish-lilac colors, looking more real than the Starets. Her head and face are covered with a thick veil, and only Her chin, which is slightly flesh-colored, is visible. On the veil there is a pattern of squares bordered with a rainbow. The figure raises Her flesh-colored arm adorned with silver bracelets and, as if turning away from something below on Earth, turns toward the Starets.*

Notes

Part One

1. This is the old Julian calendar date, which in the current Gregorian calendar is February 12, 1879. The year was not indicated in the original text.
2. In *Dreams and Visions*, Helena Roerich often speaks in the third person.
3. "Starets," literally "an elder," is defined as: 1. a monastic spiritual teacher in Orthodox Christianity; 2. (more generally) an archetypal Old Sage.
4. St. Sergius, one of the greatest Russian spiritual leaders (1314–1392); considered to be a reincarnation of Master Morya.
5. An achkan is a close-fitting, high-necked coat, slightly flared below the waist and reaching almost to the knee; it is worn by men in India. (*Webster's Encyclopedic Unabridged Dictionary of the English Language*)
6. World War I.
7. The October Revolution (1917).

Part Two

1. H. Roerich may be referring to the Alhambra Palace at Granada.
2. Old Russian (Julian) calendar date for an Eastern European pagan celebration related to the summer solstice.
3. The Kazan Mother of God (also Our Lady of Kazan or the Virgin of Kazan) is a revered, miracle-working Russian icon, a variation on the Virgin and Child theme (16th century).
4. Vyshhie Zhenskie Kursy, an institution of higher education for women in Tsarist Russia.
5. Jean-Martin Charcot, famous 19th-century neurologist.
6. "No more bets will be accepted."
7. "Number One has won everything."
8. "Number Three has won everything."
9. "N. K." is Nicholas K. Roerich.
10. "Lyalya" was a pet name formed from the name 'Helena.'
11. Ruble: a unit of money in Russia.

Part Three

1. Tarantass: A low, four-wheeled, springless carriage.
2. Caryatid: a sculptured female figure used as a column.

3. Up to this point in the manuscript, Helena Roerich has referred to herself as "she."

4. A *skhimnik* is a monk who, having taken the vows of schema, has attained the highest monastic degree in Eastern Christianity. He lives an extremely austere life.

5. Originally, the city was named St. Petersburg, but was renamed Petrograd in 1914 and Leningrad in 1924. The name St. Petersburg was restored in 1991.

6. The First Balkan War lasted from October 1912 to May 1913, while the Second Balkan War took place from June 1913 to August 1913. So "a few weeks" after August referred to in the previous paragraph may be understood as October 1912, not 1911.

7. "She" most probably refers to Helena Roerich.

8. Josef Casimir Hofmann (1876-1957), who was a noted pianist.

9. Rep (or repp): a transversely corded fabric of wool, cotton, rayon, or silk.

10. Decembrists were Russian revolutionaries, primarily members of the upper classes who staged an unsuccessful liberal uprising in December 1825 against Tsar Nicholas I.

11. The February 1917 Revolution, which preceded the Bolshevik Revolution in October 1917 (Old Style Calendar Date) .

12. A World of Art (*Mir Iskusstva*) is an association of Russian artists. Nicholas Roerich served as its Chairman from 1910 to 1913.

13. The Hermitage, now the Russian State Hermitage, is a major art museum in St. Petersburg.

14. Dogrose: an Old World wild rose having pale-red flowers.

15. All three Baltic states (including Lithuania), Poland, Bessarabia, and Finland were at that time parts of the Russian Empire. Bessarabia is now divided between the Ukraine and Moldova.

Part Four

1. Mediastinum is the space in the chest cavity between the lungs, which contains the heart, aorta, esophagus, trachea, and thymus.

2. Capital: The uppermost portion of a column, pillar, or shaft supporting the entablature.

The Fiery Experience

...the beginning of the new race is based upon the manifested affirmed principle of Fire on Earth. Therefore, creative synthesis arouses the consciousnesses. The new race is affirmed by the Fire attested by the creativeness of the synthesis of the Silvery Lotus. Each new cosmic force is transmitted. Yes, yes, yes! Thus a new force invisibly enters the life of humanity. The Tara creates! Yes, yes, yes!

Infinity, Vol. I,
para. 217

A typewritten, authorized original of *The Fiery Experience* essay is stored at the Manuscript Department of the International Roerich Center in Moscow. All entries were recorded in 1924. The dates of the transmissions are indicated in the body of the text. Questions, notes, and comments by Helena Roerich are given in parentheses. This essay was published for the first time in the Russian edition of the present book (1993).

The Fiery Experience

In "The Fiery Experience" the reader will notice italicized passages from the book Illumination, *pp. 44-108, from* Leaves of Morya's Garden, Book Two, *(New York: Agni Yoga Society, 1952, second printing 1979.) These translated fragments are used with the kind permission of the Agni Yoga Society. The reader may notice some variations in the italicized material from that which appears in later editions of the book.*

INTRODUCTION

Cooperation with a Teacher of Light was established in very early childhood. The awareness of the existence of the Teacher of Light appeared for the first time in her sixth year when the girl was enjoying the beauty of a summer morning: Intense rapture had raised the level of her vibrations, and she saw a tall figure dressed in white, standing with a blossoming apple tree behind Him. That Image aroused recollections of a distant past in her mind; the Beautiful Image of the Teacher emerged in her consciousness, and with the full force of her ecstatic love, the girl's heart longed for Him. That illumination not only awakened her consciousness, but also planted a spark of aspiration for true knowledge and a fiery love for the Image, distant, yet also near.

The intense recollections of a distant past were reinforced by the appearance of two Hindus who came to her at the times of her childhood catarrhal diseases and, of course, relieved her from dangers involved in excessive fevers. The girl was not especially afraid of Them. They would sit carefully at the foot of her bed. Her immediate Teacher, seating Himself farther from her, would pull a silvery thread out of her heart. His Companion passed the thread to the first Teacher, Who wound it into a huge ball that He held in His hand. This phenomenon was repeated several times, although less and less vividly.

In general, her childhood and early adolescence were richer in vivid visions and illuminations than her early youth.

The most majestic and vivid vision occurred in her seventh year, when in the evening sky she saw a huge, unfolding, tricolored Russian banner, which took the shape of a band with an open loop in the middle with its ends cut, reminiscent of ribbons one may see in ancient manuscripts and on title pages in old-fashioned books. The vision was so colorful and its hues, which seemed to shine with an inner glow, were so beautiful that the girl could not tear herself away from the unusual sight. But her mother, who also was there, did not see anything, in spite of all the girl's passionate assurances. She never forgot that vision, for it was powerfully impressed in her mind and memory. But its meaning became clear to her only much later, when the girl became firmly established in her approach to the Teaching of Light, and the staggering cosmic significance of the wonderful vision became a guiding Banner in her later life.

Her youth and early married life were accompanied by Precepts for right decisions. Thus the Precepts guided her entire life, both external and internal. They usually came in dreams, and, less often, as a voice heard.

After she turned thirty, or maybe a little earlier, there were new insights and two extraordinary spiritual experiences of cosmic significance.

After the age of forty, she established herself on a new level of approach to the Teacher and the Teaching of Light. The Teacher was perceived first as a Hindu, but after the consciousness of the disciple had expanded and was able to accommodate it, the Beautiful Image began to gradually change and eventually took the shape of a Majestic Image of Cosmic Significance, a Lord of Wisdom and Beauty, a Lord of the Sacred Shambhala.

The expansion of consciousness brought about a new possibility of approach to the Sacred Knowledge and of acceptance of the Fiery Experience, and finally of participation in the work of cosmic construction in collaboration with the Great Teacher, the Lord of Light.

January, 1924: (A vision of flowers—lilies, or more likely lotuses, white and light blue ones—given to me by the Hand of the Lord. In the morning there was a vision of a note written on purple paper or maybe silk. I was able to discern one term only, that of "June 27, 1927." The vision was preceded by a strong pine aroma.)

A Conversation in the evening: Urusvati has received the flowers of Blagovestie.[1-1] The ways of the world can be comprehended by the chosen ones only. Urusvati may proceed without being concerned about time, for everything has been foreseen. I deem that you can go along the path of knowledge to Our Main Home. Urusvati, do not forget about a drink of hot milk and staying warm. The gland is pressing hard on a brain channel.

Our Wind blew from the mountains and is bringing in a new stage. Gather up bits of the people's reverence for Buddha; they will be of use.

(Every night I saw around myself blue, white, and lilac flowers. I began to hear and see.... Those experiences are recorded in a separate notebook.)

Urusvati knows everything; she needs only to courageously stretch out her hand. Rare are the spirits who possess the same knowledge as Urusvati. Your understanding flows like water—with ease. Tell yourself—I know, for the terms are inscribed in myself on the purple of nerves. I know, for He writes down sacred signs on the field of my aura. I know Him Who has strained the thread of my childhood, Who has shown earthly flowers, Who through salt and ice has called to the feast of the Spirit, Who has gathered the forces of the World, Who has woven the miraculous garment. Urusvati, a Spirit covered with a veil, descends the ladder carrying flowers for an offering. O Urusvati, I will light a lamp in your destined chamber. It is Our custom to light a lamp in a predestined chamber. We place a vessel of water and light a candle to illumine the occupied room. It is better to approach while in the physical body.

Urusvati, Urusvati, Urusvati, the thread is being wound invisibly. Taking into account occurrences of the World, the pollen of the flowers falls upon the open heart. The seeds are placed at the threshold of the house, and the thorns of roses detain travelers on the path. Urusvati is coming. We are waiting for Urusvati.

My daughter will give instructions to build a number of houses dedicated to knowledge. Urusvati, *assemble the most unfortunate ones, the most obscure young students, and reveal to them a gift, the power to endow humanity. Advise them to write the statutes in the Temple.* Show them the way to help Russia grow. The World has not seen for a long time any Gathering in the Temple. Christ will bestow His Grace upon the attaining of knowledge. *We wish to see the Temple beautiful and alive. And no one shall expel those walking to Light, for ruin awaits him. Miracles will be received upon the tablets of knowledge.* Let everyone illumined with spirit go courageously to the Temple. I will select the fit ones by the laying of hands on the testing stone.

Urusvati will manifest the coming together of Earth and Heaven. Urusvati will manifest the measure of beauty by a symphony of the spheres. Urusvati will manifest a Ray of Light penetrating the walls. Urusvati will manifest the Shield that shows the course of Celestial Bodies. Urusvati will manifest the flight of the arrows of spirit. Urusvati will manifest comprehension of the density of matter when her spirit wills it. Urusvati will expose the emptiness of thought not ignited by spirit, for Ours is the path of Earth to the Palace of Transformation. Who will not wish to accept these riches?

(With great love I have laid a white khatyk on an Image of the Lord Maitreya in a temple.)[1-2] Maitreya sends thanks for the offering. *Maitreya sends courage. Maitreya will accept the gift. Maitreya feels its love. Maitreya blesses His daughter upon the joyous labor. Maitreya bestows labor upon Earth in the name of miracle.*

At the beginning of the year you may live without worry. The books that are being sent for all of you teach you. Help is available for everyone; do not bother Urusvati, Our spring.[1-3] Urusvati is a spring in a great clock mechanism that is set for a specific time.

I am writing what is needed on her aura, so do not distort its surface with your touch. Urusvati is needed; one may surely deem that she is needed very much.

Now a new understanding of the earthly path to Heaven is growing. The Temple can be established only by way of Earth. We will all heave a deep sigh when the weight of the Temple stones have been passed from spirit to Earth. Urusvati feels. Urusvati knows. Urusvati will reveal. Urusvati appeared to kindle a miracle on Earth. Urusvati shall weave a pure cover for Our Shield; so I say, "Do not obstruct Our Urusvati!"

Urusvati nourishes pure thoughts for the Teachings of Buddha. It is a necessary task to reveal a kernel of Light. The Teaching is simple and is identical with other Teachings of Light. We will give the Russian people a simple understanding of God. The Grace of Christ can be revealed in the signs of My writing. He may be seen as a True Teacher entering the homes of those who await Him. The task is to present an Image of Christ pronouncing the prayer of knowledge and the precept. Rigorous joy should resound in Temple services. There should be no frequent services. Memorable Days are to be celebrated. The Temple statutes are to be kept in a large book.

We may praise you. For a month, an important realization was firmly established—the realization of building the Temple with earthly hands. Never before have I seen so clearly the Temple defined by the prophecy. A hearth invisible to them is growing amongst the crowds. An inaudible precept is leading the travelers. Do not be surprised at My speaking repeatedly about the Temple. My Voice, as a trumpet, reaffirms daily the precept of time. I do not repeat it for you, but, together with you, we are laying the stones of the foundation.

Urusvati hears guiding thoughts issuing from Our Tower. Do not be misled: this is not accidental. True, the dates are sometimes delayed, but at other times they are brought closer. Our Mountains have such a high rate of vibration that you will be thrown out of balance even at a distance—so take the time to catch your breath. I suggest an exclusively vegetarian diet. The nerves have a fierce temper. The blood fights with the nerves. It is better not to overburden the stomach. The amount of blood is reduced. Every woman passes though it, but one needs to sense the right amount of food to consume.

I rejoice at you, I rejoice at you, I rejoice at you! Urusvati, Guardian of Justice, and Fuyama, warrior, write down a prayer of the future Temple: "In the Name of Christ, in the Name of Buddha, in the Name of Maitreya, in the Name of Mahomet, in the Name of Solomon, in the Name of the Great Teachers and Prophets, in the Name of the Brotherhood Earthly and Heavenly, accept what you wish from Us; not for harm or killing, but for cognizing Light. I am washing My spirit with the miracle of *podvig* and silence. I will receive the Radiance of Truth."

Next, the lives of the Teachers are read. This is followed by the offering of gifts. Everyone brings the best of what has been accomplished in deed or in thought. Then those without tasks are assigned a job. At the end there is some music and a brief closing speech urging everyone to derive courage from their own spirit. After that, designated brothers sort out the offerings. Some are stored away, others are distributed to people. Regarding inventions, the rights are retained by their inventors. An artist's gift is accepted with the approval of a spiritual voice. Also, the final decision is affirmed by a sign of the spirit. Disagreement is eliminated by a sign from Above. If I am present, the decision is Mine.... Dear Urusvati, do what the spirit says and you will never err.

I feel all that lies before you will be good. Urusvati will sense the ray, and the eruptions of blood will end. All will be normalized. I will speed up this process as much as the organism allows. The awakening will come as soon as possible. We will draft a successful program for the next year, but until then, there is enough labor for each of you.

Urusvati, write a service to the Mother of the World. "Thy Veil hides the Mystery of the Universe. Seraphs sing of Thy Ray. Thy Ray is the Lamp to the World. Children sing Thy Name! You conceal Thy Name from us. The people countless times appeal to Thee and offer the greatest Names. Celestial Consonances call for Thee! White Sisters, let us raise the Image of the Invisible Mother on the White Mountain! Who is able to see Thee? But Thy Light penetrates into our hearts, and a rainbow clothes the eyes that seek Thee. Joy follows Thee, O Mother of the World!"

Next, amidst flowers and music, lives of prophetesses and *podvizhnitsas* are read.[14] At the entrance, there are Images of women martyrs of both the Old and New Testaments. Russian women bring in woven items and especially produced items related to the emergence of a new life through the instrumentality of women. Organize women as participants in the state structure, which will be concerned with their needs. The women's intuition tells them how to decorate the Temple with flowers. Music and a women's choir. At the beginning of each year, hold a service for the Great Spirit. Urusvati, dear is your flower to me. (I laid the first blossoming freesias at the portrait of the Lord.)

Every vision puts some strain on the nerves. It is especially necessary to protect the nerves during their fight with the blood. Today I showed [Urusvati] an ocean of blood. It is necessary to know that in order not to torment oneself with visions. It is inappropriate to divert the nerves from their struggle with the blood. It is useful to reduce the amount of food consumed. After their fight with the blood, the nerves may be given a task. But it is better not to accelerate the treatment, for all forced measures are harmful. You may be absolutely sure, I will not miss the opportunity, not even for a minute. Your growth and ascent are normal, but I have had to protect your heath, otherwise I would be a poor physician.

When it is possible to touch without overburdening the nerves, Morya comes immediately. You sensed a blue light, but it had to be stopped when the nerves became excited. You may help yourself by lightening your diet and by refraining from irritation, even if temporarily.... When you notice the visions have resumed, do not say, "Too little!" But say, "Here they are at last." However, you already had quite a good respite.

Merging into the summits of Cosmos, one must find coordination with Earth. Each moment We are ready to forsake everything of Earth, but at the same time We love every blossom on it. Therein lies the wisdom as to what remembrance to cherish: whether about the crown or the fragrance of freesias, the shouts of victory or the songs of shepherds. That which is the most dear but least of all belonging to us is the best load to carry on the way. Song brings us health, and color will heal wounds. Therefore, I say, happy are those who understand sound and color. From the very beginning the prophets have noted sound and color. The ancient instruction about the ringing of bells is full of meaning. Wreaths and garlands recall the understanding of healing power. According to the color of his radiation, each one is attracted to certain flowers. White and lilac have affinity with violet, blue with the blue; therefore, I advise to keep more flowers of these colors in the room. One can do this with living flowers. Plants wisely selected according to color are more healing. I advise to have more freesias. I love them too. Let these flowers serve as My Sign. Our Ray, with its silveriness, is more reminiscent of white flowers. Urusvati brought her flowers as an offering to Me. Color and sound are Our best repast. Urusvati, keep reading Isis in quietude.[1-5] Do not worry. I have made a decision—they will not precipitate a deluge. The world's attitude is different; many crowd you, therefore I say—do not be distracted by the external; strive to Me, only.

Urusvati shows the right grasp of the expansion of consciousness. *Not treatises, not logic, but the channel of spirit brings the perception of Cosmos. The tenor of contemporary life has severed from humanity all understanding of the Universal Power. The perspicacity to penetrate the Supermundane spheres is manifested only at the boundary line of sleep. He who can appreciate this sacred moment has already begun to lift the veil.* Urusvati from her early years discerned the transition to the World of Light. *Not visions but awareness is important. Not what is compelled by training but what results from uncontrived revelation is valuable. The approaching time must put at the disposal of every sensitive spirit the tripod of Pythia. A kind of democratization of the features of aristocracy. But everyone inescapably bears in his bosom scales impossible to cheat. Each one measures out immediately what is deserved. This conforms with the New Era and easily reaches people's psychology. Understanding the flow of people's thought, it is easy to foresee the consequences.*

...The recompensing for bad and good actions must be accelerated. The primary concern of religion should be to provide a practical solution to life's problems. The heavenly reward is too remote; the return should be brought within the earthly span. People can now understand as universally accessible the miracle of the renewal of possibilities. Hence, either the hand of the Invisible Friend or a Sharp Sword. And, remembering the advantage of immediate reward, people will find a new path to the Temple. There is no need to implore Divinity. One should bring to oneself the best deed.

You saw flowers and instruments of the Laboratory of the Brotherhood. Fragments of Our life envelope the nerves, as threads of a cloth, and help one become accustomed to vibrations of Our Abode. You saw Our Instruments, and their image conveys a part of the aura of Our experiments. Rilm-Aer, blowing from the mountains, brings knowledge of the black stone.... I will figure out how to delicately whisper in your ear.... Direct your thought to Our Abode.

Part Two

I feel that all of you have to take care of your health, and We will take care of the rest. There is one earthly organ that does not lend itself to healing by spiritual means. It can be treated by rest and with plenty of prana. If potions can cure, is it possible that the sun is not better? As regards the heart, all medications are definitely harmful, and only a direct bridge to the sun cures the heart that has accommodated so much. You will all come to the Festival. Slander can never reduce the size of the aura as shown. (On a film my portrait came out surrounded by a circle of light.)

My Ray penetrated the spirit of all of you. Hence Urusvati feels as if her organism was shaken. Urusvati is like a wound-up clock. So much is accumulating at this time. All is astonishing; therefore, I ask that all of you take care of your health. If tired, take a rest. Let your thoughts wander without strain. If thinking, think only about directing a current in the atmosphere of your home in this way: success, success, success—thus send your thoughts. Your thought will acquire a special power imperceptible to you. (There was pain in the pit of my stomach.) It is the center of the nerves of the solar plexus; when S. touches, it feels like a current flowing. Lie down immediately; you may put your hands into hot water.

(It was said about the Stone): "It contains a fragment of the Great Breath—a fragment of Orion's soul. I revealed the meaning of the Stone. I indicated the Treasure of the Great Spirit. Urusvati, it is necessary to link the Stone to your essence. The Stone, being near you, will assimilate your rhythm and, via the constellation of Orion, will reinforce the link in a way that is destined. Know, all of you, that the Stone was sent to Napoleon. The Stone was taken back when he departed from the path of unification by leaving his wife. Urusvati, I truly say that if you will express your feelings in a direct manner, you will pronounce the best prophecies—without reasoning, but by grasp of spirit. Prophets never could give a reason for what they were saying; they just knew, without a mirror or a Voice. A fragment of Orion accompanies you as a guiding star. So write down today that you can prophesy, much more than it may seem to you. One should never belittle a gift. It grows naturally, but one needs to remind oneself about it. Keep firmly in your mind how you used to know the events as if you knew the happenings of life. Beyond the worlds, this can be said:

The greatness of Cosmos precludes scrutiny; it overwhelms and exalts. The path to spiritual knowledge is through spiritual knowledge itself. Pay attention to the silver thread that connects one's spirit to the spirit of the Guide and extends its silvery manifestation up to the Ruler of the Planet. There results a network of conduits from the Supreme Spirit. The highest Individualization does not fear union, and the gifts of revelation are sent along the silver thread up to the highest spheres. Similarly, at the birth of a spirit a lofty Spirit sends him his conduit. Remember, every kind of occurrence is possible in the world of spirit. New possibilities are molded not by an invented formula but by an indescribable power of spirit. It is both difficult and wondrous! (I was not allowed to write down a talk on Neophytes and Hierophants.)

I rejoice at your prophetic possibilities, for only through them can the best evolution in the future be secured. Knowledge of the past without foresight does not lead onward. Only the path of a great Teacher is left to Urusvati. Orators and singers are not fit for our evolution, for they appeal to crowds. Now, however, it has been decided to conduct all actions and bypass the crowds. Even My Friend, the Teacher K. H., supported action by a relatively small group.[2-1] Urusvati has heard His Voice indicating the success of experiments involving only a few people. Note this number, for this decision is important. I share with you all important decisions. Even He Who loved mass actions has joined the ranks of adherents of small groups. Even My Friend has acknowledged that the experiments with crowds failed. A change of psychology in the World will follow. Acceptance of democracy should be furthered by those few entrusted people scattered throughout the world. You were right not to write down the end of the talk (on Hierophants and Neophytes).

I will relate to you the story of a Courageous Spirit. An Old Spirit decided to bring three gifts to the people. The first one, the union and purification of religions; the second one, the glory of the Feminine

Principle; the third one, the arming of man with the power of air. "How will You proceed?" asked Buddha. "Boldly," answered the Spirit. The Spirit proceeds on the waves; we discern how he strives to attain power. The door will open soon, but a poison severs the thread. And then another life is given for knowledge, but the gathered signs are stolen by an evil priest and are not understood. But the signs are preserved in their essence and will burst into radiance when their term approaches. So where is the union of religions? One–two–three! I see bold attempts. The last priestess guards the tomb of religion till the resurrection. Where is the glorifying of the Mother of the World? One–two! I see a wise sacrifice. The bold Spirit did provide for the three gifts. Christ spoke, "Let the fires of all three offerings be kindled at the same hour." Not in anguish, but in the joy of the completion of the courageous path. Not in a royal way, but through a traveler's bag will royal gifts emerge. Silence will be a guardian, and the lightning, a messenger. So the dawn will lift the veil for a few only, and the magnet of the spirit will draw the human heart. Ancient spirit, you will reach it soon! I tell you, Urusvati, that even before the departure you will receive my letter speaking about the affirmation of the path. (What signs were stolen by the evil priest?) A formula of universal energy contained within an ancient image from the time of Solomon. (In response to my remark on the insignificance of my previous incarnation.) Rokotova's task was not a small one: providing a due place for woman, instead of freedom for husbands.[2-2] She brought to the Mother of the World the problem of the peasants' condition; she worked on the destiny of woman. Let us judge how you will achieve the attainment. Prepare your questions. I am ready to answer them in detail.

The purification of religions predicates a new direct relation with the spiritual World. Christ, Buddha, and their closest co-workers did not use magic formulas but acted and created in full merging with the spirit. Therefore, in the new evolution the former artificial methods must be abandoned. Cause and effect. The mechanics of yogism are no longer suitable for the regeneration of the World. A Teacher who sits under a tree and forbids does not conform to the need.

Whence does one derive strength and wisdom? In union with the Great Spirit, recognizing cause and motive, we build an im-

mediate consequence. We evoke those who earlier did set out on the great path of personal realization and responsibility. And our appeals, through thousands of raised hands, reach Them. There is no need to implore, no need of terror, but unity moves mountains. Desiring the good, we accept the heritage of the great Carriers of good. We leave our spiritual vessel open for reception of beneficences. Nothing of evil will touch us, for we desire only that good which has been affirmed by the spirit. And carefully shall we deliver the web of writings into the treasury, because we are going to the Sources.

To be prepared, to be renouncing, to be abused, to be calumniated, to be joyful, to be jubilant, to be silent, to be the bringing and the bestowing one, and to be in this life taught by the light of the sun, is to be as We wish to see you; and as such We are dispatching you. Thus has your spirit accepted the mission.

Not with a royal domain, not out of the alchemist's cellar, not with conjurations of magic, but in the midst of life do we go and come to You, our Elder Brothers and Sisters, to receive the treasures preserved by You, accumulated by us, because we go into the simple Temple of the Supreme Spirit. Thus we shall return to You, because thus do You wish to see us; and the load imposed by You we shall safeguard as the Chalice of Immortality.

I foresee pure thoughts on Urusvati's lips. The spirit of the Stone will not sleep for long. Morya knows the habits of the Stone. The spirit of the Stone, like a wave, flows in and again ebbs, returning to its Source. It is impossible to deflect it, except in the case of a fortunate course of celestial bodies. It is the case of a world magnet. After the Stone becomes dormant, it may awaken only at its destined time. A Ray from My Star will come in time. The conjunction of celestial bodies necessary for the Ray will bring about a needed combination of earthly events, making a closed circle, the Stone being a focus of the vortex. The relationship remains effective until the Star leaves its orbit.

When We were building the Temple of the Sun in Atlantis, enemy ships tried to prevent the completion of construction. Then We stood by the sea and repeated, "O Sun, do not allow it!" And a flow turned the ships back. Similarly, in the desert when We were laying the foundations of the Temple, fainthearted ones tried to escape the intense heat, so We appealed to the stars, "O stars, quench our thirst!" And the next day brought floods of rain.

The same happened when the treasure of Israel was in the making and traitors tried to provoke a popular uprising. We repeated, "O Stone, shelter us!" And a stone dome covered the rabble-rousers.

In the same way, when novices rushed at superior enemy forces, We asked repeatedly, "Do not allow, O Holy Spirit!" And an Invisible Shield concealed the warriors.

Now about the Visions. You have already seen My garden. After the wise flowers, you were given the best remedy—cedar resin. Learn to take a simpler approach to your work. The main thing now is rest. You ignore rest. If you feel the need to sit in silence, do not resist. To receive messages from Us is the greater work. Remember, nothing happens without a reason—you repeated My Words. Why do you send a few arrows? Do what you wish, for the spirit knows better. I repeated frequently about a sword. You will feel great relief if you do what your spirit suggests. I charge you with learning how to manifest the spirit-knowledge.

Just as you felt loneliness before, so now you must feel the spirit-knowledge. There is a bidding to each new step. Permit your spirit its desires. Exercise caution, testing yourself against your spiritual consciousness. Ask yourself, "How does the spirit know?" The main thing is to transmit it to the spirit and then manifest it in life. *The level of the spirit is important. Approaching this level, it seems that the spirit is quite remote. But this is only apparently so; on the contrary, the spirit knocks powerfully. It is important to act directly, to grasp the spirit-knowledge. As one wishes, so should one act. One had better apply it to details than risk using it in a massive way.*

Let us compare now what the spirit knows and what the will commands. The spirit-knowledge blossoms, manifesting protection and illumining the fundamentals. The command of the will is directed to the auras of others, and conquers and annexes. The command is denoted by the symbol of a sword and arrow. The symbol of the spirit-knowledge is a flower. The command can be communicated to the disciple from outside by a swift sending. Whereas, the spirit-knowledge blossoms from within and cannot be evoked. Like a flower, the knowledge blooms in its destined hour. How, then, may one assist the flower? Place it in a quiet spot, give it sunlight, and forbid anyone to touch or pluck its leaves. The symbol of white and blue flowers reminds one of an approaching hour.

Why is it important for Urusvati to grow in spirit-knowledge? She deviated several times by moving toward earthly knowledge. Without spirit-knowledge, she unwittingly passed the fruits of knowledge to an enemy. *Without spirit-knowledge one cannot raise to the heights the knowledge predestined for humanity.* While having incarnated this time, her spirit did not want to forget the spirit-knowledge. And that gift had already been manifested in her early years. Every spirit having certain right traits can evoke them before incarnation. Hence, in order to bring experiential knowledge to the people, allow at least a short time for the blossoming of spirit-knowledge. Predestined knowledge will be easier to grasp if some time is allowed for the blossoming of the spirit.

You showed today an understanding of stars. It is necessary to be careful.... We will arrange everything, but now I ask for at least physical rest. The pressure is great when the organism is changing. Trust Us—We are doing Our best.

Today you began to see something important: a shrine into which we put all Our unfinished manuscripts. Gradually there will be gathered together a whole inventory of the items used in Our Abode. All things, seen even remotely, will help you to approach the aura of Our Home. Additions to [the inventory] may be made gradually, but it would be better to record many of the details so as to better remember them. Little by little We reveal the numerous details that are needed by you and instructive to many others.

Let's assume that there is no end. Why should one return to diapers if one can continue living in the two Worlds? Everyone of the White Brotherhood can change Their appearance at will, as needed for the tasks undertaken by Them. It is easier to continue on one's path than to wait till the next battle. The time of My Coming will require not babies but friends with tried and tested spirits. I look at you from within every flower and want to help. A strong wish to return to Us as soon as possible after short but intense work is quite feasible. I think a life with Us can fulfill all the aspirations of the spirit toward knowledge. So begin to stack in a box all the seemingly small things. We do not send foolish trifles. You saw a cover for the shrine, saturated with an aura, which would preserve the flow of thoughts that had begun. You may ask about all the points that are unclear.

The Altai Sisters will bring salutations and help from the throne of the Mother of the World.[2-3] We rejoice at the decision to gather the Sisters together. When the dream is implemented, a new enveloping layer will grow. May it begin to grow with the first rays of the Stone. Tomorrow the day may be spent in quiet. It is good to go tomorrow for flowers, keeping in mind the Instructions regarding colors. Let the house dog bark when great works are being accomplished. Urusvati can look calmly at the wonderful future. During the year three works were accomplished, and in the last day a beautiful new layer was ignited. My own, do not forget: a word, as a torch, gives body to a thought. The thought was expressed fully, exactly as it should be implemented. It is one of your tasks that you direct from afar. Two gatherings on the 24th were successful, manifesting a shield of one work and the birth of the new layer of another one. *The growth of the works is similar to that of lilies. Near a garden wall one white sister has hidden herself. She has no companions, but the lily stems already show signs of the emergence of new ones.*

Urusvati, ancient is your name, and the early life of your spirit manifested twice as flowers. *Incarnation as a flower happens seldom. Some strive to the more massive forms of trees; the charm of flowers is not always accessible, and one may not easily turn twice to them. There is no forbiddance against circumventing one of the animal incarnations by way of the plants. I would not say that the consciousness of many insects is superior to the consciousness of beautiful flowers. It is wise to live through certain incarnations by sojourn as a flower: "You may hasten, but I will wait under a beautiful dome, and I will still be ahead of you."*(What kinds of flowers was I?) A lily and a rose. *Thus, a path of beauty shortens the road.* The hand, bringing the tablets of the future nearer to you, leads you along a trustworthy road.

Why do you follow Them? It is easy and useful to proceed with Them. It was impossible to tell this five years ago. But now this pillar has been established. *Swift as the flight of the falcon; unexpected as the transformation of Jonah; inexhaustible as the flame! Only by renunciation, in spirit and upon Earth, do you attain the manifestation of Light and Truth. Inexhaustible is this Source! On Earth, amidst threats, deprived of help and seemingly abased, they give, offer, endow, and follow the star. And, therefore, We rejoice on the anniversary night. And not only do they proceed to illumine the aura, but they go decisively, unrestrainedly. Therefore We rejoice!*

How should the Altai sisters be referred to by the people? "Into our village one of our own came." Let them be as one to the people.

My Hands held a Chalice with a list of future works (a vision)…. *Let us begin with labor and end with a day of rest. Let us determine what to do. To act. In this eternal action is Our holiday. But you, following Our example, should act without distress.* We do not like cut flowers. Let them grow, and, if they manage to blossom, reflecting God, the gardener will take them for the enjoyment of others. *Resolve to act in calmness, bearing in mind that Our spring flows through you incessantly. And when you ask yourself, Where are They Who made promises? We are standing behind you; and We rejoice, measuring the growth of the flowering of your aura. We rejoice because this is Our Garden!* And We see from here how blue and lilac petals unfold. *Beyond the bounds of what can be seen or known, the Light unites the hearts.*

Part Three

Many seek to approach you, but you should stay seated, as if under an umbrella, and deal with everything as your spirit suggests, from a speck of dust to a mountain.... There is no more wonderful fairy tale on Earth than the one now around you. Our Sisters admire the growth of the spiritual tree. Catherine is with Us in spirit, as are Ursula, Oriole, Teresa, and Mary Magdalene.[3-1] Mary chose the life of an obscure nun in the 13th century. She copied and rescued many useful Teachings. All workers of unity and peace join Us. Sail in peace; one billow has already passed.

Christ showed Catherine how the high spirit descended into Mary for the sake of rescuing the Teachings.

Here the Blessed One transmits: "All is for all and forever. Note the four laws: The Law of Containment; The Law of Fearlessness; The Law of Nearness; The Law of Righteousness." Later We will consider their meaning.

Now let us read from Our book where the course of events is not distorted: "When the time came for departing, the Blessed One said to His Wife, 'Let us go.' And thrice he said, 'Through the darkness of night, in the midday heat and in the ray of dawn.' But at night the tigers roared and in the heat the snakes crawled forth and toward morning the monkeys came in hordes. 'I am still afraid now,' said the wife. 'This is also for the good,' said the Blessed One. 'Without a call, but by your own steps will you be bearer of the Teaching.' And the elephant trumpeted seven times, proclaiming the date of the next meeting."[3-2] Now, something else: "Well I praise thee, Ananda. Because without a call walks She who affirms." Do not avoid the predestined, no matter how many obstacles are put before you. "And the Blessed One perceived in the Heaven upon a veil the destiny of the Light of the Mother of the World." [3-3] Now you can see how the meaning of the Teaching was distorted. Such was its destiny, however. If someone were to decide to paint a picture of the Blessed One, it would be better to show Him under the tree where He saw the white veil of the Mother of the World. Now the time has come to lift that veil, for a woman is supposed to bring the power of the World. Armed with four laws, carrying the white veil on her arm and guarding the sword, she will enter the Temple that is marked by a date not of human designation.

It is not necessary to explain the Laws of Fearlessness and Righteousness, and it is easy to understand the Law of Containment, but the Law of Nearness must be elucidated. At the approach of dates ordained, a specially saturated atmosphere gathers, as if clouds of smoke were overcasting Heaven and Earth. That which had been clear begins to crumble, and, as if in a whirlwind, falls to pieces. Even physically this period is difficult, but during this period certain dates are being pronounced which stand as milestones on the road. However, knowing that the predestined people belong indefeasibly to the ordained dates, We must calmly pass through this period, like one becoming acclimated to new gases. Remember that during this period not only the Teacher but the whole Brotherhood is watching, and if individual voices are heard you need not be astonished. It is good to have flowers near during this period. The flowers are most important.... It is right that you have remembered valerian. You may take it in the evening and in the morning.

Now the events are becoming mixed up; the great disorder of currents influences many things.

I believe certain dates may come sooner. Preparations may be made for departure. My breath is around your place. Now, how to make preparations. Make arrrangements for a quiet summer. Strengthen your health through sleep. Receive the Teaching without letting yourself become tired. Take walks and surround yourself with flowers. I urge you to endure attacks courageously.... The cloud is broken, but the dust is still in the air. Let us proceed further. The first condition of Our Brotherhood is to not regret the past and to master the future. One morning you will awaken: The Teacher, the Teacher, the Teacher has arrived. We know the blessed Plan. The spirit is yours. By the time they depart, We will have strengthened your ability to hear. My own, take enough time for rest. Do not be afraid to take an hour from the play of time. It is necessary to leave this kind of knowledge at the door. People come to Us with a stock of all previous accumulations, which are ignited at the threshold. Every priestess has brought in much. Do not forget about Iskander Khanum.[3-4] Nothing has been written about the land-owning lady of Ryazan, but her achievements were significant.[3-5] Do not forget that in Russia there were the best connections with the East and the accumulation of both forms of magic. The best people absorbed the ways of the East and were making preparations for the predestined path. And it is no mere chance that the Decembrists came to Siberia.[3-6] Vorontsov's dagger was in the East.[3-7] Try to get it.

In the ancient books of magic can be found the term, Illuminacio Regale, which means the Royal Illumination. It is such an important principle that Hermes ends his treatise with the words "Blessed are Those Who have chosen the path of Illumination." The symbol of the anointing of kings has the same basis. Absolutely all initiates into the Power of the Mysteries agree in the assertion that the Highest Harmony is in the manifestations of the Power of Illumination. Therefore, the king is symbolically the anointed one, because without estranging himself from the earthly he expresses the will of Heaven. Above the conventional formulae that are congealed in the crust of prejudices there is knowledge, diffused, as it were, in the air. Erect a lightning-rod and attract the heavenly arrow. For one it is dangerous, but for another it is the best weapon. And the whole future is based upon attainment of Illumination. A most difficult telephone will be in the hands of man.

Its Wire is already in your hands, Urusvati! Think about it—the Wire connecting with Our Home! Number seven, according to the number of years. The wires may at first be tangled, for the tension is great, and one must use every available fragment. But the experiment is so important that one should apply all patience—it is nothing other than Illuminacio Regale of the ancient ones! And it can be achieved in its perfection only through experience and after a sufficient period of time. A connection of low voltage may be achieved easily, but the Higher one must be achieved gradually. You understand that access to Our Wire can only be granted with discretion. (Shall I exercise it also during the daytime?) Yes! But let us agree—without tiring yourself.

March 29

(What does it mean,"Terpignor's horse"?) In the Middle Ages, the miracle of the horse, when Konrad was unable to catch the one who was fleeing to the monastery.

(What is the meaning of the appearance of a male figure in strange garb who said to me "Tripitaka"?) This was Our disciple who reminded you to translate everything about Maitreya. This is the second time you have seen him; he has greeted you before. (On the road to Darjeeling)

Afterwards, Urusvati, as well as the entire White Brotherhood, will need to begin to deal with the new planets. A completed round will not come again. Members of the White Brotherhood, as They are, will come to the aid of the races. There is no need to be reborn for one who is willing to take part in eternal, constant labor. Urusvati will have an opportunity to participate in the most formidable attacks. Now gather together all the details of Our everyday life. Keep in mind that Voices of those under other rays arrive distorted. The ray is a kind of resonator. The voice transmitted under one's own color sounds clearly. But use of someone else's resonator is impossible without causing some kind of dissonance. (Rakoczi's voice) Fragments of Our talk cover various fields. I will make corrections if necessary. He wants there to be no assault upon your heart; he wants you to proceed on the hard-won path. Sister Oriola will never become accustomed to human turmoil. It is possible to translate into different languages; it is something like a multiplication device. The spirit may reflect thoughts as it likes. We may not like some languages, but we may still use them. Everything goes successfully. It is necessary to exercise at different times.

April 1

You need to know this news. Urusvati is conducting a tremendously important experiment. It is a new step—to hand the Wire of the Brotherhood to someone who lives in the midst of ordinary life. The guidance of one Teacher is one thing, but confiding the Life of the Brotherhood is quite a different thing. The Wire opens a door to the Life of the Brotherhood. Our plain and hard-working Life may be disclosed only to one who can find the power of true fearlessness.

This kind of experiment is being conducted by Us for the first time. To assimilate what you hear is difficult. It is as if you were in the editorial office of a major newspaper; so handle it with care and save your forces. Do not tell children about it, as it is a sort of State secret. Details are always simple, but they may be heard only under the Ray. Gather together a collection of revealed fragments. Know that the experiment is important before you come to Us, for afterwards it will become routine. It is important to Us. But handing out the Wire in life is a new achievement for humanity.

You volunteered to take part in a most dangerous experiment that is very important to humanity, and it is a great responsibility for a new participant. In it, Higher Forces are brought down to Earth, and a new channel of Good is established. Again the analogy of an editorial office is relevant. One may receive news from the editor, but it is more important to be present when the events are occurring. That Cosmic knowledge available from Us will be given for your use.

You do not realize that you have initiated the greatest achievement of the World! I grieve though, because instead of the joy of hearing about having confidence in the Brotherhood, there is a dispute. (It seemed to me that I did not hear well enough.) If you heard about the eve of a great war, you would not believe it. Shall we return to the very first stage of symbols? I Myself opened the Wire; would I Myself obstruct the new achievement?! (I wanted to hear more of the Lord's Voice.) You know My voice and ought to know that the present experiment is under My Ray. In the future, having returned from the area of planets beyond Uranus, you will say, "I went just outside the gates." But now let Me entrust you with the Great experiment of contacting the Central Wire of the Brotherhood. The main feature of the experiment: it is to be conducted in the midst of life. Quietude is a necessary condition, as unusual currents may fatigue the body. Meals should not be excessive. The experiment is distinguished by living an ordinary life. Do not allow petty irritation to occur. When you reread past Conversations they will become clear. Only an experiment confirmed by life is Light. Just do not let yourself become tired.

More about the experiment: It is conducive to sharpening new centers. It comes close to the chaos of first sensations. *Not in jest are*

*the planets beyond Uranus mentioned. Often the spirit struck by
the cosmic whirl cannot acclimate itself and make observations,
but this is only a question of time and technique. Our prolonged
experiments will prepare for a great deal, as also for lengthy labor. Many of Our experiments require centuries.*

Not without reason did I present the cradle of growing achievements. Ideas for experiments are deposited in this storehouse, and
though all time is filled, there is an awareness that nothing has been
accomplished. *So if you feel the endlessness of labor, you know
one more of Our feelings—all time is filled. Sound and flowers
become a necessity for further flights. The sounds of the life of
the spheres and the vital emanations of flowers truly enter into
the recipe for Amrita.*

Just bring forward the Chalice of experiences without overloading
the nerves. Allow yourselves quietude as a safeguard. Indignation of
the spirit against those who obstruct is right, for it is an expenditure of
energy for the sake of humanity. Many approached this kind of experiment, but the conditions were not fitting. Now Aurobindo Ghose
was closer than others, but nevertheless he lacked simplicity in life,
and then withdrew from life.

*It is of great value to approach the highest ways without being
a medium and without renouncing the earthly life. Where there is
argument, where there is fear, where there is the germ of prejudice, there it is difficult for the white flowers. Simply, simply, simply, applying love, courage and readiness. This is no time for in-
flated bubbles; out of place is conceit, especially when compared
with Christ's washing of the fishermen's feet. In simplicity of life,
in realization of the dignity of service to the New World, love for
the worthy opens the gates.*

Another detail of the experiment: if you do not hear anything, do
not worry; but concerning the Wire write down: "Nothing was heard."
A silent Meeting will be held, when the will of the Gathering is directed at counteracting the evil. So far everything is going very well.
But it is better to miss something rather than get fatigued. First of all,
about the number seven; in seven years humanity will feel the outcome
of the experiment.

April 2

It was not My voice. We know the essence. Just guard your health; everything else is filled with light. The spirit knew when it spoke about the beginning of the experiment. The Direction about the experiment has been issued by Chr[ist]; He knows the best solution. A place is ready. (In the Wh. Br.)[3-8]

Part Four

April 3

The rainbow is the best sign; each hint of a rainbow indicates the development of the third eye. Now back to the experiment. (In response to my remark that I fear having made errors in the records.) I will have enough time to make corrections. So far all is well. Your sensitivity is to be praised if you noticed the Ray of the Brotherhood. A touch of the Ray is a live touch. Put all these details in the book *The Inner Life of the Brotherhood.* This is a requirement for every experience. (What if I make mistakes?) Then I will correct them. Do not forget to record any feelings in your brain and spine. Do not miss the effect of noise. Indicate what kind is more painful. Notice accompanying waves of light and sound. The rainbow is characteristic. Discerning the voices is not important now. It will come gradually. (I constantly see something like a rainbow circle.) This is the aura of the Ray of the Brotherhood. Without the former, one cannot see the latter. The date may be vaguely set at 1928. After that, three years with Us. We will not diminish your opportunities even for a single hour. Make allowances for 1927, 1928, and 1929. Consider that 1927 will be a rather difficult year in a physical respect, as always is the case with the new ones who come in their physical bodies, but 1928, 1929, and the first half of 1930 will be a celebration. The experiment will make many things easier. Upon entering the atmosphere of the Brotherhood, one will be able to avoid suffocation. If the Ray of the Brotherhood seems to be dense, then one can imagine the heaviness of the entire atmosphere. We will carefully prepare for it. Therefore, resting the heart is necessary. Do not let yourself become tired, for there will be many remarkable things happening during that time.

April 4

You should have paid attention to some sentences that sounded ordinary or even childish; it is a very characteristic detail. *Just as We watch over you, so do We watch the development. We watch the development of children throughout the world from the cradle on, weighing their best thoughts. Of course, the spirit does not often reach its best development, and the number of deserting ones is great, but We rejoice at a pure thought as at a beautiful garden. Therefore, do not be astonished that the Great Teacher repeats simple sentences, because by fixing these thoughts We sometimes provide opportunity for an excellent flower of spirit to become stronger. Therefore, along with great cosmic discoveries and world events, We just as carefully cultivate the flowers of the spirit.* Sometimes Christ Himself repeats simple words because their effects may be great. *Thus diversified is the labor of Our Brotherhood.* That precise phrase was said by the Teacher Christ. It was said originally by a little girl to her sick father. But her wish was better than those of some adults, so Christ affirmed the will in space. I tell this to explain why there are various strata. A ray that is destroying cities is as colorful as a ray that brings help to a little heart. And how many of your thoughts are repeated by Us with delight. Among Our records of thoughts there are also your thoughts—strong and shining. (This is in response to my question, "Are there thoughts that cannot be read?") I will explain everything: *There is thought which leads inwardly, leaving the surface of the spirit unruffled, and there is also thought which flies into space as a projectile carrying an explosive charge. A ray accompanies the flying bullet. Every spirit knows when thought flies like a boomerang. It is especially desirable that the thought be tinted by one's own color. But it is only opened centers that do not give color to the thought, leaving it enwrapped in the color of the person; and then true individuality has begun. Instead of the thought's being colored by its contents, the whole sending is permeated by the color of the individuality. Thus is the ray physically formed.*

I consider it important that you heard how a bell rang and a door closed, for complicated sounds are less accessible. So far the recording is going very well. We are surprised by the penetration in spite of the extraneous sounds. These days, your organism is greatly advancing and has learned much. You might be given all the remedies, but they would constrain the experiment by bringing in prejudices and flooding the entire, available field of perception. Let your spirit adjust freely and keep watch as a soldier on guard. This imparts to the Experiment scientific character. The experiment is not for Us or for you, but for the World. Notice when I tell you the names of the Brothers whose voices sound unpleasant now due to improper resonance. If a tower is very tall, the voice may be very shrill. It was Brother Cheloma, Our Brother from Mongolia. If a tower's ceiling is high, the quality of the voice is changed. (Why do I seldom hear M. M.'s voice among the voices?)[4-1] I am often in solitude, for the sword is close now and the blood again must be averted. Messages from the North are not good. Do not let yourself become tired, for there is much ahead.

April 5

Think about it: never before has it been possible to initiate such a valuable experiment, and also now to engage in conversations, confident that you are free of prejudice. There were never before such faithful records of the Brotherhood. It was remarkable for you to hear Sister Oriole playing the lute, and to endure the laboratory ray, to see the view of the door, and to receive the reminder of the image of atoms—all that during the fifth night and without going beyond physical consciousness. The next stages to come will be the most valuable. It is a very refined achievement to discern the crackling of rays refracting in the places where the aura accumulates and to grasp an accompanying symbol without any mediumistic activities. Remember this before your final departure for Our Abode: A young girl named Helena [Elena] will come to you to join the sisters. You shall ask her, "Were you Nellie, the little girl who loved her father so much?" and reveal to her the day when Christ blessed her. You will also rejoice; your garden has its fair share. And how many fragments will fit into a harmonious necklace! Do not let yourself become tired; this is important. Being awakened is not bad, but afterwards do not burden yourself with excessive thoughts, for the centers are exposed and the new epidermis has not grown yet. Your sensitivity is high. The task is to grow the valuable matter rather than burn it. Keep away from the experiment all unrelated thinking, and also all that is fatiguing. (In response to my remark that walking makes me tired.) It is true: do not agitate the open vessel. Do what your spirit wishes, for peace and the right condition of the spirit are most valuable for the experiment. You feel the heaviness of the ray from the Laboratory. (But why does M. K. H.'s voice, even raised, not bring any painful shocks to me?)[4-2] Because the room is a small one. We await shockless application of the ray, but only time will show what is best. You should not burn or chill your nerves. (In response to my remark that I see no progress in visions or in hearing words, for earlier I saw a formula for atomic energy and heard whole phrases as well. I also saw the functioning of nerves in a cell of the solar plexus.) You saw the cell in yourself. The greatest pressure is exerted by the combinations of the voices of different Teachers. You were accustomed to the two Rays of M. M. and M. K. H. from childhood, but you have not experienced the pressure of all of the Teachers. That is why care is needed. Progress is already evident. But notice the waves surrounding the current, just as you began to do.

I have already said you need rest and must avoid becoming tired. Short periods of rest will lead to better results in the future. Above all, do not rush, otherwise abandoned centers will continue functioning and you may feel pain. Some earthbound centers fight against the rise of their spiritual rivals. One needs to let them quietly become dormant. Get enough sleep; wake up when necessary. Everything goes so fast that you need reserves of strength. You need to avoid insomnia. The Ray of the Brotherhood constantly envelopes and brings vigor. It is better to take a bath in the daytime and valerian in the morning and the evening. It would be better not to develop photographic films; let your children do it. You would hardly believe how carefully We watch after you all to prevent overloads and to guard you.... It would be wise now to go to bed.

April 7

We are so glad to see your joint constructive work and know that the experiment is in trustworthy hands. Your exaggerated reputation as a woman of high society and as a clever man are precisely right. *Indeed, through life one must attain. It is precisely the conventional religiosity that is not needed. The facts of conscious communion with the Abode of Light are needed. Let us say we wish to bring help, so we proceed consciously, without magic, to the practical Source. In this simplicity is contained the entire current secret, as yet so inaccessible to those who walk up to their waists in prejudice. It is difficult for them to understand simplicity, beauty, and fearlessness!* Dear ones, walk like lions with Us in constant work. Urusvati, recollect the picture of Heaven that you saw in your fleeting vision. The top of Heaven was darker than the aura. Do not let yourself become tired; everything pleases Us. At night let yourself fall asleep, but develop in yourself a joyful alertness. This is a special kind of joy; it may be called "possibilities." Just keep your inner windows open. The first stage is to learn to listen and become accustomed to the play of the waves of the ray and their accompanying radiations. The second stage is conversation with Us. Do not overstrain the centers. There were two nights. First you need to familiarize yourself with the Voices. I intentionally do not let My voice predominate in order to allow others to be heard.

April 8

Do not be surprised, for the Ray touches upon the ray of the centers, and a high tension ensues. The Ray was known for a long time, but there was neither time nor opportunity to make use of it. Except for the one in the spine, all centers below the waist are inimical to the experiment. It should be subordinated to the Solar Plexus. There was no damage, but do not overstrain the strings. Look not at today, but to the future. A diver should preserve his supply of oxygen. Look only toward the future, for judging by the number of sensations noticed, this is an experiment of high importance. As regards diversity, the records cover a very wide circle of Our pursuits, and here My satisfaction is beyond expectation. I repeat again: just do not let yourself become tired; do not forget how to sleep.... Urusvati may take the valerian medicine—it is very good. (Who is participating in the experiment?) Many participate, for the whole of the Brotherhood is interested in the experiment. (In response to my remark that it is hard for me to be the object of observation of so many Individuals. Can it really be true that all of Them watch me?) Where My Ray allows, it also guards. (Whose cough did I hear last night?) Vaughan's. He burned Himself with the Ray.

April 9

Urusvati may calmly accept everything. *Inasmuch as self-confidence in action is blessed, so is self-conceit ruinous. Self-conceit is hostile to simplicity. Even great minds are subject to this malady and must return an additional time to labor until they eradicate this husk.* No member of the Brotherhood suffers from this. *One of the impeding conditions is lack of simplicity. One can wear bast shoes and still not be simple. In simplicity one can build the greatest Temple. Simplicity, beauty, and fearlessness—Christ and Buddha spoke of nothing more. And it is a blessing if the spirit vibrates to these Teachings.* (It was said in response to my remark that those three Teachings are most dear to me. One day Lama M. brought in an image of Buddha and told me he had a dream: a Tara came to him and ordered him to take to a lady living in Potang the image of Buddha, which was standing on an altar in his room. Great was my joy, for I could not obtain such a large image of Buddha.) Do not distrust the lama, for he was sent by Sister Oriole at Christ's order, so that a new flame of Buddha could be kindled near Christ. The lama is right, for Our Eastern Brothers call the Sisters *Taras.* They carry the Principle of Motherhood. In general, considering the symbolism of the East, one can find details pertaining to Shamo and Gobi, even though there are more than enough that are worthless or trivial. There are always those who will try to spoil everything.

Do not neglect your sleep; it is better to miss than to overstrain the centers. The Ray became a bridge. It is now to be assimilated in everyday life. *An apparatus is a first step. The true conquest will be achieved when the spirit has replaced all apparatuses.* It will become habitual for you and then through you, for a hundred people. *For man to be fully equipped without a single machine—Is that not a conquest!* (In response to my question, "It seemed to me that last night I heard cracking sounds above myself. Is this true?") The rays crossed. It was a struggle of the rays of the body and the spirit. It is a common phenomenon, but it is very good that you have already noticed it. (I heard also a strange, squeaking sound, when I was listening to incoming words.) A gardener was moving flowers. (Why did the voices seem muffled?) They came from an underground chamber; it is also a remarkable achievement (Why do I not hear long messages?) Listening to a long message, you would be distracted from the various voices and perceptions, and the new experiment of cosmic proportions would turn into personal instruction. (Does it make sense to write down formulas of cosmic formations if they cannot be applied to the earthly plane? Which position is better for listening?) Not lying on your back, for you now need to avoid over-burdening the spine. (When will I clearly see M. M.?) When the situation is better, I will knock, for I am always near you. It would be a pity if My Rays were to interfere with the experiment. (Is it not possible to alternate the Rays of M. M. and the Rays of the Brotherhood?) Then we would shatter. (I do not understand.) Again it is simple—one may fill a glass only to the brim. (I understand that it may be dangerous to me, but why for Others?) There are many other reasons. It is easy to undermine the Great Date, considering all the particulars that have been gathered during the millennia. After a millennium the thread of a plan is outlined. A yarn is perfect when its threads are appropriate. It will be better for us to continue tomorrow.

April 10

I saw a Tara who loves you very much. Her name is Bh. Po. Our mapmaker in China is preparing a path for you, just as Ov. is doing in Japan.

Many watch you with dedicated love. Ask yourselves—has there ever been a person who approached you with friendliness without being uplifted? *For the reason that Our pupils bear within themselves the microcosm of the Brotherhood, there is not an indifferent attitude towards them. In their mode of life the same details as of Our Life are gradually revealed. There is endless labor; absence of any sense of finiteness, even of knowledge; loneliness and the absence of a home on Earth; the understanding of joy, in the sense of realization of possibilities—for the best arrows so seldom reach their mark. And when We see the hearts of people who strive toward one and the same garden, how could We not manifest joy? But courage in the face of endless labor is especially important. It is true that from the realization of the infinite possibilities of the human apparatus one feels relief.* (In my vision

I was shown a sample prepared for examination under a microscope—a solar plexus nerve on a thin glass plate colored in rose and green.) *The serpent of the solar plexus helps to overcome the confusion of the centers; that is why the serpent was a regal symbol.* I showed the microscopic sample of a solar plexus nerve. *When the coils of the serpent begin to curl, the organism becomes especially sensitive. Flowers transmit their vital emanation through the fibres of the tissues of the white blood corpuscles, which defend the citadel of the serpent. In nature, serpents love flowers; similarly, the serpent of the solar plexus is nourished by them. Pigs also trample upon flowers, but without any effect on themselves. Therefore, without conscious consumption of the vital emanation one can miss the best remedies. Hence the desire to see flowers unplucked.*

Your wish to let flowers breathe comes from a sensitive source. Your spirits already manifest many qualities that were previously hidden. Your experiment is difficult, and what has been achieved is remarkable. Nay, the coordination of centers is much better. Your new acquaintance is startled by the results. One may be given a vision, but to pass into the earthly consciousness details of the complicated Life of the Brotherhood is something unheard of. Visions from Us plus your attempts to approach Our Life from Earth—thus does one bring the Higher Planes nearer. Think about the difference between [efforts made] from here and from there. Instead of [ascending] to Heaven and detaching from Earth, it is better to attract the Higher Forces down to Earth; and it is this opportunity that will bring in a new life. You are charged with passing on this opportunity to the Altai Sisters. Let this Fire-Blossom bloom in Altai, but keep it in the utmost secrecy.

Part Five

April 11

The result was striking; even a disturbance of the spirit and a room filled with denials could not interfere. The Ray was knocking, for one needs to let prana freely in, especially after irritation. (Strokes and crashing sounds at the window) You have heard about the condition of Tib[et]—under siege. You saw our underground chambers and can understand how difficult it is to catch the sound of a voice. Now absolutely quietly accumulate details of the experiment. (I heard a crystal sound.) *The refraction of rays yields sounds that enter into the symphony of the music of the spheres. One may picture their crystalline quality of subtleness coupled with the power of the whirlwind. There is a center in the brain that is called the bell. Like a resonator it gathers the symphony of the world, and it can transform the deepest silence into a thundering chord. It is said: "He who hath ears, let him hear." Similarly the spinal chord is called the spear, because if We wish to parry the blows We must strain this channel. Similarly the centers of the shoulders are called wings, because during a self-sacrificing podvig their rays intensify. The legend concerning wings is highly symbolic. Likewise, it was a favorite custom of the ancients to wear a round metal plate upon their breasts. The crown of the head is termed the well, because the waves of outside influences penetrate by this way. Everywhere in antiquity we see the covering of the head connected with the symbol of the priest, whereas now this symbol is replaced by the name of a business firm. So men have become spiritually bald.* Urusvati heard voices from a locked, underground chamber, which was kept separate from the hands of those who were not chosen for an important task. I have sent a vision of L[hasa] from Our mirror, for T[ibet] now constitutes a knot of difficulties.

April 13

As to Purmayan, He also knew Isk[ander] Khanum. He will play a significant roll in the revolution in I[ndia]. He knows the people, for He walked as a sannyasin for a long time. The people did not abandon the religion. Urusvati will gradually learn about all friends. Gradually the entire Assembly of the Brotherhood will be revealed. Urusvati does not need to be irritated by birds, for every sound contributes to the experiment. One could spend seventy-seven nights to learn [all] the names [of members] of the Brotherhood. Everyone will be introduced, but without knowing Their Rays the acquaintance will not be useful for the future. I consider that the experiment is going perfectly well. It is better not to strain. It is possible to attain a better coordination of the centers without avoiding the manifestations of life. After becoming accustomed to [extraneous] sounds and petty interferences, it will be possible to hear at all times. The main thing is not to rush, for every achievement should take root. You have already seen the windows of the Tower and [experienced] the resonance of Its height. Now you will learn about the voices from the underground chambers. Some on high towers, others underground—all utilize the best conditions for Their work.

The most important is not recorded in the book—the varieties of activities and the telegraphic method of work. Let your experience build. You see for yourself that even birds seem to interfere. Realize two fundamentals: First, in order to come to Us, you need to acquaint yourself with the many things that will be accumulating during these years. The second foundation is related to the world, for you will bring to the world constant conscious Communication. It is necessary to have possibilities of communication in different areas. *When many earthly apparatuses will have to be destroyed because of their harmfulness, it will then be time to bring humanity nearer by means of a natural apparatus. The literate in letters can act only upon the surface of the Earth, whereas the literate in spirit can operate beyond all boundaries.* There is some knowledge of the Brotherhood, although less than half has been given out, but now it is important to know Those holding the solution to the present Task. The Brotherhood works in groups, and growth of the Task harmoniously joins together [the members of] the Council for new combinations. Do not yield to the heavy rays of Earth. Leave a particle of Earth to K[onrad]. He has strained the ray of his laboratory knowing that the year 1936 will bring him a personal battle with Me. But in

America his ray has already been assembled. I mean to say that the waves of air carry rays that are unpleasant, though harmless. *The construction of New World combinations does not flow easily. The discarded centers attempt to obstruct the efforts of the new ones.* A new memory is formed. *We shall withstand the storm and downpour. Our mirror is bright.*

April 14

Sharka also is Ours. He has an assignment in Tibet. Our work is divided into three departments. First, search for ways to better the earthly plane. Second, search for ways to pass those results to people. Third, search for ways of communication with the far-off Worlds. The first task requires diligence and patience; the third one, ingenuity and fearlessness; the second one, such selflessness that even the most difficult flight would seem to be a rest.

There was a sensitive feeling that one should gather all cour-age to attain. There are tiresome and dangerous crossings, which may be endured only by trust in the Guide. He must lead you to the goal and not overstrain your strength. If He should overtax your forces, with what would He replace them? I understand this stage of the experiment is boring, and how difficult it is to become enthused over a scattered necklace. This phase is simply to be lived through.

Let them understand that *the lofty mission of women must be manifested by women, for in the Temple of the Mother of the World should abide the woman.* The Temple should be connected with the Temple of the Spirit—it is an easy architectural task.

The manifestation of the Mother of the World will create the unity of women. The task now is to create a spiritually sovereign position for the woman. And the transmission to woman of direct communion with the Higher Forces is necessary as a psychologi-cal factor. It is necessary as a practical impetus. *Of course, through the new religion will come the necessary respect. I feel how strained the current is, how strained the atmosphere,* but do not forget that an attar of roses was considered in ancient times the most soothing remedy. Roses are in bloom now, and their presence is helpful. Flow-ers are the best remedy. I pray that the knots of the world fall to pieces, for the chalice is very strained. The chalice is a name for the center in the middle of the chest. *Soon the pressure of the stars will be altered. Even the approach of the friendly planet brings difficulty, because its new rays are piercing the new strata of the atmosphere. Certainly, they are better than those of the moon, but the new pressure is not yet evenly distributed.*

As to your last vision, it needs to be explained how a tissue covering [the materials of] unfinished experiments is woven. You saw how live cells were added to the tissue in order to impart to it genuine impenetrability. In ancient records one can find the mention of a live tissue. This kind of tissue exists and constitutes important equipment in Our Laboratory. A simple covering constitutes perfect insulation for research objects. Live cells, extracted from plants, yield fibers that continue to live and form a live fatty substance that serves as an excellent preservative. The people of the future Russia will greatly appreciate this resource.

April 15

Lao Tze, Kiumbe, and Shoruman are Our Brothers and members of the Eastern Union. Urusvati may take part calmly in the experiment. If there are going to be gaps in the records, just make a note of it in the morning, as in: heard a lot, but could not write it down. Because the main thing now is to refresh yourself physically. The wild ones are having a celebration now, so it is better not to strain during this week. It is better these days to take only what is easy to pick up.

The main channel of the experiment is happily established. Indeed, it is uniquely difficult to receive in one year all the voices and discriminate between them according to their tasks. Only in childhood is it possible to have easy access to this choir. Only by restoring that kind of integral consciousness is it possible to gain access again. *Just as simply let us approach the Gates of the Great Knowledge. True, We compose complicated and exact formulas, but the method of discovery lies in the spiritual consciousness. Precisely in this consciousness We find the means to make new spheres of the worlds accessible to thinking, thus extending the boundary of thinking. The consciousness thus merges into a bottomless ocean, as it were, embracing new spheres. Thus great and powerful is the creative work of Cosmos.* And you yourself will discover new Worlds. This is so shiningly beautiful! It all depends on the spirit.

April 16

Transmitting a very important message. You have heard today an exclamation—*Urusvati! It is time to say that this is the name We have given to the star which is irresistibly approaching the Earth. Since long ago it has been the symbol of the Mother of the World, and the Era of the Mother of the World must begin at the time of Her star's unprecedented approach to the Earth.*[5-1] Nephrite has already read this prophecy, and, when near death, when she wanted to be present on Earth to witness its coming, she looked at her ring. *The Great Era is beginning, because the spirit understanding is linked with the Mother of the World. Even to those who know the date it is marvelous to behold the physical approach of the pre-destined. The approach of this very great Era is important; it will substantially change life on Earth. A Great Era! I rejoice so much in the Tower, seeing how the new rays are piercing the thickness of the Earth. Even though in the beginning they are hard to bear, yet their emanation brings in new elements, so needed for the impetus.* We want the Icon of the Mother of the World to be finished at this time. It is time to remove dust from the image. Someone is very opposed to seeing it. I am also glad that the experiment went quietly this past night. In this way it is easier to enter the atmosphere. Do not be distressed when the *new rays are reaching the Earth for the first time since its formation.* But write down that *today is the beginning of the feminine awakening. A new wave has reached Earth today, and new hearths have become alight; for the substance of the rays penetrates deeply. It is simply joyous to feel the approach of the New Era.*

April 17

Galileo still calls astronomy "geography." Right now He is busy with a new celestial body, which appeared behind the morning star.[5-2] First, He thought it was a comet and so announced it to Us, but yesterday He realized that there is an entire planetary body speeding behind the planet. It is not clear yet whether it is pushing the Morning Star or is being pulled by it. But it is already clear that we have double rays. The heart area receives them, and, acting along the spinal cord, they produce contractions of lesser occipital centers. The greatest sensitivity occurs when the centers move—the fall of a rose petal may be perceived as a peal of thunder. Therefore, We are so concerned about quietude. Therefore, getting over birds' cries and dogs' barks is a victory. Galileo will give Urusvati excellent instruction in geography. She has already heard His voice. He has already expressed His wish to show practical results, especially the application of planetary rays to organisms. He works in a densified astral body. This is a [method of manifestation] of the Brotherhood. Some Brothers come from Earth, having an opportunity to manifest an astral body; others come from the astral plane, having an opportunity of densification to an almost physical degree. This makes a practical interface between Earth and Heaven.

April 18

Ureitos, an Egyptian Hierophant, the last to know the Mysteries, works with Us. He completely agrees with Urusvati about giving out secrets to those who are deserving of them, even though He was poisoned for it. *The necessity for deceit compels the priests of the old religions to push the people into the abyss of darkness. Yes, one may leave them at the foot of the mountain, as did Moses, but the tablets of the Commandments must be manifested.*

"How perishable everything once seemed!" It is told to both of you. *Our disciples, when on Earth for the last time, experience a feeling of loneliness and estrangement. Only in consciousness does one understand the value of Earth, but nothing compels one to look back if the spirit has already filled its treasure chest.*

I will cease to serve as a Teacher; soon we will be coworkers. I am speaking about Our feelings, for soon you will have to grow accustomed to them. *The chief requisite is modification of the human feeling of joy. And what joy can it be, when one realizes the imperfection of life? But when the spirit faces the greatness of Cosmos, then this joy is replaced by the realization of possibilities. And when I whispered, "Thy joy will depart," I had in mind the transformation of human joy into the cosmically manifested conception as if by entering into a vacuum. The rays of the new life enwrap one better than mosquito netting. And one need not strain oneself toward the Earth; in this, when we are working for the Earth, there is harmony. For outsiders, this seems sheer nonsense, but you understand how one can grasp and develop each pure earthly thought beyond its contemporary import.* Not abstract good, but the knowledge of the laws forces Us to say those simple words that so burden you, but which must be written down. *For when one has traced the thread from Christ to the blade of grass, then only has the scope of the work been covered. Great is the knowledge of the absence of death. All has been forgotten—otherwise men would live differently!*

April 21

Urusvati, as her name indicates, is close, most of all, to the work of searching for new worlds, where there are indeed unlimited possibilities. You need not burst into tears when all goes well. Do not forget about caterwauling. (Why is it that all I hear these days is colorless, and the timbre of the voices is almost imperceptible?) Stinking threads reach out for you; many arrows are temporarily aimed at you. To some extent they discolor space. Your personal state is already in contact, so they disturb you no more than cold drops thrown on your back. But it is also for the better, for the experience should withstand the most varied conditions. Soon birds and cats will not affect you anymore. Be assured that unwise acceleration may cause a brain stroke. We rejoice at your progress and wish that you would enjoy the air and rest. It is better to skip a day. (Shall I listen if I am tired?) I suggest that you go to bed earlier; do not write down the conversations in the evening and hasten to go to sleep. It would be better for you to go to bed earlier. It would also be better not to influence the experiment. (Shall I listen in the daytime?) For a very short while. All proceeds at full speed.

April 22

When would it be possible to expel all the cats from your house? When missions like this are taking shape, when the experiment begins to acquire sonority, then one regrets every speck of dust....Today the experiment was very successful. One more beautiful encounter: Radegunda, one of the most active Sisters.[5-3] In her earthly life she was engaged in running labor houses and schools.[5-4] Nuns of her monastery had to learn some kind of handicraft. *Thus, each useful thought finds approval. A plucked string produces sound. A clear and courageous formulation of thought brings benefit.*

You have a gramophone; We also have our own musical recordings. *We can appreciate a medieval lute as well as Wagner's "Die Walkyrie." Also fine is the ancient Chinese crystal instrument. The purity of its tone corresponds to the purity of colors. It is called a rainbow harp. The rays produce excellent trumpet sounds, and the vortex rings are irreplaceable, as when striking a chord on strings. Verily, it is worthwhile living with such perspectives.* It is so sad when they add a drop of bitterness to you.

It is useful to notice weather conditions during your experiences. At the end they will not matter any more. All will come; just do not let yourself become too tired. Do not even think about it. We ask you to accept, simply and quietly.

With your whole spirit you have accepted the most difficult collaboration. You are your own laboratory. A world experiment is impossible without your kind of background and self-command. Hearing Our voices in different rays, noticing the feelings and even writing them down is an iron-clad achievement. The main danger and difficulty is in the change of voices. Your organism will become accustomed to the change of the rays that accompany the voices. You rejoice in the most difficult. It is time to go to bed.

I approve of your paying attention to your pulse. It is symptomatic when the centers adjust so as to expand their functioning. Do not let yourself become tired—this will guarantee rapid success.

Part Six

April 24

Urusvati has experienced My Ray for a long time, but it still causes contraction of her nerve centers. Right now only voices similar to My Ray can reach her without causing disturbance. You can imagine how different are the actions of the rays: yellow, ruby, and apple-green. These colors have a strong effect on the eyes, even on a painted picture. Kumakami belongs to the yellow ray. He manages the library. But the Eastern group is closer to you. (In response to my remark that we were given the names of others than those who were in the early days of the Theos[ophical] mov[ement]. Henceforth Konrad's hands shall not reach out for you, for his impertinence oversteps all limits. His experiments with teraphim cannot be tolerated. Strange! He never made any attempt upon Urusvati's life. His ray was not so bad long ago. Maybe in the final hour a miracle will happen. By that hour Urusvati will already have returned to Us. Her wish to protect the greatest enemy is worthy of a Sister of the White Brotherhood. But the essence is the same (in all incarnations). Otherwise the World would be drawn into a catastrophe. Konrad would misuse the formulas. The last experiment did not take place. If it did, it would have resulted in the coupling of Urusvati's good and Konrad's evil. She strove for the highest benefit, and only her physical beauty impeded his attempt. The goal of the experiment devised by Konrad was to obtain from the Brotherhood the formula for atomic energy. But before the experiment had ended, Our messenger knocked. And it is predestined to end only now.

One evening a nun asked for overnight lodging, and when the hostess emerged for dinner, the nun blessed her and said, "Run along now; the monastery is waiting for you." (How could the nun know?) She'd had a dream. The same night the miracle with the horse had occurred, when the horse turned to stone before the bridge, and the bridge was raised. (Would it not have been simpler to destroy the bridge?) But then some people would have been killed, and Konrad would not give up the pursuit. Whereas when the horse reared up and turned to stone, the rider was shocked. The horse remained as stone for three days. If Konrad had had the time to burst onto the bridge, much blood would have been shed. Our Ray prevented murders. Nothing happens wiser than in life. So far your ray is unpleasant to him, for it reflects your closeness to the White Brotherhood. When you are testing your forces in a personal battle, then you may dress the wounds. Thus far he gloats.

Let us proceed with the experiment. (Why did M. M. write to me, "Stand firm"?) You will comprehend it with your spirit. (Are there inaccuracies in my records?) I do not see them. Be on guard. Indeed, to reconcile the different rays is not an easy thing. There are many new voices. (Shall I write down what I heard in the daytime?) Yes. (What does the strange word "Peku" mean?) A technical abbreviation for the name of one of Our underground chambers, "Pekere." (What does "the Star in Allahabad" mean?) The Star of Christ—His Path.

April 25

The spirit of Urusvati has to assimilate the Common Ray. The feeling of the entire orchestra is still new. But if you notice a rotation near your solar plexus, it means the beginning of the assimilation. Of course, after that, *in conformity with the rhythm of World Motion, repetitive accrual is needed. The display of haste is adverse to the World's creation. The process of formation of crystals and flowers indicates how perfection develops.* How is the life of Christ to be pictured? By multicolored crystals and the radiance of flowers. His Thoughts will remain as blank pages. But between them, the lightning of His unexpected appearances flashes and the thunder of his sparse words bursts out. More should be said about the thirty years than about the three years of Service. "For thirty years He walked repeating the word so as to impart it to those who would not receive it. The Teachings of Buddha, of Zoroaster, and the old Sayings of the Vedas, He learned upon the crossroads. Perceiving pure eyes, He asked, 'Know you aught of God?' By river barges He waited for the travelers and asked, 'Do you bear aught for me?' For it was necessary that He cross with earthly feet and ask with human words. When He was told of the starry signs He asked to know their verdicts. But the ABCs held no attraction for Him; people did not exist for this. 'How can I calm the devastating storm? How can I disclose the heaven to men? Why are they rent from the eternal existence to which they belong?' Such teaching of the essence of life effaced"[6-1] Our magic techniques, and I learned from Him to abandon "methods of magic because instead of winning the subservience of the minor spirits of nature, He razed all obstacles with the sword of His spirit. His teaching guided the people to the possibilities of the Spirit. Therefore there were no Magi near Him; only by the stars did one know of Him. We knew much," but He could do everything. "Then we resolved to serve His Teaching...."[6-2] Thus shall We begin the Story of His life, that the unmutilated word shall be inscribed upon Earth. My best writings were destroyed. And your records of Christ cannot be given out yet.

While in the experiment, you should notice when your pulse is too frequent or too loud. Let us continue in this way. Now it is time to go to bed.

April 28

Let us finish talking about the experiment. It is not only the different nature of the rays that exerts an influence, but also their intensity. Switching between rays of different intensities is similar to connecting a lamp to different wires. After the crystal Ray of Christ. (This was an explanation for the sparks I felt on my shoulders.) If the ray of the newly invited specialist is in tune with a ray of higher intensity, the former is absorbed, which results in soundlessness, causing troubled perception. The main thing is not to let yourself become tired; give your organism enough time to assimilate the new fires. Old Derky is a former servant of Thomas Vaughan, who was called in to help with the experiment, in the densified body. Sometimes specialists need to have familiar conditions. They worked together for forty years. Union is a great thing.

Half the sky is filled with an unusual manifestation. Around an invisible Luminary an immeasurable circle has begun to radiate, rays rushing along its perimeter. The furies of terror have hidden themselves within caves, suffocated by the radiance of this sign. A path opens before the people going to the West. *The best abilities have been borne by the people. The Giving Hand lives wisely. And let the old lands rest. To whom to give the new land? To those who will bring a small portion of the old Knowledge. The knot of peoples is taking root in a vacant place. Let the departed ones come. Since seas can cover mountains, and deserts can re-place sea-bottoms, then is it impossible to imagine the miracle of populating a desert? A ploughman, a simple farmer, gives rest to his field, permitting it to be overgrown with weeds. Likewise, in the Plan of Construction the places of harvest must be alter-nated. It is befitting for the new to be in a new place.*

Asia was covered with ice, then ice was replaced by flowers, which in their turn were covered with a soft carpet of barchans.[6-3] It is time to raise the carpet! Therefore, thinking about the New Country, let us seize all old places and say, "Resurrection! It is befitting for the new to be in a new place. Treasure of Poseidon, come into view![6-4] Do not serve a small cause!" Breaking the solitude of Our City, We shall put Our trust in the chosen ones; only in accord with them is it possible to preserve the predestined possessions.

Departing for Our place, Urusvati will say, "I am going to my an-cestral estate," since, indeed, as Urukai, she owned these lands. After putting into order the Center of the World, We will move to new places with all of you, but that will not happen soon. Before that time Urusvati will discover a great many useful and beautiful rays coming from new Worlds. And now, prior to the new worlds and the miracle of the desert, one task remains: ring in Zvenigorod.

Do not overindulge in the experience. Be the first to ring. Give your solemn promise, otherwise the desert will not flourish. Much has been done, but far more is to be done. *I feel the human spirit will rise; but welcome the most unfortunate ones: "Come, ye naked, We will clothe thee; come, ye little ones, We will rear thee; come, ye dumb ones, We will give thee speech; come, ye blind ones, and see the predestined estate in Our place." Whose hand is stretch-ing forth to the bolt of My House? Traveler, thou art without belongings; therefore thou shalt enter! Thus will we attain.*

April 29

Three Instructions: First, it is necessary to explain why Urusvati should suffer from the experiment. Urusvati has to become accustomed to the laboratory's rays. If you wish to bring exact knowledge to people, you must not stay in the halls of the general Teachings, but must go upstairs or downstairs to the rooms of specialized investigations, where physical and spiritual rays may sometimes be unbearable. Therefore, bringing the Great Experiment to humanity, you earn an entrance ticket.

Second, today you were shown how We push through in L. ideas of the future structures in Zvenigorod. Remembering nothing, suspecting nothing, he has already expressed his delight over what he has been shown. In such a way he gradually will assimilate principles of modern construction coupled with the utilization of Russian architecture. It is necessary to preserve the Russian character of the city; I do not like featureless cities, for any true offering to the world is based on the best in personal expression. Of course, we will not tell that to L. It is only his spirit that knows the towers. *It is time to do away with the imperfection of matter. For this the people must become conscious of the spirit; otherwise the general condition tends to reduce the individual possibilities to its own level. It is as the waves of the ocean preserving a common rhythm. Therefore, it is time to arouse the nations, whether by sword or by lightning, in order to evoke the cry of the spirit.* The experiment goes well. It is impossible to notice the dates of the awakening of the centers without keeping records. It is boring to record your temperatures, but without records it is impossible to know the course of an illness.

April 30

Today we will talk about creation and experiments. But let Me first explain the meaning of a dream-vision. In the Region of the Brotherhood, a worker was carrying grains collected for experiments. They were [wrapped in] a gelatinous tissue, in which grains will not lose their vitality. This is a special kind of prismatic dream-vision, refracted and intensified by Our Ray, which caused the violet coloring. Note especially the importance of the tissue that preserves vitality.

Could you but see the clichés of the first creations, you would be horrified.

The chief obstacle is that matter can be acted upon only through matter. To bridge the gap between the spirit and the Brotherhood is not so difficult, but to establish a normal link between the Brotherhood and the people is unspeakably difficult. Men, like parrots, repeat the remarkable formula, "Death conquers death"—but they do not care to ponder on its meaning. Various means of action were attempted. Christ considered heightened ecstasy to be the best method, but this beautiful measure just led to saints' relics and idols. The resultant harm prompted Christ to stop the action. And Our little experiment with the Theos[ophical] Soc[iety] has shown that matter yields with great difficulty. Therefore *We have decided that the future destiny should be shaped by cooperation of the spirit under practical conditions.*

Of course, Urusvati was right to notice that leaving the physical body enhances the phenomena, but that artificial state only hampers the experiment. Even hearing half a word in the normal state is better.

The result is remarkable indeed, for penetration into underground chambers is very difficult, even in a heightened state. We Ourselves are looking for the best conditions for the Life-Principle. The Supreme Instruction is to realize Communion without changing the conditions of life. The Order is to establish direct communication between separate specialized fields. *The difficulty lies in the new differentiations of humanity. The former primitive divisions into castes, classes, and professions are being replaced by a complex distinction according to light and shade. Such a system, like a purified communism, will select the best groups of humanity. Without details, one must trace a general demarcation line of light and shade, as if recruiting a new army. How difficult it is to select without resorting to special measures!* And now Our Laboratory is particularly busy, for a destructive ray is penetrating to Earth. (How could it be possible for such a ray to reach people?) The resourcefulness of Our "friend" again. It is better to find an antidote. But the same ray, if modified, can be constructive. After having added an ingredient, We will create the means to change the surface of the Earth. Deserts will flourish under the action of this Ray. Careless are people who have chosen that path. Measures are being taken. None other than Vaughan will restrain his compatriots, the Englishmen. Earth is approaching the New Era.

May 1

Of course, it was Vaughan. Combining telephone and vision capabilities is not easy. Indeed, We share everything, both good and bad. Indeed, We watch all those who participate in the movement. Is it not sad to encounter a thoughtform like that received from M. in your conversation with her? Is it possible to expect success if such thoughts creep in? Not only external action, but also inner talk can cause great harm.... The Teacher has shown you the image of her thoughts. There is danger in it, and it is difficult to move such heaviness. Everything should help rather than do harm to the common cause.... and Mor ... must put Service above all, then it will bring him success and opportunities, for there are no secrets. Light illuminates, while darkness burns holes....

The experiment goes perfectly well. You need to know all that We hear. Our words accompany the most diverse works. Do you remember an exclamation, "Their staggering death!"? (Did it refer to the heat ray?) No; in such a way you acquaint yourself with the different rays and form an idea of the dispatches from Earth to Us. What remains is the color of what was said. (Yesterday I was hearing in full quietude.) A good sign. (A sound of a dropped object?) Of course, I dropped My pen. It will be possible to quietly see and hear at all times, as you wish. At the same time you also need to take care of your health. Waves of currents grow in a spiral fashion; the principle of the spiral vortex is found in everything. It is time to go to bed.

Part Seven

May 2

Today we are going to visit Our cemetery. We too have Our cemetery—a storehouse of records of spoiled plans. It is a very sad chamber for Us all. Let us choose something. Here is a plan based on Bonaparte. The one called St. Germain directed the revolution in order for it to renew the people's mentality and to unite Europe. You know what course the revolution took. Then a plan was brought forward to choose one person to serve as a symbol of unity. Napoleon was found exclusively by St. Germain. The star he liked to talk about brought unexpected opportunities to Napoleon. It is true that many members of the Brotherhood did not believe that war could lead to unification, but We nevertheless had to admit that the very personality of Napoleon, intensified by the Stone, allowed him to absorb all details.

You already know that the appearance of the Stone is always connected with the feminine principle. Napoleon, following the advice of the evil forces, extinguished his own star. The Stone then was left for a while in the possession of the Jesuits, for Its general mission had been obscured. The Stone was brought to Napoleon in Marseilles by an unknown person, and Napoleon gave it as a gift to Josephine. The plan was then broken when Napoleon recklessly attacked Russia, for he was not supposed to interfere with Asia.

Let Me remind you about another plan—the unification of Asia and Europe. After Alexander the Great began his great deed, he, in the same way, broke the pattern of his fate by sending away his beloved Melissa. Napoleon and Alexander the Great were both foretold about the Stone, but the clarity of the task was obscured by human nature. True, they gave the Stone to their beloved ones with the best of feelings, but then they were clouded by savage outbursts and thus lost their connection. The Stone must be worn by a woman who has evoked the best feeling. Yabuchtoo guarded It, and Kurnovoo wore It for the Feast of the Sun.[7-1] We speak about true feeling, not about the custom of the time. I plead for understanding, for even Konr[ad], after having learned about Urusvati's connection with the Stone, took all measures to attract the Stone through her.

There is a way of mystical connection with certain objects. When Napoleon gave the Stone to Josephine, it was given with the best feeling, but it is wisest when the path of the Stone goes along the line of age-long ownership. *The Mother of the World is a symbol of the Feminine Principle in the new era, and the Masculine Principle voluntarily returns the Treasure of the World to the Feminine Principle. While Amazons were the embodiment of the strength of the Feminine Principle, now it is necessary to show the spiritual perfection of woman.*

Is it possible to protest against Christ? He has already told you that He grieves about the harm done by those ecstasies. Furthermore, the church sought to emphasize that aspect. I repeat: the Roman Church is harmful. *In the name of Christ great crimes have been committed. Therefore, Christ nowadays clothes Himself in other garments. One must discard all embellishments. I am not speaking of slightly embellished works (such as those of St. Teresa of Spain and St. Catherine of Siena), as even through the volumes of Origen changes were liberally made. Therefore, it is time to change conditions in the world.*

Let us continue with the experiment. Tomorrow write down your questions. I promise to give exact answers. *The spring cannot act before the appointed date, and to hasten means to cut the wires.*

May 3

I would like to tell about an unfinished experiment: Sister Isar, a native of the Orkney Islands, undertook explorations of far-off worlds and did not return after one of her flights. Even now there are several theories regarding that puzzling phenomenon. I believe she went beyond the gravitational field and was drawn into a vortex of an unknown group of [celestial] bodies. Unexplored are far-off worlds. I believe she still exists. That's why We call the unknown regions "Orkland." (How many years has Sister Isar been missing?) Thirty years.

Now about the Stone. The Stone, which has fallen from Orion, is kept in the Brotherhood.[7-2] A fragment is sent to the World to accompany world events, and due to its inherent magnetic power, it maintains its connection with the Brotherhood, where the main body of the Stone is kept. This is a simple magnetic principle. This is not just symbolic; it is physical affinity that keeps the connection taut. By means of this "wire," it is easy to protect those who are called. You were shown the kind of labyrinth into which one falls if one loses the Stone. The labyrinth can be severe. Napoleon knew [about the power of the Stone], but, due to his human weakness, attributed everything to himself.

You also have heard about Masculine and Feminine Principles: when they are linked by spiritual feeling, the circuit is closed, and materialization of the Higher Forces on the earthly plane becomes possible. Later it will become clear to you how Zvenigorod should be built. You already have information about altitudes and the arrangement of levels.

Here is an example: You are living at a height of approximately 7,000 feet; such an altitude is suitable for the Temple. The altitude of 12,000 feet, above the Temple, is proper for Meetings. Therefore, you have three levels of life: below there is a city of the New Era, and above it, the Temple of human achievements and, still higher, a meeting place of Earth and Spirit. The Stone will be deposited in the Temple. Udr[aya] will know about that place, for after you leave, he may be protected through the same "wire."[7-3] Jason the Hierophant accepted Orion's gift when in Asia. Jason is among the Brothers. Accumulations during several incarnations facilitate one's approach to the main body. Having broken the circuit, he (Napoleon), of course, deviated from the straight line of thought.

The Stone is sent by decision of the Brothers; that is why some Teachers possessed it. Although He knew about the Stone, Christ's task was to open people's eyes to the spiritual plane. We wrote together, for it is now that forces of the spirit are to be brought closer to Earth. When in a house, one does not see it. We like the simple attitude that you both show toward Us. However, the main thing is that there is no treachery in your house. We see the Light; the dimensions of your auras do not allow for treachery.

We cannot know the limits to the possibilities of conquest by the spirit. The seed of the spirit is self-contained, and the direction of its striving is indicated by the aura. (Are there unconditionally hidden thoughts?) Yes. *There are thoughts directed inwardly and absorbed by the potentiality of the spirit. There are thoughts that are not manifested upon the earthly plane.* There is no need to manifest them, for they are not applicable to Earth. It is better to devote a separate talk to this topic. Make your questions crystal clear, but do not necessarily expect immediate answers; they may come later. (During the day I do not have the time to think, whereas in the night I have to listen, though I want to think.) It is too bad. You are not exercising your apparatus. We like crystal-clear questions. (But M. M. did not like it when we asked questions.) It is not permissible to interfere with urgent messages. But, writing down your questions, remember that there is a country called "Orkland," which no one knows.

However, Udr[aya] heeded the nightly request and brought in an Image of the Mother of the World. It represents the most ancient image based on an ancient archetype, existing since the times when the desert was flourishing. For that, We will send good luck to his future book. Urusvati is quite right in wishing to add material related to Buddha. Describing images of Taras, one may point to the Feminine Principle of the Mother of the World. I well see the importance of the book. Information about the importance of Asia in the history of humankind may be added. One may indicate that neither China nor Persia, but indeed an empty region was the place where the spring burst forth. Thus new books have been started by the anniversary of your departure. An Image of the Mother of the World is started. Udraya's book is started. Lum[oa] started his approach to My pharmacy—musk.[7-4] It cannot be said that this year was not full. The beginning of the experiment of a future life and the beginning of the Museum as an anchoring of the past will indicate the scope of the beginning. Now it is time for your hearts to take rest. Every day something of importance (in the experiment) comes, but it will fit into its right place only later. Do not hamper the excellent beginning of the experiment.

May 5

One can build a city, one can give the best knowledge, one can provide clothes for the guardians, *but most difficult of all is to reveal the true Image of Christ.*

Indeed, you hear remarkably. For when We speak Secrets, a special receptivity is needed. You heard about a remarkable date. These kinds of secrets are imparted with precautions, for they are isolated from the other "wires." Let Me explain this in greater detail: when We intend to transmit something that should not leak into space, We create some kind of air channel; of course, it takes much energy, but the message is transmitted in its entirety, and even the Hierophant [of Evil] cannot penetrate that channel. It is difficult to know how, but it saturates space and creates new records for the future. Of course, it is not always possible to resort to such isolation, for a large amount of electricity is needed. But sometimes the very atmospheric conditions help. We wanted to demonstrate the possibility of absolute isolation. Of course, no one will interfere with Our Talks. The isolation is not a megaphone; it is an inherent quality that attracts your attention. You should know why it is not good to resort too often to this: it forms a kind of invisible air pipe, and the strong tension can crush it, which could result in a brain stroke. It is to be used with especial care after a thunderstorm. Besides a mystical date related to the Temple, Christ communicated about preservation of the treasure. It is necessary to remember that on the indicated day Christ will visit the house, for that is the day of His initiation. Thus let us turn to purification of the Teaching. Let the little ones think in whatever way they can about Zvenigorod. But you yourselves think how to cleanse the body of Christ. It is inappropriate for Him to ring in Zvenigorod; it is you who were told to do this. *Gathering the crumbs of the people's concept of the Savior and replacing the chiton with overalls, one can find illumination.* By human hands the Temple shall be built. Old Believers, Molokans, Pashkovists, and Stundists will help.[7-5]

Udr[aya] is on the Path; let him also think about Christ. Let him remember about the cross not of human making. Let him think about schools where the name of the Temple will be pronounced in connection with the true history of humanity. The name of Morya (repeated seven times). Courageously carry the consecrated Shield. If leopard skins could guard one from the enemy in the mysteries, then how much more will My name always shield you. A sevenfold sound has been put at the foundation of the World, therefore, the sealing is sevenfold. This is a simple rhythm of nature. Take Us and, knowing the path, build broadly.

The centers move not easily, and "the Chalice" is especially vulnerable. I expect [you to use] valerian; you may lie down in the daytime; a short ride would be useful. It is a very difficult task to weld the links of the Teaching. Yusna knows how difficult it is to touch Heaven when on Earth. She works with Us and knows how to protect Urusvati's heart. Urusvati can be confident in one thing: everything will be easier when the situation with the domestic spirits improves. Also, appeal to Christ in that Image that is dear to you and in which He wants to be depicted. One may hold for a while the wish to simplify Christ's Image for popular use. However, very soon everything will fall into place, but it is necessary to preserve forces. Soon it will be possible to ask particular questions, and soon specialists' answers will follow. Be fair: many questions have been answered already.

May 6

The Star of Allahabad pointed out the way. And so We visited Sarnath and Gaya. Everywhere We found the desecration of religion. On the way back, under the full moon, occurred the memorable saying of Christ. During the night-march the guide lost his way. After some seeking, I found Christ seated upon a hill of sand looking at the sands flooded by moonlight. I said to Him, "We have lost the way. We must await the indication of the stars." "Rossul Morya, what is that way to us, when the whole world is awaiting us?" Then, taking His bamboo staff, He traced a square around the impression of His foot, saying, "Verily, I say, by human feet." And, making the impression of His palm, He surrounded it also with a square. "Verily, by human hands." Between the squares He drew the semblance of a pillar surmounted by an arc. He said: "O, how Aum shall penetrate into the human conscious-

*ness! Here I have drawn a pistil and above it an arc, and have set
the foundation in four directions. When by human feet and human hands the Temple will be built wherein will blossom the pistil
laid by Me, then let the builders proceed on My way. Why should
we await the way, when it lies before us?" Then, rising, He effaced with His staff all that He had drawn. "When the Name of
the Temple will be pronounced, then shall the inscription emerge.
In remembrance of My constellation, the square and the nine stars
will shine over the Temple. The sign of the foot and the hand
shall be inscribed on the Cornerstone." Thus He Himself spoke
on the eve of the new moon. And the heat of the desert was great.*
When I lived in the body of Akbar, due to bodily forgetfulness I
began to build a Temple with a pistil in the middle of a square. I
consulted the stars, but the dates eluded me. Pisces is His physical
sign, but the sign of His *podvig* is Orion. *The Star of the Morning
is the sign of the Great Era which will flash as the first ray from
the Teaching of Christ. For who is to extol the Mother of the
World if not Christ, the One so demeaned by the world? "Give
Us the Arch of the Dome, wherein to enter!"* Christ will show to
Urusvati a sign of the foot and the hand nailed down by the world.

Our Yusna examined your heart and found out that the experiment may develop brilliantly in a few months, but you need to spare
your health. It will change soon. ([This is regarding] my agonizing
spiritual condition.)

This kind of condition is known very well to Us, for the gates are
already opened, and the spirit knows all that is predestined. When
We touched Him, We were filled with presentiment. Of course, bodily
forgetfulness took over.... Let Me add that I was called Morya by
the name of My lands. Urusvati saw Yusna in violet with a white
shawl. You will recollect—it happened two days before the call,
and Her face is not especially beautiful.

Part Eight

May 7

We ask you to conduct a much needed experiment tomorrow. My Ray has blended with those of both of you to such a degree that talks may go easily. Now We decided to try the Wire of the Brotherhood by the evening talks. Therefore, tomorrow the experiment should be started at nine o'clock. We ask you to notice all peculiar details and finish by ten o'clock. We will do this for three evenings. The first will be devoted to the general wire; the second, to the laboratory ray; and the third, to the station of the world patterns. I will be absent so as not to dominate. I ask you not to be confused by any unusual occurrences. Sometimes one ray is totally different from another one, and even tiredness may result. Therefore, finish at ten o'clock. I will not be surprised if F(uyama) tires more than Urusvati, for Urusvati is already accustomed to hearing different voices and has passed the stage of early confusion. We would like for you, without being harmed, to come closer as soon as possible and become Our full coworkers.

I feel how Urusvati's spirit is bursting to go forward; her aspiration is such that neither feet nor even wings are sufficient. What an unbounded striving! Trust Our experience: Christ knew when He sent a call to Saul. Everything is successful if only you do not overstrain your health. It would be alright sometimes not to record our nightly exchanges. Discern causes in full chiaroscuro. Our eyes know where and when the rays dart out.... We are pained when you experience hardships. You see, I even must withdraw for three talks, if only to help you expand your possibilities. Do not be confused by interruptions. It may be better to start in the dark. Along the way you both will discover various details. You see, the Pharmacy of the spirit is so different from that of Earth. As soon as ossification of the spirit occurs, all conditions change. Now it is time to rest. You see that I even have to withdraw. Everything goes well, as you will see by events.

For three days I heard via the Wire of the Wh[ite] Brotherhood, the Wire of the Laboratory, and the Wire of the Station of World Patterns.

May 11

Urusvati should not worry: the experiment is organically consoli-
dated. At the same time *the touch of the Ray of the Brotherhood
increases the depth of perceptions. Therefore, one must take into
consideration every sensation. Small as well as important events
strike upon the aura, as upon musical strings. The growing aura
has its advantages, and these Aeolian wings in many ways resound. The burden of the world plays its symphonies upon them.
One cannot say that a man of a luminous aura is motionless. The
outer shell of the aura is like a surging sea. What a task for the
scientist—to trace the nourishment of the aura from within and
its reflection from without! Verily a world battle! Therefore all
complex sensations are increased to the point of pain. The symbol of the burden of the world is a man carrying a sphere.*

Judge for yourselves, since from a horseman's fall, to worldwide
reconstruction, to the Ray of the Brotherhood—everything is to be
noticed and accommodated. *An impression can be received of being between the hammer and the anvil. Therefore, the attainment
of a rainbow aura is so practical, because it carries within itself
the means of assimilation of all that exists. Even the best monochromatic auras must quench the conflagrations by drawing from
their own ocean. Whereas a rainbow aura easily reflects and takes
in the rays. Therefore, podvig is a most practical action.* But sometimes it is given to one to perform a complex action.

Dear ones, take it correctly—the ocean of *podvig* is great. There
never before was such a time when the whole world was the arena of
action. Thoughts of reconstruction have encircled the entire planet.
What previously filled a town or a country, now floods the world. In
acquiring awareness of this scale, the reservoir of your ocean is filled.
And what was emptied yesterday is easily filled up tomorrow. Just do
not worry; you will not be late, for the gates are open. And when you
say with a smile, "I will postpone it today to preserve it for tomorrow," it would mean then that you think strategically, by distributing
the troops. If the channel is open, the message does not slip away; but
the difference is not great if it stays in the spirit. Let Me explain this.
The experiment itself penetrated certain centers to such a degree that
a year's work was done in two months. The most important thing is

not the messages themselves but the fact that your organism has withstood the alteration of rays. Now let the spiral of nerves settle. Of course, it is not a small burden; but any added obstacle just makes your [progress] even more valuable. Your sensations are varied, and the apparatus is full of input, but everything will go to its appropriate place without the receiver being overloaded. Who called you my own! (Is it possible to postpone some part of the talk until...?) Yes, it is, but let us first strengthen your organism. You already receive colors of groups of rays well, but there are those that can still shake you, and it is necessary to provide protection. Let us continue tomorrow....

May 12

Truly, I am glad that Urusvati has some notion of the sacred rhythm. Our nightly Service is very important. During those Services Our heads are always uncovered. Think about how far your centers have imperceptibly progressed so that you can now cross the threshold of the Sanctuary without experiencing spasms. It is [often] possible to hear the music and enter the Temple, but the place of the nightly Service is far less accessible.[8-1] Even an impressed hint of the nightly Service around the Stone is a high achievement, for no one, except Us, can be admitted. Yes, the Stone rests on a cushion, which lies on a marble foundation and is separated from it by a disk of lithium. After establishing the rhythm, We silently saturate space. This Repository is located deep underground, and many people do not suspect that, during their sleep, the White Brotherhood descends through the galleries for the nightly vigil. Good Vaughan advised how to further reveal the Gathering to Urusvati. In all matters related to combinations of rays, We always ask for His advice. Rays are sometimes like flowers and sometimes like swords. We reinforced space in order to extinguish a war.... Now it is time for you to go to bed. You need to refresh your forces.

May 13

We praise Urusvati for her decision to take a rest yesterday. After experiencing the rays of Service, a rest is needed. It is amazing that those rays reflected by lithium did not cause any shock, for they are linked to the available rays. (Why is it so difficult for me to bear children's voices? Which ray causes the greatest shock in my organism?) The yellow one, but now it will become easier. Let us return to the children. The period when the voice breaks is also the time when the ray forms. With small children a ray of their previous incarnations struggles with a new one, hence discord that strikes the perfect ear. The main danger of the experiment in real life is to be pierced by false sounds. Therefore, in the daytime the rays should be admitted very cautiously. The wire works in an automatic way, but it can be muted. In the same way, a musician can use a pedal, but if he overuses it, his instrument will be destroyed. Of course, it is possible to know how the Wire touches. You yourself will check your entries in Our records.

May 14

Fire burns away imperfect thoughts. How else to fill the cradle with authentic achievements? The experiment of filtering a thought through Our Ray is very important. Everyone expresses the essence of his aura, but single thoughts can be of different value depending on their spiritual consistency. Then the substance of the thought can be tested by a special ray. The presence of inner spirituality illumines the thought with the color of the aura, but if the thought is a base one it is burned away by the ray. Thus, there results not only a testing of thought but also a disinfecting of space. One may imagine how the ray penetrates space and reveals wonderful treasures, but also little red and orange flames, which are like criminal poisoners.

How could We not purify the layers above Earth, when even to the eye they are of a smoky orange color? The invention of the ray transmitted through a lithium compound does honor to its Inventor. It is possible in considerable degree to render the atmosphere more healthy and thus contribute to the salvation of many people. Through the same ray it is possible to increase the detection of nascent spirituality. *The main thing, though, is to destroy the germs of base thoughts, which are more infectious than all diseases. One should be careful not so much about uttered words as about thoughts.*

Uttering one word, ten thoughts are born. Discussion of this invention marked the end of Our manifested Service. This is when the best discoveries are brought to the Gathering. The same will be in Alt[ai]. Three men worked on the invention: M. M., Vaughan, and Paracelsus. You saw Him watching the action of the ray and heard in the laboratory a discussion about the final experiment. Truly, We share Alpha and Omega.

I do not envy people who emit base thoughts, for the flame will touch their hearts. Add this talk to your letter, for after reading it, they will say to others, "It is not practical to have dark thoughts," and, besides that, it is good to give them some joy. Those who do not understand will at least be cautious about it.

Let Christ be presented as if clothed in laboratory rays. Do not be confused if mundane impressions come along with great ones. Our work encompasses everything. The Ray of the Mother of the World is what We call the new Ray. Let us not speak in base terms about this New Era.

May 15

[A] visit to Our Museum is significant in that that Era is represented in the lowest galleries. But in My eyes this is a great achievement. Not phantom astral accumulations, but a whole link [in the chain] of a Great Culture. Sensing of the Stone while in the physical body is very symbolic, for the Stone is attracted to its main body.

It is not possible to stay for a long time in the lower galleries, for the air is saturated with preserving gases. (In response to my remark that I could stay for a long time and see clearly in the galleries devoted to the life of Christ.) The difference is twenty-five floors. Let us not forget that the astral body is quite susceptible to gases. Even primitive sorcerers burn heather and verbena, the first to repel and the second to attract. We Ourselves descend below the twentieth floor with some safety devices.

Of course, I indicated the tension of the apparatus needed for a great task. (An explanation of the vision follows.) When facing the greatness of Christ, there is no shame in standing in tension. The experiment progresses in a quite unusual way. It is a joy to see how the past and the future pass before the consciousness, in the same way that clichés flash in Our minds.

Of course, besides the mirrors concentrating the images, We also have regular communications as swift as sound and thought. Their clarity and duration depend on various factors. Certainly, their volume and location are of importance. I make no secret of the fact that nonuniformity of conditions often equalizes events of unequal significance, and then we need to resort to corrections using Our mirrors. Experience in discerning differences between rays helps to classify messages. But often the apparatus rings in the same way whether caused by some accidental collision or by the downfall of an entire country. And when one hears words like "Paris" or "hand-to-hand combat," it may be difficult to decide which one is more important. This is why We have a rule that no event is unimportant. Sometimes a pattern of a world event flashes so quickly that We can use only the guidance of inner feelings to rush and verify it in the mirror.

I am glad to see how diverse are your perceptions. It is not easy to grasp the surrounding patterns, but we can see that complex things fit into their places. We avoid the astral world; We are interested in life; and therefore you, on your way to Us, master Our basic ways. Of course, you hear the same as We. Now you surely will ask, "What has the fall of the horseman to do with the Brotherhood?" If something is under special observation, then every event in that field of vision is visible, like a fly sitting on the glass of a magic lantern. (Did I discern correctly in the Museum the constructions from Shamo and Gobi?) Yes, yes, yes.

May 16

Before talking about the Museum, *it is necessary to speak about truthfulness of the foundation. You noticed that We call the Astral World a heaped-up conglomeration. We emphasize how We avoid it. You know already that astral bodies have volume and weight and carry away with them many peculiarities of earthly life. The relativity of earthly knowledge is well-known. Of course, the astral bodies carry away with them not a small share of this relativeness, but, being freed from the earthly shell, they acquire creativeness of the spirit. But you can picture to yourselves how the relativity of knowledge is reflected in these structures. Alongside an imagined Olympus, one may encounter a monstrous factory, unrealized on Earth. There exist harmonious oases, but in general there prevails a fantastic cemetery of human experiences. It is inadvisable to delve far into the astral patterns, because only an erroneous presentation will follow. In this the usual mediums are harmful.*

Let us not enumerate the consequences of the fumes of the earthly kitchen, but it is more important to understand how one can mitigate the consequences of relativity. They may be mitigated by truthfulness; but truthfulness can be realized only through spirituality, and therefore the awakening of spirituality becomes a cosmic requirement. We gather grains of truth, and thus Our Repository acquires fundamental importance. This enables Us to correct fantastic clouds of misunderstood facts. The Ray of the Mother of the World may help remove unworthy images, but for research to be positive Our Collections in life provide the best aids. This is why the best spirits from the Astral World are eager to approach Our workrooms. Thus We preserve truthful signs of all events. The order of the galleries of the Museum is based on the principle of practicality of preservation. The Museum was founded in a very ancient Era. The underground facilities of the Temple go down into a granite mass.

The name of the First Builder is known. (The name was given, but I was not allowed to record it in my book.) He laid the foundation like those in the Egyptian Pyramids. An ancient riverbed among basalt strata made it possible to significantly lower the lower galleries. There are stored primordial forms transferred from the Himalayas, which are the forms of the very first creations that were stored in caves. We are now considering what relates to the peoples of Shamo and Gobi. A continental belt linked the submerged Atlantis with a flourishing high-altitude country called "Gotl." Its wise system provided the country with a religious law governed by the Feminine Principle. Thread, string, and serpent constituted the sacred link. The thread represented the hearth; the string, evocation to the Deity; and the serpent, knowledge. The Ray can penetrate to the foundation of the Temple through an opening in a semiconical roof. Buildings were designed in a circular style. There were a Temple of the Sun, a Temple of the Moon, and a Temple of the Serpent. Women wore a semblance of the serpent, braiding their hair with plates of sacred metals. Of course, the dimensions of the Temples were enormous. Babylon might give some idea of the dimensions involved. One can imagine how diverse the metals were! Records were made on metal surfaces in cuneiform characters.

The experiment goes fast; you are about to enter a new phase; you hear clearly, and many Voices that caused shock now do not pain you.

Part Nine

May 18

Joy is a special wisdom, as Christ said. (Those were the words I heard.) Our Garden is similar to people. Urusvati is growing a garden by a room linked to a certain date. Our collecting flowers in the morning is no mere chance. We greet the mornings amidst plants, for *nothing gathers the essence of prana as well as do plants. Even pranayama can be replaced by contact with plants. And it should be understood how assiduously the eye must fathom the structure of the plants. The pores of the plants are enlarged not only by the advent of new leaves and flowers, but also by the removal of dead parts. The law of Earth's nurture affords, through the antennae of the plants, the possibility of drawing out of this reservoir by means of smell and sight the precious quality of vitality, the so-called Naturovaloris, which is acquired through conscious striving.*

Just as living plants that have not lost their vitality are of value, so can preparations made by drying them in the sun also be useful. But the stage of decomposition should be avoided, because decay is the same in everything and always attracts imperfect spirits. Therefore, one should watch the condition of cut flowers. The smell of decay must be sensed, as it is not the external appearance but the smell that indicates the symptom. When it is not the season for flowers, it is useful to keep small evergreens. Like a dynamo they accumulate vitality, and they are more effective than pranayama. Instead of by ritual breathings one can thus receive a most condensed supply of prana. Of course, a state of rest also increased the effect. Vital understanding of the power of nature will provide, without magic, a renewal of possibilities.

Besides short flowers, My Garden is full of long and stretching plants. If We are concerned about the weather, many plants are moved inside. Flowers are on balustrades of the stairs, and the old gardener takes away decaying plants. Truly, Urusvati grasps many details. The reddish-yellow Tower is connected by passages with the rest of the structure. From afar, the buildings may be taken for slightly sloping rocks weathered by time. Windows in the outer walls may be taken for birds' nests. The surrounding desert is intact. Often a traveler goes by without ever suspecting anything, but wondering at the behavior of his horse or camel. The animals turn their heads to the seemingly lifeless stones and even try to turn to what seems to be piled heaps of stones. Some people even saw inscriptions on the walls, but, of course, thought they were signs of deterioration. Of course, an unwelcome traveler will always be led away. Everyone feels something. But a desert dweller is accustomed to voices and fires of the desert. (If this is published, then won't many rush there, and disturb Your peace?) It will not be disclosed, for since they cannot recognize even you, how can they find Us? They will speak [about it] for a long time. When they were in Lhasa, did they find anything?

Time here is a factor of tremendous importance, otherwise there will be no opportunity to come closer to the experiment, to compile a book, to finish paintings. (Will we live here for the second year?) I do not think so, for the main thing is mobility. Let us sit, if only for a short while. Harmony between you is very useful.

May 19

It is impossible to separate the conditions of Earth from those beyond it, because the mental world has no boundaries.... Again one must speak against the astral world, because it will be desirable in the future to shorten considerably one's stay on this level. It is unavoidable now, but upon development of the spirit the manifestation of the mental world will be more attainable.

Devachan is the place of pleasant realizations. But at the same time it is dangerous, because a weak spirit is reluctant to leave so pleasant a place. This station encourages an unwillingness to return for more labor. And when the time comes to leave this Valhalla, while the mental body impels one to podvig, *the astral body finds the place most comfortable.* (Do densified astral bodies have any advantages in exploration of the far-off worlds?) As regards projection of the subtle body, [conditions] are similar. Of course, a particularly leading and penetrating mental body is typical of old spirits. Overall, there is a lot of mechanics and chemistry. But the mechanics is based on the individual seed of the spirit. *It is precisely the spirit that does not permit one to stop, for the spirit in its innermost self remembers the beautiful worlds. Beyond all the recollections lives an inexpressible, firm awareness of the possibility of return to the Light whence emanated the spark.*

Our dear, *how can a sensitive spirit avoid an attack of anguish?* Soon you may write to members of the Circle that they gradually should accustom themselves to paroxysms of world anguish.[9-1] *There has never been a case of a man being able to detach himself in spirit from the earthly plane without contraction of his [psychic] centers, exactly like that of the daring aviator who feels a singular tremor in his heart upon detaching himself from the Earth. The goal and the meaning of existence is to strive Upward beyond the limits of the Known and to help one another.*

If, without any mechanics, we recall the sensation of standing on a rock before a phenomenon of nature, does not the heart contract with rapture? After this stage, the sensation of embracing boundlessness will be realized.

Some people accept easily the luxuries of the Astral plane, but there is nothing for you there. Only Our abodes of knowledge will provide the path. For now, with the ray set, let us continue. Later, if My presence is difficult, you may choose, according to the ray, those who are best fit for joint work. Right now, with time so short, tension of the spirit is quite understandable. I may give an example.... I assure you: when you will come to be tested by the Ray of the Mother of the World, you will forget all shadows. You are on the threshold of an individually unique task of discovering new worlds for Earth and on Earth. Not due to the achievements of others, but thanks to your own laboratory work. But the sum total of knowledge emerges very fast.

May 22

Now it is necessary to talk about the experiment. The experiment may be gradually shifted to early mornings, with the view in mind to later shift it to midday. For that purpose We will have to find a quiet house for the next year. The main thing is not to take house servants with families. In the future be certain not to have people crowded around you.

Now you may let your centers strengthen in their new state. Let your nerves rest, otherwise tension makes them oversensitive. The fact of transmission has been established. That is the most impor-tant thing now. It was also important to notice that the rays of rainbow, lilac, and blue auras were received much better than all the yellow ones...

May 24

Each ray can provide protection only within the limits of its own range of colors. If a bright yellow is discordant for a violet ray, then how much more injurious the crimson-toned range to the outer shell of that aura? Through perfection a new defense is attained, whereupon We shield ourselves, as it were, against fa-tigue caused by the various colored flashes by our own gamut of colors. For instance, someone possessing a violet aura begins to see everything in waves of violet and blue tints. This means that his shield is becoming stronger. It also means that instead of re-ceiving stings and wounds, by immersing all around him in his own ocean, the alien colors are seemingly drowned in the accu-mulations of his aura. But the difficulty of these accumulations is that they cannot be superimposed from without and can be only developed from within. Therefore, it is a good sign when the flame of the spirit radiates its own color.

The family of green colors is the most changeable: when in the proximity of yellow, the waves of green turn yellow, in the same way a pink may easily turn red. There is a yellow tint that, like a well-known tint of topaz, does not tolerate impurities. Violet ones, dark blue ones, and some yellow ones possess certain steadiness. As an example, I may mention Our Brother Rak[oczi], whose Ray is of a particular yellow color that, although very high, nevertheless is not always com-patible for joint work with Our [Rays]. It is to be understood that this relates to joint experiments. This is why in the present experiment tension increases when different rays proceed in sequence or simultaneously. Indeed, it is a good sign (i. e., that I see everything in violet) as it shows that the basic color begins to "drown" others.

Of course, an aura is always a combination of three tints. *Each monochromatic aura contains within itself three frequencies, corresponding to the three chief aspects: physical, astral and mental.* So, in your case an artist would have to paint the aura as follows: a dark blue-lilac circle around the head, then a purely lilac circle encompassing the space from the top of the first circle to the knees, and finally a large violet oval. The violet is a fighting tint protecting against touches from the outside, and the head circle corresponds to the spirit and must be protected while in the lower stratas of Earth. The outer oval is studded with purple sparks, which impart to it steadiness at random encounters. But in order to convey the general impression, it would be necessary to paint a silvery-lilac circle around the head, a large lilac circle of a darker hue, and a barely noticeable mistiness to the oval. Therefore, it is very important to strengthen the basic color of the aura before departing from Earth. It is a manifestation of the lilac ray. What we call violet is closer to purple, and the lilac has a strong dark-blue hue. But soon the aura will become much broader, its color will be more silvery, and the large circle will be bordered with a rainbow web. (Those on Earth have centers that allow them to penetrate into spiritual realms.) That is why the Prince of the World impedes development of those centers. (But why can those centers not be developed by chemical, if not mechanical, means?) These centers cannot be developed without conscious participation of the spirit.

A dream showed the meaning of one's final missions. *We see the march of predestined events and note the appearance of quiet figures who, though seemingly detached from life, are valued by Us for their* podvig. *But their lives flow on in a kind of detachment, through which* podvig, *manifests like a spark in the darkness. Subsequent as well as earlier events pass utterly unnoticed. A throne, or a monastery cell, or a cobbler's nook have no importance; one's previously accumulated aura accompanies this ultimate path. Of course the aura expands and shields the unusual sensitiveness; but its quality no longer changes, and from an early age one can distinguish singular children, who carry their own world of manifestations of the spirit. Very rarely, almost never, do they limit themselves to a single specialized profession. Actually, the absence of specialization is characteristic; hands seem to be stretched out to the Chalice. Looking into past lives, one may see representatives of religion, kingdoms, science, art and mechanics waiting and prepared for the journey and ready to depart at any hour without regrets.*

The combination of a correct appreciation of the beauty of matter with a readiness to fathom the attainments of the spirit, brings the podvig *to maturity. The turmoil of life no longer attracts, and of course there comes the realization that it can proceed no further in the same way. The* podvig *may be of short duration or even instantaneous. The realization of the necessity to express a definite action is brought from the past, and it is accomplished as simply as any daily deed. And so, the most difficult thing is to encompass both the rapture of matter and the manifestations of spirit. And how many wondrous quests have been delayed by a regret concerning matter, or by spiritual isolation.*

Sometimes the affinity of the spirit with matter is easily achieved; then one should look for the cause in the past chosen lives. The most exquisite ascetic, who curses the beauty of the world, closes the Gates before himself. Likewise, the scientist who forgets about the Source deprives himself of flights into the domain of higher conquests. Children will grasp this simple condition, but many adults reject it as nonsense. Only by special ways of communication can those in the train of podvig *move on. And to await that which the spirit believes and knows is timely becomes so painful that it is as if time had stopped, and some sort of conflagration had destroyed the accumulated wealth.*

Someone said: "Why was it necessary to be first a king and a priest in order to afterwards waste time as a landowner? Is the very difficult task of successive experiences needed just to know the measure of one's estate?" This is what someone pondered in his forty-fifth year, two years prior to the end of his entire earthly path.

Truly did Christ say: "You know neither the day nor the hour."
He also revealed another truth in saying, "Why hast Thou for-

saken me, O Lord?" This refers to the knowledge of the spirit. At the last moment, before the consummation of the earthly cycle, we sink into a seeming vacuum, in order that all the accumulated fires may flash out at once. By restraining the consciousness of the past, the leap over the abyss is achieved.

Let us record tomorrow a few more examples of feelings before the change of incarnations.

Part Ten

May 26

"I am a simple nun; what do you find in me? Do not kiss my hands; I cannot work miracles. Father, why do they rush into my cell? I have nothing but books. They want me to put my hands on their heads, as if it would cure them, but I myself feel nothing. Sometimes the page of a book is illuminated by a faint blue light, but it cannot be that this light comes from my fingers.

As far as I can remember, nothing remarkable has ever happened in my life since I was brought into a convent school, except perhaps that the needed books are already pulled out for me when I come to the library, and I sometimes see dark-blue sparks near them. It often seems to me that I am about to go somewhere, and perhaps these people have come to bid farewell to me. I am ashamed to say so, but their reverence is burdensome to me; they take from me something irreplaceable, and only touching these ancient manuscripts brings fresh forces to me. Just before my coming here, my mother had a dream: I was in a kind of white garment and there were swirls of flame behind me." Thus confessed a nun one year before a fire, when she saved unique books and died from heavy burns.

And here is the last talk in a 17th-century laboratory: "Why is it so stifling today? I cannot understand how to conduct the last experiment; quick wits fail me. I remember that in Nottingham my hand reached out itself for the needed retorts.[10-1] It is necessary to deliver my records to Oxford as soon as possible. Durkee, I will go by sea soon, and I cannot take my books with me. Tell my people: it is time to start a new experiment. An extraordinary force will help move the most immovable objects. The most heavy objects may be made almost weightless by surrounding them with an essence of a gas from Jupiter. Imagine the stupefaction of a tavern keeper when a boy will carry a whole column right before his eyes; horses will be grateful to us. The only needed thing is clean air; iron debris and metal dust are destructive to the gas. It is necessary to clean up the whole room, even leaving no rust on the nails. Remember: it is like gunpowder is to fire. After the experiment we will go overseas—it is stifling here." Thus spoke an alchemist four months prior to an explosion.

Let us give one more example: "How can people treat a priest like a sacrificial animal? I must recite the same thing to them every day. One could find new ideas, but they want only repetition. Every day they want to stab with the same knife. These steps are so familiar to me, as well as every shadow on the wall. I have nobody to tell: 'You are gone, I cannot communicate alone. You promised we would go together, why is this solitude necessary? I forgot something very important, and I am waiting, as if knowing nothing.'" Thus strove a man of very high position one year before an unexpected moment of clattering horse hoofs. The ways of the Teaching are diverse, but the time just before departure shows similar signs. (Why am I so tired by this talk?) It is clear why: we are talking about the moment of transition. The currents of old records are being transmitted, and these records all have a similar, suffocating quality. The last of these records is less than three centuries old; it was when My Friend was in a hurry to go. We will talk tomorrow about the effects of the rays of records.

May 27

Now you will ask why one's last incarnation requires solitude. This is a condition very difficult to explain from an earthly point of view, but simple and immutable as soon as one crosses beyond the line of earthly existence. Even in the ordinary approach of a ship to a harbor, one observes a similar phenomenon. Life on the ship ceases; the journey is ending; the passengers are busy with the matter of disembarking, and the recent group activities seem no longer to exist.

How much more so is the feeling of any organism approaching a complete change of state. The flow of striving toward the means of expression of one's last action is guided by the intuition.

Of course, both of you have noticed two ways: working either in the [physical] body or in the densified astral body. Each state has its own advantages, and it is only the spirit that can decide which way is closer to it. Of course, from the point of view of working on Earth there is very little difference between these states. Surely, for work on Earth the body fits better, but outer communication is easier when in the densified astral state. Communication is possible between the two states. The body can easily project its astral [vehicle], but the densified astral cannot assume all the characteristics of the body.

Of course, the tissue that preserves vitality can also preserve the body. Even some densified astral bodies remain under the protection of that tissue during distant flights. Sister Isar's "little home" is still waiting for her.

Everybody can change between these states, but to venture farther, one must pass through a still lighter state. I, and the Group that assumed the work on Earth, must stay in physical bodies, and I can tell you in a whisper that the last battle requires that we be in that state, for it makes it possible to overtake Our enemy more quickly. He would like very much to destroy several bodies.

Do not fatigue yourself with the experiment—better to treat the messages just as you practice your scales. The recording of them may be resumed later. A better [position] of the spine is desirable. (I had a very bad bed with a depression at the center.) The Kundalini center may glow with a warm fire, but without affecting the nearby organs. Heaviness, bodily aches, and tiredness are undesirable, so you need a more comfortable bed. There is some advantage in plumpness, though, which for now is not to be feared. Also, you need to avoid lying on your back, for it increases pressure on Kundalini. (But I hear better while lying on my back.) The bed must be straightened. It is impossible to proceed at the same pace as in the early days.

Sure, but I am hiding for your good. However, new achievements are needed for success. As for Me, I am always close, but many other rays must be introduced. Spoken words are accompanied by a ray that echoes them. But also you hear about events in Turkey. A discourse will be given later, but now the sparks of words are more useful.

May 28

Urusvati senses how people must be raised by raising their level of understanding. Is it possible that We will have the joy of seeing the serpent's head crushed by the human heel! Indeed, the great decision indicated by Christ grows. All Heavenly Forces cannot gather as much flame for the last battle as human *podvig* can add. The offensive cannot be started from Above only. A new stronghold on the mountain will provide a foothold. The support for My foot is the construction, which rests on that very Stone. A small fragment may be taken from it for a ring that you will give to your successor before your departure. Let the tradition continue, unbroken.

And Urusvati in the Snows will continue encouraging the work. Help Us, help Us, help Us in all ways. We create a new link between Earth and Heaven. Christ the Builder wore a mason's head scarf. Christ will build the roof of the Temple. The rays of the message penetrate Earth like multicolored threads. A vision during the Temple's construction: A Luminous One entered and began to test stones with a little silver hammer, and upon finishing it, He soared to the vault and shone like silver. A new truth will descend upon the building on [   ]. It is a joy to Me to tell you how it will be. You are interested in the structure of Our Hierarchy, but I would prefer to tell you about the miracle of Earth. When I can do it, I love to talk about the coming times. You can imagine how intensely We watch the laying of the foundation.

May 29

Although the experiment enters a quiet phase, it includes the development of the centers. We see how the intensity of visions, sensations, and understandings come into balance in a natural way. Life-related phenomena must pass into daily life in a normal way. The bridge of sleep is inevitable for some time, especially if it is difficult to attain a state of physical quietude. Regard with attention all that comes to you.... Now the experiment shows a new phase. One needs to understand both directions, one being when the rays can turn into waves of fire, burning out the coverings of the centers. We know cases of so-called ecstasy when good organisms were uselessly reduced to ashes. Physical unpreparedness resulted in inflammation of the centers, simply because of imperfection of the apparatus. (Perhaps one modern mystic burnt out in ecstasy through her leader's fault.) Therefore, the way of [slow] accumulation is better; transmission without inflammation is like an open channel without obstacles.... One need not kindle the centers if the organism is not open to the ecstasy of harmony, but then openess to beauty would also be impossible. But if ignited, the coverings of the centers are to be protected. Now it is impossible to advance without beauty. All can be endured, if the foundation of beauty is preserved.... The manifestation of fire is to be guarded, otherwise the fire of the spirit may burn away, to no benefit.

How is it possible to achieve cosmic conditions earlier, if people cannot take part in Our work before the age of fifty? They may be Our instruments, but creative work in the framework of Our Plan begins at a later age. In the case of Blavatsky, the difference was that at an earlier age she perceived her own actions as clearly distinct from those given by the Higher Guidance, but later she merged both in her consciousness.

Ramakrishna made an irreparable mistake by admitting Vivekananda to Samadhi, which shortened Vivekananda's life. He might otherwise still be living, a true spokesman for India. However, everything comes enveloped in its own atmosphere; the first phase, in London and New York, produces the so-called miracles, but there is no *podvig* in this.

An understanding of the sorrow of this Era prompts sensitive organisms to hasten. If We had shamelessly allowed the rapid pace the first days to continue, there would certainly have been a conflagration within one month. If it were possible for a long time to avoid anguish in conditions of quietude and a comfortable bed, then the coverings of the centers could have acquired immunity more quickly. We would like to find better conditions. We do see images of consequences, but conditions of the path are yet to be discovered. Of course, work and anticipation of dates are particularly painful.... Only to you can We entrust the cause of women in Russia. Celestial bodies determined the approach of the Era, [which will come] if the path is protected. We will shift the date and find the most quiet house.

May 30

Horror flies over the World. Only a serene place of retreat can help gather power. My warrior can be renewed by quiet. I teach how to find quiet. My House is now in the Desert where We have come together for building the New Era. Everything is to be collected in one place. Manifestation, manifestation, manifestation triple can restrain the Beast. Christ pacified the Beast with unsparing courage. The Teacher repeated the words that He put in the foundation of His Teachings. The Furies could not understand that He was already laying the foundation of the New Era. After learning about the purity of snow, have no regrets about the blossoms in the valley. It is only at the summit that the boundary of the World is drawn. *It also happens that before departure all voices become silent, and, even being aware of this law, one becomes awed. In the Egyptian Mysteries there was a fixed moment when the neophyte, having been placed before a threshold in absolute darkness, had to enter into the Unknown without slackening his steps. ... Especially nowadays, since Christ has renounced the miracles, this moment into the Unknown must be passed by special means. Because the future Era must erase the boundaries between the Worlds. And the Egyptian Mysteries have been transformed into the formula, "by human feet."* The achievement of human Power can light up the underground chamber where it will be inconceivably easy to walk, and where one finds treasures rather than darkness. (It is related to my dream.) Before beginning a complex work ... one needs to find quiet.... The pain caused by uninvited shouting is understandable; it is less painful to drive a nail into the hand than to have nerves pierced. Therefore, We will find a quiet house. Now, if possible, both of you retire to bed earlier. All that has been skipped will be made up for quickly, for the vessel is open. You are carrying a blessed miracle; you just need to protect your state. The waiting will not be long; there is no need to agonize. While waiting on the scorched sands, Christ repeated: "I am impoverished." But the sun in its transit shifted the shadows of tents, and the emerging cool brought freshness. There were no flowers, but there were waves of hope and expectation.

June 2

Urusvati, do not worry about the experiment; the morning will come when the new stage is achieved. You see how even weak voices can pierce through the disharmony. There was never a human apparatus that was not in need of great care at certain times. Let Me mention the case of Ramakrishna and Vivekananda. If you knew the absolute silence that they needed for a long time you could imagine what mortal pain could pierce them. But later a luminous cornea-like covering forms near the solar plexus, and even though pain continues, deadly danger is gone. The only important thing is to go on until the end. One must spare and protect the accumulation destined over centuries. (But what if I die?) Then the building of the Temple would have to be postponed for one century. Dissatisfaction is merely awareness of possibilities. There is no room for satisfaction in Our Brotherhood, for it means death of the spirit. (But I am in anguish!) It is earthly sorrow; it has already been said that not One of Us could avoid it. But when Ch. the landowner felt this same readiness to break the vessel at any moment and was tormented by vague recollections, that was his last stage.... It is possible to easily avoid another incarnation.... You ask about F.; but earthly labor lies ahead for him, while you will be working in the densified astral body in far-off spheres. It is possible to easily move from the physical body to the densified one. Therefore, the place of meeting with the Sisters in the future will be at the summit of B[elukha].[10-2] You will have time for everything. Just enjoy nature and keep in mind that legends about the communication of hermits with the spirits of Nature indicate times of the growth of the centers. The right amount of food is what is needed to replenish forces. The right amount of warmth is also what is needed to replenish forces. It is possible to reduce the amount of food as long as the physical forces are not in decline. Excessive food causes pain, just as the loud shouting does. You need to eat only farinaceous, non-fat, and vegetable food. I assure you: your body will soon aquire immunity.... All these statements are necessary to describe the current stage of the experiment.

Christ knew when he touched. Chr[ist] kindled a blue fire. Chr[ist] sent a cross. Lilies never before smelled so strong, and Buddha donned His lilac garment. Urusvati's celebration is Our Celebration.

June 6

Truly, it is right to guard against shouting. There is a transition time when the vessel is open but is not yet protected. What hurts are not words but rather discordant tones. The consciousness is right to defend itself. It is necessary to more securely lock the windows, but just for now, as, indeed, sounds increase a hundredfold. One must protect oneself. Even ordinary concentration requires complete quiet; but when the opening is uncovered, it is like trephination of the skull, and a light feather then feels like a one-pood weight.[10-3] It is dangerous to permit the piercing of a center. Offer a few rupees, and all will quickly change.[4] It is better to purify the air. Give them (servants) five rupees per family so that they will go to their village.

Part Eleven

June 7

The motion of Urusvati's centers occurred in response to some need in America.... Udraya was almost right when he spoke about movement of the astral body. It is like a phone call. (There were repeated sensations of the skin crawling and of contraction of the nerves in the back of my head close to the top, and then a strong rotation in my head that caused loss of balance but not of consciousness.) It is the place where the astral body emerges. *Before it comes out there is a sensation of an outflow from the vertebrae.* You are right to wait for a quiet house, for the time is coming to stabilize achievements.

The various centers unfold differently, and the time comes when this difference must be normalized by rest. ... You may stay for a while without exertion.... *just as a tuned piano should not be touched for awhile nor pounded with any metallic object, an entire rock can be split if knocked upon by metal in a discordant tone. Although this manifestation is well known, it is difficult to imagine it in connection with the human organism. Only by experience can one sense how much more shocking than an explosion some whispers are. It must also be remembered that the combinations of nerves are so diverse that it is difficult to determine the effects by any laws. The physical condition and the spirit are so closely interrelated that only by personal experience can one determine how to safeguard the correct approach of the fires. Fires are the wells of the rays.* ... Both of you affirm understanding of the force related to Us. When you strive toward Us, feel yourselves leaning against Us.

June 8

Chr[ist] says: "You may use My Name if the motivation is sufficient." Buddha says: "You may use My Name if the motivation is sufficient." And I, Who temporarily keep watch on the Tower, say: "You may use My Name if the motivation is sufficient...."

Urusvati rightly observed that world decisions are conveyed by world thoughts, and the building of the New Country can take place only in the framework of world understanding. We hardly need eloquence; the way of touching the spirit is much more powerful. When one sees how important decisions are made with one gesture, it becomes clear that the value of words lies not in their quantity and outer form, but in their inner essence.... A blacksmith should not play with his hammer. Christ's Teaching can be written down on one palm....

June 9

Three years ago My Hand heralded the beginning of the Experiment. On the small table between the beds, there was a dark-blue light, and the Hand wrote on the black bench in the same way you are writing now. The result is good, for the signs can now be given not only at night. The point is not the duration of the contact, but its vitality. It is necessary to achieve simple connections in all the circumstances of life.... I repeat it—We like the result, for several voices have already been included without causing shock. It is now possible to tell what Tara Urusvati will be called in the future. Every Sister and Brother has a descriptive name, depending on the kind of activity; yours will be "She Who Inspires New Ways and Liberates from Prejudice." Not only in the Brotherhood, but also in A[ltai] will you be called by this name, when you will meet the chosen sisters at the Summit of B[elukha]. Therefore, your work will be related to the far-off worlds, for new ways calling Earth to the circle of spiritual ascent will come only from there, and prejudices will fall in the face of the grandeur of possibilities.

Of course, it is work within the White Brotherhood, for flight of the spirit is not measured by hours; it is a phenomenon outside of time, when the spirit flies between planets; it takes one moment that cannot be prolonged, for otherwise there would be a separation between the densified body and the mental body. But it is necessary to remember that the spirit, acting outside of time, cognizes also without the help of measures, and thus reaches up to the fourteenth level of hearing, whereas in the earthly sphere it is possible to attain only the ninth one.

Right now there are no more than three such (people), but with the A[ltai] sisters it can be developed up to the ninth. But the A[ltai] sisters not only will walk on Earth, but also will master the many threads of the earthly sphere.

Urusvati saw an image of the future, when the strings of a violin and a small chain wove a part of a symphony. The sound of rain is also not without significance. There are many ways to enrich earthly creativity.

The crowning of Tara Urusvati will afford new ways to the earthly sisters. When the circular Crown of the Brotherhood touches, it always causes rotation of the centers. Urusvati, Our Crown with the Stone is over you.

Your spirit receives rays and currents—not only K. H.'s and Mine, but also those of Ter., the Chinese Tara, Moh., Lao Tze, Vaug[han], Confucius, and of course Buddha and Chr[ist]. (So it is still difficult for me to receive other rays, right?) Not difficult, but rather that you cannot discern them. (How does the Ray of Teach[er] Rak[oczi] affect me?) It strikes you on your knees. (It is disappointing to me that I cannot yet discern by sound who is talking to me.) Not so important... (During the talk I felt a rotation of the centers in my head.)

June 11

I Myself will give an Instruction about the Temple. Our Directives will be exclusively in this regard. I see how a lama beholds a sign: A luminous woman carries a chalice down from the mountains. Her face is covered with a veil given by Me. The radiant violet aureole shimmers. I open the gates to the luminous Temple, and the fires in the Temple ignite. A long white scarf is spread down the steps. Female disciples approach carrying lilies. I, I, I—I call thrice the spirit of Urusvati. I and Urusvati, before her arrival are like two stars, Urusvati and Uranus, seeking a new orbit. This orbit may be drawn by hand and the life-giving spirit. The dark ones would yield to the formidable Ray of Buddha's daughter. Urusvati, the Ray of Buddha followed Him on his path as Gautama. [She is] a flower of spirit who was charged by the Mother with the responsibility to guide the first women's community.

When completing the earthly cycle, it is not proper to speak about its insignificance. Look deeper, and you will see beautiful strivings. I see no one ahead of you. Your close approach to Buddha was begun long ago. You laid many beautiful foundations, but not connected with any name. Whence came this possibility to be a Tara with a mission to be an inspirer and a liberator? There is awareness of the predestined! And when the end to ways is close, the spirit begins to constantly strive. We three are waiting for you: I, Whom you inspired to My best thoughts, your former spiritual Teacher, and your uncle Who reached Us via an unprecedented self-sacrifice. You will learn from Him Himself about it. You should wait until the Day of the Mother of the World, when you will tell your female disciples: "Here we are, the earthly ones; here we are in simple garments; here we understand the praise of greatness of Russia, shown on a Cosmic scale, and now I may go, and the mountain will become the Place of Trust. Now I may leave to you the white scarf. R. may find a path leading up to the Mountain. Do not reject the predestined R. Bethlehem.... The unprecedented is predestined to you."

I rejoice to see how unusual it is in life to go truthfully and sensitively. I rejoice to see how Urusvati's experience is accumulated naturally. (But I am doing so little!) Let Us judge; your organism senses the limits of possibility. It will blaze and cannot be put out! And if you meet a tiger, tell him: "Do not eat us, there is so much work ahead!...."

Urusvati heard Buddha's voice: "Allow yourself courage!...."

June 17

Today Urusvati heard the voice of My Friend and Brother who talked about debts that He took upon Himself. My Friend filled an entire purse to pay these debts. For now I am more lucky than He. Forming a circle carries an obligation to pay for it. I shall pay for you.... I will pay in full. I have no fear and will pay what is needed.

June 18

I sense Urusvati's love for Buddha. Urusvati senses the Ray of Our Great Brother. (During the general Talk there was heard a noise, as if the sliding door to the lower terrace were opened and then closed. After a few seconds footsteps and voices were heard on the lower floor. My son George went downstairs to find out what was happening. Upon his return he told me that the servants also heard the entrance door open; and the team consisting of a butler, bearer, and night guard went to see to it, but everything was in order. The Lord said that He Himself had opened the door for it was He Who was in the house.)

June 19

Urusvati, take care of your chest; do not damage the crystal marked by Christ, when the Lord was examining the stairs. (What does a sensation of the consciousness being outside the head mean?) This is a very characteristic phenomenon—consciousness signified by a flame above the head. It means growth of the astral. Every time notice the new sensations, for example, a flame over the head. The astral knocked at the toes, but since the lower centers were closed, it went in the right direction. Otherwise there would be a downward outflow, which is a sign of delay of spiritual development. (Is this the beginning of the projection of the astral?) Of course, yes, as the astral grows, its outflow becomes more natural. (What kind of book did M. M. show me?) A book of defense—a book of human ingratitude.

Just think about how much you give away in the nighttime! The mere exerting of influence over Tam ... takes much energy. (Did George see me?) Yes, and more than once; sometimes you retain in your memory and recall fragments of talks upon your return from flights.... Now it is necessary to improve the general results. Let us not close our eyes to what is happening, especially because as personal successes in the experiment grow, many voices come, and their effect is lighter.

I admire Urusvati's reliable intuition.... It is necessary to manifest stern affirmation.... Urusvati resembles more an Egyptian priestess, while F. shows the character of a Dalai Lama. Your missions correspond to those characters. Knowledge of past events may help those who are awake in spirit, but to those who are sleeping it is unadvisable…. It is remarkable that Urusvati is tense, like a spring, at the coming of a wave. The waves are strong but the ship withstands.

(How soon will I receive answers to my questions?) Soon. (I heard a voice that has answered my question. Whose voice was that?) Buddha's.

June 24

The flights of the subtle body can be of two kinds: either it flows out of the feet and wanders aimlessly, or it passes through the upper centers and embarks upon spiritual missions. It is instantaneously transported across oceans, it teaches people, it nourishes auras. It must be said that only extraordinary strivings and resourcefulness impel the subtle body to concentrate its touch upon a physical object. It is noticed as a right and unexpected shield strengthening the result. *For usually the spirit strives to act upon spirit, overlooking the fact that physical objects can be excellent conductors. (If it was produced by the mental body, does that mean that what I recorded left no trace?)*

It remained there, as far as the mental body could compress energy. We are glad that *not only your astral body but also the mental body is active. Of course the astral body is also projected, but We do not value the actions of the astral body. We consider the consciousness of the mental body more important.* Especially valuable was that, for the first time, you applied your influence to physical objects. This is a very practical step. *To sharpen the point of this force is not so simple,* and this resourcefulness will be of use for future flights. It is necessary to become accustomed to new sensations. Indeed, you climb mountains without oxygen, and this makes a difference. The experiment resulted in great achievement. Is it possible that you consider [hearing] Buddha's voice a trifle?!! (But I have already heard Christ's voice!) Christ's voice is easier to hear, for the red and yellow tints are weaker in His rainbow. Buddha's rainbow is much harsher. When Urusvati saw it she could not accept it at once. (Why is it harsher?) For He passed away without destroying the Sheath of His Spirit, as Christ did. He was even burned, whereas Christ destroyed His Body by action of the Spirit. Christ's Spirit, by Its own order, decomposed Its Body into atoms. It was a remarkable achievement of Christ. She who hates cemeteries should approve when earthly baggage is carried away by its owner. The Bodies of Christ and Buddha are similar, but Their tints are different. It is easy to understand that burning cannot achieve such a degree of decomposition into atoms as the fire of the spirit can. Cemeteries and saint's relics constitute the lowest level, burning is higher, and the fire of the spirit is still higher. But on Earth only Christ accomplished that.

I can tell you both some important news. My Friend is going to pass to the densified body. (Is Teacher K. H. going to help the Plan?) Yes, but not here. Let Me describe the essence of His experiment. He is trying to bring the quality of the densified body closer to that of Earth, without being burdened by the earthly envelope. Hir[onius] also would like to join that experiment through Me. For F. there will also come time to remain with Us, like you. Hironius' time has not come yet. But we see your constant readiness to pass, and this quality, coupled with vigilance, is very much needed. However, departure should take place without betraying the Plan of the Lords. Maybe I also would like to leave for other worlds, but I live on Earth instead. You see, it is Christ's Plan that is carried out.... He may choose a Plan, while We and Our coworkers stand guard. Even hunger and pain will not hinder those who are with Us. The whole field can be seen only after the battle. I also may need a rest for a moment, but instead new messages arrive and half of My warriors ask for a temporary withdrawal from the battle. They intend to improve on Christ's decisions! Everybody believes that he or she would do better if they were in His place.

Even the manifestation of the Christ's Plan does not make them understand that it is impermissible to betray the Plan. The first condition of the Brotherhood is obedience to an accepted Plan, and the One Who offered the Plan assumes responsibility for it. Is it possible that We will obstruct Christ's Will? And where the Lord chooses not to disclose His Will to Us, We say: "We will not increase Your burden, for You are in command this day."

I would suggest to you to write [letters] at two-week intervals, beginning next year. They should become accustomed to receiving your letters less often. I Myself will tell you when to write. I Myself know how necessary it is to stop this flow soon. You are in a special state of the spirit when enormous sendings are projected not only through your aura but also through your limbs. It may be felt as a beam of light in your hands or a pulling sensation. (This night I suffered from pulling sensations in both hands.) This is why I tell you: do not indulge in giving too much.

...This last night a secret mystery of Ishtar was used, when, to strengthen the neophyte's consciousness, the supreme priestess in complete darkness, invisible, touches with her lips the solar plexus of the newly-converted. It is a most ancient Mystery originating in Egypt. You both remember from the talk about Neophytes that if the Neophyte crossed the threshold of darkness and progressed only up to the most finely spun veil, and due to his spirit being dormant, he was invisibly stopped, then he received a kiss from the Mother of the World. Nephrite played that highest role. It was magic then. Centuries passed, and the spirit can apply this powerful action in life. (I saw myself as a priestess in a white garment kissing the solar plexus of my son George.)

Notes

Part One

1. Literally *Blagovestie* means "Good Message" or "Announcement of the Good News."
2. A khatyk is a ritual scarf.
3. The term "spring" may be understood to mean "a moving force."
4. Plural of *podvizhnitsa*, which means a female engaged in *podvig*, who is a devotee, a zealot, a heroic woman utterly devoted to a noble cause. In the context of Eastern Christianity, it may stand for a female hermit or ascetic. The masculine form is *podvizhnik*.
5. *Isis Unveiled* by H. P. Blavatsky (Wheaton, IL: The Theosophical Publishing House, 1972).

Part Two

1. The Master Koot Hoomi.
2. Rokotova was Helena Roerich's family name in her previous incarnation in nineteenth-century Russia.
3. Altai, or the Altai Mountains, is a mountain system in Central Asia ranging from the Gobi Desert in China to the West Siberian Plain in Russia. The highest mountain in the range, the Mount Belukha, or the "White Mountain," is hinted at in the Roerichs' writings as a sacred mountain of outstanding importance.

Part Three

1. These may be identifications of previous incarnations of some Sisters based on the information herein and on other writings by Helena Roerich, especially *Letters of Helena Roerich* (New York: Agni Yoga Society, Inc., 1954): St. Catherine of Siena (1347-1380); St. Ursula (4th century); and St. Teresa of Avila (1515-1582), who is mentioned in *Letters of Helena Roerich* under the name of St. Theresa of Spain.
2. From the book *On Eastern Crossroads: Legends and Prophecies of Asia,* (New York: Agni Yoga Society, 1992) p. 9 .
3. Ibid., p. 10.
4. One of Helena Roerich's previous incarnations. H. R. published a partial

Russian translation of the *Mahatma Letters* to Sinnett under the name of Iskander Khanum. It was customary for H. R. to use names from previous incarnations as pseudonyms.

5. The original Russian edition (1926) of H. R.'s *Foundations of Buddhism* (New York: Agni Yoga Society, Inc, 1971) was published under the name of Natalia Rokotova (alternative French spelling: Natalie Rokotoff). Ryazan is a Russian city situated southeast of Moscow.

6. Many Decembrists were sent into exile in Siberia. Decembrists were those who participated in the conspiracy and insurrection against Tsar Nicholas I on the day of his accession in December 1825.

7. Count Vorontsov was a Decembrist.

8. The White Brotherhood.

Part Four

1. M. M. refers to Master Morya.
2. M. K. H. refers to Master Koot Hoomi.

Part Five

1. & 2. The star refers to Venus.
3. This may be a reference to St. Radegunda, a Merovingian queen of the Sixth Century who became a nun and founded a nunnery at Poitiers, France.
4. Sister Radegunda's service to the poor was to maintain communities that would provide housing and sustenance in exchange for productive labor.

Part Six

1. & 2. *On Eastern Crossroads: Legends and Prophecies of Asia* by Helena Roerich, (New York: Agni Yoga Society, Inc., 1992), pp. 41-42.
3. Barchan is a crescent-shaped sand dune with the convex side in the direction of the wind.
4. The Treasure of Poseidon refers to a submerged island that was a part of Atlantis.

Part Seven

1. Kurnovoo: a ruler of ancient Atlantis and one of Master M.'s previous incarnations. See *Leaves of Morya's Garden, Book I*, para. 353, for a partial listing of Master Morya's past incarnations (Agni Yoga Society, 1953).

2. See *Agni Yoga*, Afterword, and *Supermundane, Book I,* para. 134.
3. Udraya is Yury (George) Nikolaevich Roerich.
4. Lumoa is Svetoslav Nikolaevich Roerich.
5. The names of sects in Russian Orthodox Christianity.

Part Eight

1. Perhaps it is this kind of Service that is depicted in Nicholas Roerich's painting *Treasure of the Mountain*. See Jacqueline Decter's *Nicholas Roerich* (Park Street Press, 1989), p. 202.

Part Nine

1. The Circle refers to an inner group of the Roerichs' coworkers in America.

Part Ten

1. A retort is a vessel with a long neck turned downward, which is used in distilling liquids.
2. Belukha is the highest and most sacred peak of the Altai Mountains in Siberia.
3. A pood is a Russian unit of weight equal approximately to 36 lbs.
4. A rupee is an Indian unit of currency.

Letters

*H*ere are thirty-one letters of Helena Roerich, which were written between the years 1945 and 1949. They were sent to America to Sina and Dudley Fosdick, the directors of the Nicholas Roerich Museum in New York City. Some portions of the letters were omitted.

Letters

My Darling Sinochka,[1]

Thank you for the detailed letters. Thanks to them, we can more or less orient ourselves to the situations that have been created and to the moods of our old friends, as well as to those newcomers visible on the horizon. Of course, there are difficulties everywhere, and there is a decline of interest in that which is most urgent, the culture of life. Everywhere irresponsibility is on the rise, and I await the changes, especially in everyone's consciousness. People think least of all about cultural progress, when they should be preparing for the coming new step in evolution, not with empty dreams about a rosy future, but with harder work, expansion of consciousness, and with thoughts of ways to bring enlightenment.

Value those coworkers who prove themselves in action. Though there are not many of them, if there is but a spark of love of the Teaching burning in their hearts, their labor will be a hundred times more productive.

Apparently, America has more luck with books and materials getting through. But here, things drag on very slowly. Sometimes telegrams are delivered within two days of being sent, but letters, if they come through at all, can take from three to six months or more. Often they do not reach us at all, disappearing in space without a trace—at least this is what a local TASS representative claims. Sometimes he sends us newspapers, pamphlets, and records of the activities of different educational groups.

There are many things in this material that are touching and joyful, but also things that sadden one; apparently, there are great privations and shortages of intellectual force.

I was touched recently when I was reading about the activities of Russian scientists, of whom many of those mentioned are women. But my joy for them was short-lived because, for some reason, the author of the article decided to reveal the scientists' ages, and I, to my great disappointment, learned that some of them were older than I. As for the rest of them, they were about my age! Well then, "zhivy starym zhirom."[2] Thus, imperceptibly, the field of knowledge may turn to desert. It is necessary to put some time into strengthening the staff of teachers. When will the time come when it will be possible to adjust to the increasing rhythm of the right accumulations of knowledge?

I write in these days of VICTORY. How much happiness as well as sorrow!

The war with Japan is undoubtedly going to end by autumn, but for how long will there be quiet? With Roosevelt's death, another page of history has ended. The new one is going to start with difficulties; the pattern is complicated. But let joy be with those who are ready for heroic deeds in the building up of culture. The eve is always difficult. A little more patience, and there will be possibilities of new rays of hope. No seed is lost where the Earth was plowed by the nations' suffering.

It was terrible to find out from R. Pel's letter about the death of friends in Paris.

What kind of death? Can it really be of starvation? It is impossible to understand a crime so horribly committed against such an old and wonderful man as the scientist Metalnikov.[3] The brutality of the Germans is going to remain matchless in the history of the nations. Magazines that our local English friends send to us from London are full of descriptions and photographs of madness and mockery, sadism, and acts of brutality against human individuality. Our local English magazines also tell about horrors that happened to the unfortunate prisoners and captured townspeople in the concentration camps. It is disgusting to look at these brutalities, but they have to be known. It is impossible to educate a new generation without the knowledge of past madness; there is no way to educate in the greenhouse of the delicate a generation that is destined to create a new Earth.

Heroism of the spirit is strengthened by a stern knowledge of unvarnished reality and by the courage of a life lived in the name of the true meaning of man—creator of the worlds—and not by the pictures of a rosy prosperity. It can be said to those who, as Sinochka writes, consider barbaric the actions of the nation that selflessly defended itself and brought victory to the motherland, that wished to open friends' eyes to the destruction that occurred in the country, to the 'historical' property, and to those principles that created and supported the nation's heroic spirit; not only is it not barbarism, but it is a warning to those who have not yet experienced such a terrible ravaging and bloodletting of their own country. Must one have to face such sorrow to be convinced about how much people are filled with terrible, brutal egoism? To the nation that went through such terrible sufferings and the loss of all that is most valuable is offered cold condolences, and it is expected to respond with a sweet smile, while it is reproached for barbarism for daring to show its pain and express the indignation of its spirit.

So we are happy for the developed activity of ARCA.[4] Let it become stronger. Its time will come and its wonderful activity will expand. Sinochka and Dudley, like an ancient priestess and priest, maintain the fire entrusted to them in the Temple.[5] We value, dear, truly value your love and selfless labor in the name of culture, that poor Cinderella of the rich sister, civilization. Where is that prince who will pick up her shoe?! He is truly going to be crowned with a world crown. As to your question about paintings, you should have a little more patience. The traitors won't be able to get away from the heavy karma built by them. Circumstances hasten and will show the hour of the reverse blow. Watch the traitors and their patron as much as you can, but have patience. I hug you, my dear, and I rely upon my faith in you.

August 14, 1946

My Darling Sinochka,

If one can trust the newspapers and radio, I am writing this letter one day before a general postal strike. I want, my dear ones, to assure you, firmly and calmly once again, not to be disturbed by any approaching confusion and events. Preserve in your heart steadfast trust in the Hierarchy of Light and joy in the service to the Common Good by introducing the great Fundamentals under the Banner of Peace and Culture. Indeed, the Banner of Peace covers all vital manifestations for the good of people.

This letter was delayed for a few days, for the oncoming period of earthquakes and floods, as always, affected my health. The tension in my head increased and caused me pain, and the centers of my lungs also became painfully sensitive. Whenever I moved, breathing was difficult. Since August 12, though, the pain has disappeared and only some tension is left, so I continue this letter on August 14.

I've been looking lately at the message given in 1931 about the great meaning of the Banner of Peace, or the Banner of the Lords, and how necessary it is to unfold The Banner of Peace because of all the foundations of culture contained within it. It was precisely in foreseeing the approaching wars, disintegrations, and new distractions that the Banner of Peace was raised. We know that new ideas and constructions are implemented and affirmed only in the presence of great tension and battle, and every battle has its purpose, and every pattern its meaning. But the time of their affirmation could last for tens of years. It was said: "The time when the Fire-blossom is manifested cannot be an easy one. The Banner of the World is not unfurled at the bazaar."[1]

"...During the Era of Fire, when Light struggles with darkness, the manifestation of the Banner of Peace is that fundamental sign which will give a new step to humanity. Thus Beauty, Knowledge, Art, and all nations will unite under this sign. Thus, only the highest measures can be applied to the Banner.... The great proclamation must be understood as a step toward the regeneration of the world."[2]

I also recall the beginnings of the League of Culture under the Banner of Peace. Of course, the war, but mainly the betrayal of a few apostates impeded and even stopped the development and dissemination of the good activity. With the coming new Cycle, the Banner of Peace and Culture must be raised and unfurled once again. It is said in the book *Hierarchy*: "Without culture there can be no international agreement or mutual understanding. Without culture the people's understanding cannot embrace all needs of evolution. Therefore the Banner of Peace comprises all subtle concepts that will lead nations to the understanding of culture. Humanity does not understand how to manifest reverence for that which comprises immortality of spirit. The Banner of Peace will bring the understanding of this lofty significance. Humanity cannot flourish without the knowledge of the greatness of culture. The Banner of Peace will open the gates to a better Future. When countries are on the way to destruction, then even those who are spiritually depleted must understand of what the ascent consists. Verily, salvation lies in culture. Thus, the Banner of Peace brings a better Future."[3]

"It's time to understand that the Banner of Peace, the greatest in history, is unfolding. The Banner of Peace never before was manifested as a sign of the New World. Let people understand the Sign of Salvation. The Earth trembles. Currents are scorching! The Banner of Peace, Our Banner, is as a beacon in the storm. And the sowing of culture is an antidote!"

I strongly advise you to look through the paragraphs in the book *Hierarchy* that concern the Banner of Peace, at least those wfrom #324 to #400. More than anything else, the book *Hierarchy* relates to the Banner of Peace, and that is why we have to extend our understanding even more of its significance by reading this book when we work to raise this Banner. The Banner of Peace—The Banner of the Stronghold of Light!

Let us understand the League of Culture as a conglomerate of every possible organization, from spiritual to cooperatives. Everything can be placed under the Dome of Culture. That is why one must not be apprehensive if unexpected organizations become affiliated with it. You remember, of course, all departments of the League of Culture, but I will list them so they will be on this sheet.

Let all our institutions and organizations be kept and developed, but over them let the World League of Culture come to life.[4] Let all the members of our institutions also be members of the World League of Culture. It will contain the following departments: first, the Department of Peace; second, Spiritual Development & Education; third, Science; fourth, the Arts; fifth, Motherhood & Education; sixth, Craft and Labor; seventh, Cooperation & Industry; eighth, Protection & Safety; ninth, System of Land Tenure & Construction; Tenth, Care of the Public Health. The rest will be included as parts of these departments: Justice will find its place in the Department of Peace; the army, in the Protection & Safety [department]; and Treasury, in [the Department of] Cooperation. Of course, [the Department of] spiritual development will contain Religion & Philosophy. Departments are supposed to have councils and chairmen. Let the beginning be small, without propaganda. Let the year 1931 be the threshold of the world movement. We send rays to different countries, but, most important, do not reject newcomers, and abstain from quarrels, which are born out of ignorance.

Events will help the movement for culture to develop, as a last refuge. No one should think that this movement is an old one; it is a threshold of the New World. Thus, we will collect the best thoughts near the Banner of Peace, and we will cover it with all our undertakings. Let the coming ones get used to seeing the Banner of Peace and remember the great foundations that it leads. The Great never entered the world with fanfares and triumphs, but always with labor and suffering, accompanied by ignorant mockery. But we will live through all objections to see the confirmation of culture as the head of the New Construction.

Mass consciousness will be raised to a new level and they will understand that countries cannot live and develop without an understanding of true culture. It is impossible to continue the education of new generations with substitutes for culture. Any surrogate is a lie, and false bases can't make strong foundations; this is why decay and self-destruction are inevitable.

Of course, the threshold of the New Era that brings a great world reconstruction and is escorted by incredible revelations and scientific discoveries will not come easily, but it is wonderful to lay the foundations of a magnificent Future.

Indeed, the coming era will to some degree unveil the Supermundane World. Many things will become evident and accessible to earthly sensations, and this is exactly what is bringing me joy. The boundaries between the spiritual and the material, between the earthly and the Supermundane, will gradually disappear and people still in the earthly life will be consciously preparing themselves for usefulness in the Supermundane World. The earthly life itself won't be a senseless scrap, but will become a conscious, creative work through implementation and application of the accepted assignment in both worlds! It is possible to imagine how the evolution of the Earth will be ennobled and quickened. For the present, mankind is busy with increasing self-destruction, for not many understand that within self-destruction first of all is contained mental murder. Mankind has produced a dangerous situation. People are killing the spirit and depriving themselves of psychic energy. It is impossible to imagine how ill is mankind! And this contagion goes throughout all the planet. Heavily populated places are especially subject to epidemics of self-destructiveness.

Humanity does not think about how it will be perceived in the Supermundane World. Religions were not able to explain the significance of morals, and now the religions cannot find common ground with Science. Great Unity is being displaced by pitiful division. Every breaking up is a symbol of weakness. To where will wandering humanity turn? It needs, first of all, a doctor and a Teacher. They can warn about the dangers, which are great! The Thinker deplored: "Terrible is the sight of the wandering self-destroyers. Some of the two-legged, limited by the world of the flesh-Earth, suppose that self-destruction is just physical murder; they can't even imagine another more miserable murder—psychic!"

It is so important, so urgent, to realize the salutary Beacon—the Hierarchy of Light in the ocean of madness! The Banner of Peace should remind one about the terrible times!

Sinochka is right to be revolted by the injustice inflicted by the paid opposition. Also, right are those who predict that it will justify its name, but as always, not with the meaning that is desired by some participants. Great decisions are guarded by the powers of Light, otherwise our planet would have exploded a long time ago, without the possibility of finding a better home for mad humanity! Nobody pondered over these consequences.

My darling Sinochka, I understand the sadness and anguish you feel by looking at those who apparently have the capacity for the new consciousness but can't show a constant enthusiasm of the spirit. I am so familiar with this. It could be advised to Magdalen to read paragraph 38 in *Hierarchy*.[5] I love it very much. I ask Sinochka to tell Katherine that I wish her to become imbued with the meaning of the Banner of Peace and to read the paragraphs that I have indicated.[6] The Banner of Peace is not just a Banner of Peace, but precisely that by which the world survives! I send to Sinochka and Dudley all my tenderness and love and heartfelt regards.

January 1948

It is necessary to explain to all who study the Agni Yoga books that the Primary, fiery energy is one and the same as the names: fiery energy, heart energy, mental, and psychic energy. They are all names that are, in essence, just different aspects of one and the same fundamental, primal energy, or the energy of Be-ness. It is possible simply to say that psychic energy is a higher quality of primal energy. Thus, spirit and consciousness are inseparable from psychic energy. To better understand the meaning of the activity of psychic energy, it is necessary to include some paragraphs on spirit and other subtle energies. This can broaden the understanding about its innumerable qualities.

To be sure, I would begin by compiling excerpts from paragraphs 42, 56, 63, and also 131, where is discussed the inseparability of the fate of human evolution from cosmic processes and the most subtle energies. It would be wrong to omit in #216, which is dedicated to psychic energy, the examples of the different qualities of psychic energy that are awakening every century. If Madam Dzh. is writing out #214, where it mentions Materia Lucida, the more so should she include paragraphs 144 and 145, where it is mentioned that Fohat nurtures psychic energy. It is impossible to make contact with subtle energies without the development and accumulation of psychic energy. All of our organism is in existence and its centers are active because of psychic energy. If #145 is included, then on page 79, the sixth line from the top after the words "Using the opened centers," add "of Sister Ur...", otherwise it will be impossible to understand which centers.

From #148 it would be good to write out the phrase "All experiments in the regions of subtlest energies can take place in the hours when you are easily borne from Earth...."

Psychic energy is precisely a subtle energy.

The solar plexus is also a repository of psychic energy and this should be mentioned.

And now the Fiery World. I already mentioned the unity of fundamental energy, which is the primal and fiery energy. Fiery energy is exactly the fundamental energy, because fire is manifested in everything. There is no life without fire; there is no manifestation without fire. The highest manifestation of this fundamental fiery energy is psychic energy, and the qualities of this energy are unlimited. All subdivisions are in essence different qualities of the one fundamental energy, which manifests on different planes and through different bodies through the different nerve centers or vehicles. Actually, it is difficult to separate spirit from soul, because spirit is fire, and the soul collects fiery manifestations of the energy. That is why there is no tangible difference between these energies. It is possible only to see a different degree of the fiery power in its manifestations.

The Subtle World is all around us, and its scope is much broader and in no way comparable to our earthly plane. If you wish, it could be called a step to the Fiery World. The Subtle World has many spheres and layers, and there is no other division between them than through the quality of consciousness; therefore, there are as many stages as there are levels of consciousness. Of course, the Fiery World is a specially high stage in the perfection of consciousness. That is why inhabitants of this sphere rarely, and in only the most exceptional circumstances, can come nearer to our earthly sphere. Their approaching may provoke large disturbances in the Subtle World as well as on Earth. There is too much of a difference in their vibrations from the earthly ones.

The Supermundane World is both the Subtle World and the World of Thought. What could be more supermundane than thought? Devachan is, of course, a special state in the Subtle World in which a spirit is absorbed for needed rest. This state is really heavenly bliss, because in that dream state, the spirit experiences a transcendent earthly reality of a special brightness, which includes all the happiest days and moments of its earthly life. Not a single sad or unpleasant thought darkens this state of bliss.

Do not grieve, my darlings, about those who fall away. You are working for the sake of the idea, and not for the moths that cannot yet comprehend the meaning of what is being offered to them—acquaintance with the country of the Future. Unfortunately, we must limit distribution of the Russian books of the Teaching because, apparently, many of them have perished. But the time is close when they will be needed in Russia.

"So, the wicked will flow free like lava engulfing throughout history those who take up arms against Good." Sinochka is puzzled—how is it that true evil can be engulfed by its own evil? Earthly justice, of course, is not always just, and centuries must sometimes pass before justice triumphs. But nevertheless, it does triumph. Our modern consciousness already elucidates and values events and deeds of past centuries in a different way. Don't we now condemn all the delusions and crimes committed through ignorance and self-interest?

Truly, the evil will devours and destroys its own bearer. Who are those named soulless creatures and cosmic waste? The evil will pushes them onto the slope, and in their fall, they speed into the abyss. But there is no evil will that could engulf the bearer of Good, because the tortures and even premature death bring to the bearer of Good incomparable rewards in the Subtle World and strengthen his spirit for new accomplishments, for new perfection. Exactly in this way can it be understood that an evil will is destroyed by its own harm.

January 13, 1948

With whom can I share all the suffering I have gone through but with those closest to my spirit? Who else can understand all the complexities of the circumstances that led to this New Decision, which gave N. K. the possibility to now end his labors of light with a beautiful, final chord, one more time to manifest and raise the Banner of Peace in the midst of the general madness of the world, this time in his much beloved India?[1]

Our Light, Our Beloved left as he lived—simply, beautifully, and majestically. The world truly is orphaned by the departure of this beautiful Spirit! India touchingly, beautifully, and strongly responded to his departure. Newspapers, magazines, societies, friends, and acquaintances remarked brilliantly about the irreplaceable loss to the world of this great creator of wonderful images, this giant of thought and activity, a wonderful human being, a true friend of humanity. Indeed, after meeting him, no one left feeling burdened; on the contrary, he could relieve other's burdens and direct them on a new path, a path of aspiration and courageously realized labor in the name of the Common Good. Many remarked on the great riches of his spiritual legacy, and it is the responsibility of every conscious human being to accept this wealth and follow his lofty advice.

There is now an exhibition of his paintings in Delhi. Nehru gave a wonderful speech during the reception about the significance of his work. He particularly stressed the idea of the Banner of Peace. Enormous numbers of visitors attended the opening, and [the exhibition] is continuing with the same success.

It is still difficult for me to write about his illness and last days. I will write later. But I would ask you to convey to all his friends and admirers the statement that is both wonderful and very true: "The heart could not endure the amount of poison generated by a mad humanity."

I never saw beauty as high and spiritual as was impressed on his face. We could not tear ourselves away from our contemplation of this heavenly goodness and the touching tenderness of his wonderful face. He was shining as if from some inner light, and even the white narcissi that surrounded him looked crude next to his luminous appearance.

Terrible pain wrings the heart when thinking about the loss. He was asleep when the call of the G.L. [Great Lord] came for him, at three o'clock in the morning on a most solemn day, by the Hindu calendar, of Shiva's birthday. One week before his death he saw Saint Sergius standing between our beds and saying: "My dear ones, why must you suffer here? Go with Me. Come to Me, now!" His spirit wanted to leave; he was grieved very much by the world's chaotic happenings—though in secret we kept from him all the dreadful things going on in our valley and in immediate nearness to us. He was also very worried about the growing Russo-phobia in America, because he knew where this hatred would lead. His heart could not endure the pressures and the terrible pain of seeing the oppression of all that belongs to culture, all that brings salvation for the coming generation.

The only consolation in our sorrow is understanding that a better lot was given to him. Why prolong his suffering amidst such ignorance and waste his best gifts on present generations that cannot accept or value them? He will return in a better time, to a purified soil, and will finish his sowing and service to his country and to all humanity. But the loss of such a leader is truly irreparable and will delay the progress of humanity for another century.

We are going to leave our beautiful valley, our place that he loved so much, on January 17. We are going to Delhi and will be staying in New Delhi in the house of our friends the Maharaja and Maharani Mandy. Write, my darlings, to this address. To keep you informed about our travels, I am going to write more often when we get to Delhi. We will meet the Russian ambassador there, and when the decision about moving is officially registered, we will notify you by telegram. We will move the paintings and all materials, the archive of his wonderful activity.[2]

We are courageously going to continue his work, courageously to accept this burden and carry it on, until the given goal and day.

Darlings, continue your wonderful work as much as possible, considering the circumstances, and without great expenditures. Do not be disappointed by small results, for who can measure them? This is a time of transition, and it is saturated with so many explosions that there is no possibility for pursuing the plan for constructive work. Keep the flame alive, like an Icon-lamp before a Holy Image, as a sign at the crossroads!

Your thought regarding a "Roerich Foundation" is wonderful. But how will America respond to this! We received very few letters or telegrams of sympathy from there. But India truly showed an utmost reverence for him. Many people wrote me the most heartfelt and touching letters, expressing their deep sorrow, and their feeling of loss at the departure of our Pasenka (as his sons and Devika referred to him) of Light.

I would be happy to see you both at our place, as well as Katherine and Inge, but it is not possible to rejoice right now.[3] The danger is coming closer to our place because of the war in Kashmir. Almost all foreigners, as well as the English, have already left the valley. Because of the very different (and absurd) rumors being spread, the people are very worried and their mood is far from peaceful. The whole valley could be set on fire again like straw, and then any possibility of departure would be stopped for a long time. And now, because of the terrible flood, the rise of the Beas River is higher than 33 feet, and many bridges and mountain roads have been carried away. We have been isolated from the rest of the world for several months.

Now we are faced with large obstacles to our travel because a break in the road has not yet been filled, and there is no way for a car to get through. The break stretches for another four miles; boxes have to be carried by hand, and coolies are impossible to deal with because they charge such exorbitant prices. Our luggage is huge; we are taking heavy boxes with paintings and part of the great library. We will send you a telegram on our arrival in Delhi.

My dream is to work with you and to meet also with Katherine and Inge. This dream has to come true. The work will be hard, but in the heroic labor we will find new joy, and new possibilities will appear for us. The coming time is terrible, and the madness will bring consequences on a large scale. Nineteen forty-nine is going to be a difficult year! A mad rush to destruction. Hitler's example has not frightened them.

February 7, 1948

You understood correctly that the departure of our darling and beloved Pasenka at this present time was truly the best conclusion to the life of this wonderful, selfless toiler. Truly, by this time his heart could not contain the human poison that saturates the atmosphere of the planet. So one more great spirit is gone, killed by the hand of madness, who with his blood imprinted nonviolence as his Teaching. Spirits of Light depart before the approach of darkness, and Their Images remain as the only Beacons in the blackness of the approaching calamities.

Dear ones, you are asking about the direction of your activity— of course, I consider the main directions unchanged. Now it is important to collect all materials regarding the activity of Nicholas Roerich, from the early years till his last days. Collect two or three copies of all articles that appeared after his departure. A complete collection of all his articles should be gathered, and all appeals made to different countries in connection with the Pact, and all answers to them. Keep, as well, all of his letters to you and to his friends. It is good to make a complete list of all of his paintings in different countries, including those that we have, as well as the ones you have. Of course, as soon as we are settled in a more or less permanent place, we will begin sorting through the archives and organizing all the materials that we have. We are trying to collect as many articles and notices as possible that have appeared in the local press.

There are a lot of them, but most of them are in the local languages. Besides, there is no clipping bureau here, and it is possible only by chance or through friends to find out what came out and where. But it is possible to say that not a single important town, nor a single newspaper, failed to pay its respects to the memory of this great artist and human being.

Some of the largest and best paintings were bought for the future National Gallery.

Concerning the activities of ARCA, of course they should cease as soon as the New Country's representative departs. Great caution should be displayed, because unfriendly attacks could come regarding that institution, which so selflessly worked for the rapprochement of the two great countries. To avoid blasphemy, do not put N. K.'s portrait on display. For the summer, ARCA's functions could be stopped or reduced to a minimum.

But the activity of the Pact Committee has to continue. Only the sudden assassination of Gandhi prevented the final ratification of the Pact by the Indian Government. The country is in a state of great grief, but his tragic end could well make possible what he could not achieve when he was alive. It is difficult in the world; confusion is coming, but we will make it through this knowing that the madness will not last— otherwise the world will not survive.

We will send you a telegram and tell you where to write to us as soon as we know about our way. I think that you will have to write to the address of Boris Konstantinovich's wife.[1] Also, I sent you more pages of *Supermundane* by boat mail. Guard them very carefully as I do not think that I will be able to repeat this sending. We will publish it in America when we are able to establish the date of the awaited appearance of this wonderful Revelation. I will send you *Infinity* translated by Mr. Gartner, but keep in mind that there may possibly be great inaccuracies because I didn't look through this translation.[2] We also will send a box with Conlan's article and books of the Teachings in different languages; you will be able to use them sooner than we.[3] I feel sad that I could not answer Sinochka's questions regarding the correctness of the translation of the paragraphs in *Fiery World*. I do not know if I will have a chance to answer them because our moving is time-consuming. We are in the vortex of city life now, and it is difficult because of new people; new, difficult vibrations; the valley's atmosphere; and large accumulations, clean and dirty, both good and evil.

February 23, 1948

Delhi, India

My dear and beloved, every bit of news from you makes me rejoice. You see, my spiritual loneliness on Earth is great. The loving understanding and spiritual harmony that bound me with N. K. made all the difficult situations easier and brightened the future. With his departure, my isolation from all that is personal and earthly is even stronger. There is left only a deep desire to bring forth all the collected treasures and to give whatever is possible to hungry souls.

We hope to have already moved on by the beginning of March. It's difficult to stay here. The people are showing their fangs, and of course, these latest conditions are the most destructive. The world situation could change so much in the near future that it's impossible to say who is going to be where, not only by autumn but even by summer. In any case, we are going to try from wherever, dear ones, and by all possible means, to let you know about our movements. Rumors are spreading here that are at times so ridiculous; but in general, there is a lot of sympathy expressed for the New Country. Ordinary people have begun to better understand the meaning and significance of the world's latest political situations. There is a lot that has to be solved in this last act of the world's drama. Mad humanity is rushing along in the heat of passions, but there is no place for lusts when the world's destiny is reaching a stage of completion in order to make way for the new construction. How few are those who understand that cosmic construction does not resemble the expectations of humanity.

Everyone values the art of N. K. very highly and emphasizes the world significance of his various activities and his influence, not only on today's minds but, most important, on those of future generations.

I send you, dear ones, the last pictures of him, of his shell. But his shell was so filled with light and expressed his natural essence so well

that these pictures mean more to me than any other pictures. He was
that way in the last months of his life when I was writing to you about
how he had become such a beautiful elder. Gentleness and great hu-
mility emanated from his expression. His wonderful shell was committed to the flames on broad ground, on the mountain side of our estate
with its wide view of three snowy ridges. On the site of the cremation,
a large beautiful fragment of a rock was hoisted, which bore a Hindi
inscription under the Banner of Peace. This rock was carried in a
primitive manner from a great distance. People from neighboring vil-
lages carried the rock with metal cable and on large wooden rollers
and pushed the rock with wooden levers. With frequent stops, the
people moved it a half-inch at a time, then carried it for several days.
Nevertheless, they managed and hoisted the rock onto the stone base,
under which ashes remained from the burning of the pyre.

The day of cremation was exceptionally beautiful and solemn. Not
a single puff of wind, and all the surrounding mountains were dressed
up in a coverlet of fresh snow. I had never before seen a cremation,
and I have to say that it was a great and wonderful sight. The people
built a pyre of deodar over which aromatic oils were poured. When
his bier, covered with white flowers, was placed on the pyre and the
fire was lit from four sides, wings of high flames enveloped him and
hid him from us as the flames rushed up into the cloudless blue of the
sky. There were no fumes or smoke, only the wonderful aroma of
deodar and sandalwood trees.

Two and a half-hours later everything was finished, though cremation usually takes about six hours. People drew their own conclu-
sions. The one who is gone was a great Rishi; his body was so clean
that the flames at once enveloped him, and there was neither smoke
nor fumes. On the second day we collected ashes. Part of them was
left at the cremation site, and we took the rest with us. It was terrible
to come back into an empty house. It was terrible to look at the glass
door of his studio, from which he will no longer gaze nor emerge to
admire the mountains and the sky lit by the fire of the sunset.

Our Light and Beloved One will live in the people's memory. An
enlightened consciousness will understand what a great Spirit walked
on Earth among the people and was awakening their consciousness
to all that is Beautiful, and in this way he poured the Elixir of Life into

them. After his murder, Gandhi became a Savior and the father of his nation, but even greater will be our Light and Beloved One when everything that he created and made known for the Good of humanity will be collected. Truly, he set the foundation for the New Era, the New World.

The place of cremation of his lighted shell is guarded and will become a place of pilgrimage for many worshipers.

It is painful to realize that many wonderful souls could not show love or heartfelt care for him during the last years of his life. His heart lived with a desire to reach consonant souls and share his spiritual wealth with them. By this time, loneliness began to burden him. He wished for activity and the spreading of the new consciousness among the coming generations. Of course, the retranslating of all of his work should be looked into. There is a lot to talk over and much to put in order. Our Beloved just wanted to give and never cared about what would happen with his artwork or possessions, but we have to, in all ways, guard his spiritual heritage. It is difficult to decide how to start this, because even knowing where to keep his remaining paintings hasn't been decided yet. If the whole world was engulfed in fire, what place would be the safest? We will take them to the New Country, but how many paintings will be left in the cities and museums of India and Europe, and will they survive? What will America do with all those treasures that were stolen [by Horch]? His last foul deed was to throw the treasures, acquired with donated funds, out of the Museum. No worse act has occurred anywhere else.

N. K.'s departure wasn't a simple leaving for the purpose of rest. No, our Light and Beloved One left so he could be of greater help to the world. In the Subtle World, where all images of the Future are born, there is a need for those who have highly disciplined psychic energy. There are months and years of destruction coming to Earth, to settle scores of the centuries, and the work of construction has been moved to the background. For the spirit whose Chalice is filled with achievement, it is already difficult to protect it so that it will not be spilled or trampled. During these times of madness, it would be better for those spirits to wait in the beautiful world, where they will be able to strengthen their ideas, so that later they will be better and brighter when manifested for the ungrateful habitants of Earth. And I too will not see the fruits of experience that I have accumulated. These books are going to stay in the storehouse, and it's possible that no one will have access to them before another century has passed. Will I have time to put together my notes on the New Science—the New Cosmogony—which are now in complete disorder?

Armageddon is very strong, and although we are in its last phase, there are a lot of crimes being committed by the supporters of the dark forces. In your country, terrible organizations of these supporters are gathered. We received a disgusting offer from one of these organizations not long before N. K.'s departure. Of course, we did not answer such an insulting and dishonest message, but when there is time, I will copy it and send it to you, so you can become familiar with what is going on in your country. Recently I received a letter from a victim of such an organization asking me to save him from them. But who can help the unhappy one but himself? How can I make him understand this?

April 9, 1948

Mandy House

You are right that the Roerich Foundation could bring together some of the activities, and, of course, in this way many things could be simplified. I already wrote to you regarding the order of publishing the books of the Living Ethics, but I will repeat it. The publishing of the third volume of *Fiery World* is of course, first, and then the translation and publishing of *Brotherhood*. The republishing of *Aum* or *Agni Yoga* can be done only if the yearly budget of the A[gni] Y[oga] S[ociety] is in balance, and if for the publishing of one of these books there is more than enough money set aside. The members of the Society should understand the importance of having the full series of the Living Ethics books. But rarely is someone's heart so aflame that he or she is inspired with the desire to study all of the Teaching and start on the path of self-perfection. The wonderful books, *Community* and *Illumination* could be translated gradually. And is it possible to forget the wonderful book *Infinity*? All this is waiting for the new fiery spirits who will come to replace our departing, decaying race.

Because people are becoming cruder everywhere, we should be especially careful that none of the good ones be ensnared by enemy forces. The admiration for N. K.'s paintings is a really good sign. Indeed, only hearts that are sensitive and kind can feel the beauty of these creations. It was said that there would not be a greater singer of the Holy Mountains. He is going to stay forever unsurpassed in this field. Really, who would be able to dedicate himself as much to that constant imminence, in front of the greatness and beauty of these summits, which embody and guard the greatest secret and Hope of the World—Sacred Shambhala? It is going to stay with me as one of the last impressions of his Dream, his love—"Song to Shambhala." With the majestic sunset in the background lightened by the last ray, and the Sacred Ridge sparkling in the distance, there is an impassable region that spreads behind it, which is surrounded by snowy peaks. In the foreground, on a dark purple rock, the singer himself is sitting.... All the meaning of his life, his aspiration, his work, his attentiveness and great service, are imprinted in this song to Shambhala and about Shambhala.

Dear ones, I dream to work with you, because who else would understand and feel the sacredness of the mission of our Light and Beloved One, his service to all humanity. Truly, he had outgrown the earthly limitations, and his aspirations were already directed to the stars, to space, where work is not limited to our three dimensions. In this time of savagery and the destruction of all remnants of the cultural achievements of the great past, of the general leveling of all that is original, all that is beautiful, his figure rose above all, as a strong reproach, the last Symbol of the Creator and Singer, directed to Infinite Beauty, Eternal Beauty. Truly, the world became an orphan with his departure. The exhibition of his paintings attracted tens of thousands and raised their vibrations to a much higher level in the delightful perception of the wondrous colors and images that were close to them. Many kept the memory of these wonderful uplifted feelings for a long time. How much Good was spread by those influences? Who knows how many people left the exhibition cured of the beginnings of illness, or forgotten shame, or bad intention because they had come under the influence of the new vibrations, the new thoughts?

April 16, 1948

My dear ones, yesterday I received two letters of yours dated the 4th and 7th of April, which included the "Pegleriada" and a package of wonderful articles by Mrs. Heline about N. K.[1] How wonderful is the possibility of such a fast letter exchange. Today I sent Katherine a telegram asking her to send, via airmail, ten Pact brochures because of a request from the Government. Apparently, there is new activity regarding the Pact, but all the brochures that were given to different ministries and to different people have disappeared without a trace. All day yesterday Svetik was running through the city trying to find these brochures, but found only one copy, which belongs to a distinguished local scientist, Prof. Batnagar.[2] Isn't it always the same, and so familiar, for the dark ones to lay obstacles down before each new endeavor of Light?

In any case, whether the Pact is going to be accepted here and ratified now, or some obstacles will later appear and everything be postponed, we will continue to have a calm attitude, because nothing can diminish the later significance of this Pact. Anyway, it's sad to see how difficult it is for people to accept the best ideas, and how narrow is their understanding of every benevolent signpost on the path of progress. I wish very much that India, which is so loved by us, will accept and protect itself by the shield and the Banner of the Powers of Light.

The article by Pegler that I received, with the three portraits placed in a row, is revealing. All three images were amazingly selected for the expression of the inner essence that was imprinted on each of them— truly, Christ crucified between two robbers! I wish to have another copy of this sudden witness of truth. It is useful to collect all the material—for the sake of history—that is characteristic of our terrible time and of the demoralization of all foundations, everything by which humanity lives. One can see almost everywhere walking corpses covered with masks. Truly, the world is putrid. I appreciated the answer, the article by Fluke.

Sinochka is right; it is appropriate to subscribe to a clipping service in connection with Roerich's name. It's possible that the unexpected sum of $150, about which Maurice is writing, could be used for this.

My dear ones, I am touched to the depth of my soul by the help you are offering, but by our own means we are going to be all right. In the Motherland everybody must earn his keep, and if there are possibilities given for that, then we'll be materially secure. But with all my heart, I value your care.

The heat is already approaching; yesterday afternoon the temperature reached 100, but I'm still all right, in spite of visitors every day. Strophanthus is my support.[3] Svetik and his wife are going to Bombay on Saturday and will be looking for lodging for us in the surrounding hills. The embassy promised that the ship will be directed toward Bombay, therefore we decided to go a part of the way. But before getting a telegram from us, continue to write to Mandy House, New Delhi. I am worried about the fate of the articles about N. K. that were sent. It was so difficult to collect them, and having to duplicate them would be almost impossible. Also *Supermundane* was sent almost at the same time as *Infinity*. Is it possible that all of them have disappeared?

I have read the letters to the ARCA members and I do not see anything to be changed or removed. One can't become sad that none of the members respond or comment. These letters are useful as information regarding the society's activities and could replace the yearly report. Rarely do members of any society comment on its activities, and usually most of them never read their own society's reports. This uncultured attitude can be encountered almost everywhere. Therefore, dear ones, act on circumstances and possibilities, and don't become strained; one must conserve one's strength. We are on the threshold of great events.

I am worried about N. K.'s paintings being in the hands of the apostates. It is important to keep watch on their actions as much as possible. I would like to have the advice of a clever and gifted lawyer as to what to do in order to keep at least a small thread [of ownership], which would leave us with the possibility to claim that justice be restored in the event of a change of circumstances. According to N. K.'s will, which was made at home and was signed and certified by our local administrator and witness, Colonel Mahon, all paintings belong to me, and it places the responsibility for their destiny on me. Svet has arrived, and he says that the Pact is going to be ratified in a few days. The Minister of Education has signed it and the Ministry of Foreign International Affairs responded positively. But, dear, do not notify your committees about our joy. We have to wait till there is official notification of the Pact's acceptance. We know about the course of events, but premature notification could damage the case.

I've read the paragraphs that were sent of *Leaves of Morya's Garden.* They sound good, and I did not notice any errors in the translation. Now I will try to explain the paragraph from *Fiery World.* It is, of course, difficult to translate. The pyramid was often considered a symbol of the Macrocosm and, consequently, of the Microcosm; hence there is a separation of the three natures, or the Three Worlds—physical, astral, and fiery. The Essence, or substance, of the nature of each of the worlds is different from that of the others. The Summit is the Fiery World; the middle of the structure symbolizes the Subtle World; the bottom, or foundation, the dense world; and, of course, the nature of these three worlds differs so much that it's possible to say they are separated, or there are boundaries between them.

You know how difficult it is for people to master the manifestations of the subtle nature, and with what difficulties signs of the subtle spheres are grasped, and to what deathly dangers and shocks people are exposed when in proximity to fiery beings or fiery energies. Given the coarseness of the dense world it is difficult to imagine that all three essences could merge, but for this exactly one should go through refinement, harmonization and an uplifting of our substances, or natures, or bodies—the physical and the subtle—in order to merge in the fiery Apotheosis. The fiery principle is the sculptor of all that is real, and a fiery summit could be considered as a fiery seed, or spirit—the one that lifts every existing thing from the depth of the dense world to the fiery Apotheosis. The "rib" of the pyramid I think could be translated as "edge." To be exact, the Subtle World could be divided into many spheres, but the major three worlds can be considered fundamental.

Take into consideration, dear ones, that in primitive physical man, his natures, or shells, particularly the subtle ones, are only slightly developed, but as his moral and intellectual characteristics develop and his inner shells become more definitively outlined, they finally begin to separate one from another and act independently, each in the sphere according to its nature. The conscious separation and conscious action of man's three natures is an achievement of the Arhat.

April 18. It was 103 degrees yesterday; today it is going to be higher, but I am still all right. Maybe after ten days we'll be able to move to a cooler place. One must be convinced that the inexplicable delay results from ignorance, from fears and bewilderment in coping with circumstances. So we are waiting here for the uncertainties that obscure our ship to clear away. Regarding future correspondence, we will take all measures and will try all means to create a normal working relationship through regular correspondence, as it was with Grabar.[4] But any correspondence with Grabar ended with the departure of our Pasenka. It is difficult for me to understand how to explain it. Of course many letters could have disappeared at the time of the second flood, which occurred after we had already left. A few telegrams that were sent by Devika's mother were never received, nor were Devika's letters.[5] The road to our place in Naggar is not usable yet, and at our place, walls have collapsed; but the area where the rock is, which has the sign of the Banner of Peace, was untouched.

Our dear ones, do not be confused by any seeming failures. Everything is now so transient that nothing could have a final conclusion. The world is confronted with decisive happenings, truly "to be or not to be" will confront all countries. The "Roerich Foundation" can be created later, and for now will exist in our friends' hearts, who should now devote themselves to collecting materials. So, dear ones, cultivate calmness and carry out the programs of your institutions in accordance with circumstances and possibilities. I sympathize with Dudley very much; I know all the burden of his incompatibility with the vibrations of surrounding people. I recall truly the life of Christ, and what a total horror it was from the moment of His coming into the crowds to deliver to them the Treasures of Heart and Mind. Was it possible to expect refinement and a just attitude to the true spiritual treasures even among devoted fishermen? Complete loneliness.

June 8, 1948

My dear and beloved ones,

I'm trying to write my first letter after a two-month interruption. Your precious messages of April 26 and of May 2, 7, 11, 16, 21, and 25 with all the enclosures were received. Thank you, dear ones, for the much needed information about the affairs, and I also value your reflections on the mood of current happenings. I will try to answer your questions. Of course, we are not expecting any polemics with Pegler or lawsuits with Horch.[1] The elucidation given by Pegler as to some actions of Horch and Wallace was very helpful and should be remembered.[2] But I would also like to have the opinion of the experienced and gifted lawyer regarding the rights to the paintings by N. K. that had been sent from Naggar to America and were received by the "Roerich Paintings Corporation" for exhibition in the museum, as well as for sales.

From the very beginning of that flagrant crime, N. K. dreamed of finding an honest writer or a lawyer who could elucidate clearly the meaning of the destructive attack on the Cultural Creation, for the ideas pledged in it had already gained world significance, and the Banner of Peace was already signed in the White House by all of the American republics. In Europe and Asia there were cultural departments working in complete accordance with the main activity, which was blooming in the museum in America. Let us try not to overlook such a writer, but he has to come himself and be inspired with a strong desire to shed light on the crime committed and to restore the truth. As usual, nearsighted people do not yet see the consequences of the destruction, but it does not mean that they do not or will not exist. In the predestined time they will appear with mighty power. We should not expect from Weed and Bolling more than they can give.[3] Your wish to put my name in as an honorable Chairwoman I accept with all my heart.

Now to paragraph 597. "Therefore, know how to speak to everyone about the most joyous, in the simplest words and in the expressions most fitting for all...."[4] This means to have the ability to speak about the most joyous in the simplest words, in the most acceptable expression for everyone, because joy has to be available to all; and our Teaching, first of all, manifests and opens the gates of joy. Maybe Sinochka will have the time to send me the paragraphs that need explanation.

Gubareva's articles are wonderful; I approve very much of her second article.[5] It is necessary to awaken the minds of the ordinary person. Only developed thinking will provide solutions for the New Era. Encourage and treat kindly this nice, gifted writer.

Now as to the information about the sick old woman who has been receiving messages: it is very interesting, and if the content is as beautiful as Sinochka describes, then why not publish them? Of course, not all wonderful messages come, for certain, from the Great Stronghold. There are many wonderful spirits across the border that have the possibility to transmit their thoughts to earthly inhabitants. As it says in our Teaching, "We do not stamp every line attributed to us."

But of course, Great Teachers sometimes use unexpected channels for sending the needed ideas. I would like to have an example of the old woman's messages, especially about Buddhism.

Now another thing: The Thinker, so often mentioned in *Supermundane*, is a collective concept. These thoughts were manifested and repeated many times by the Great Lord in many of His incarnations, and that's why for me the Thinker and the Great Lord are one individuality. It is occasionally possible to recognize words said by other Teachers, but who knows? Haven't these thoughts been heard by the original Thinker?

Now about my illness. Of course, it is caused by yet another inflammation of a group of centers. If my strength hadn't been so exhausted by N. K.'s illness and passing away, of course it would be easier for me to bear this new inflammation. The inflammation of the vagus center is a very dangerous phenomenon because of its closeness to the heart; but the power of the fire was weakened by the activity of the solar plexus, which drew to itself a part of the fire. Nevertheless, I had to resort to a reflex inflammation of the nerve stems that go along the ribs, and provoke an illness named by the doctors as [   ]. But the local name for it, "the cobra's bite," reflects the meaning of the illness much better. Now, although the major pain caused from the vagus inflammation has gone, the pains connected with shingles still continue.[6] They treat me with tablets.... Switzerland's product is very good for all nerve illnesses. Try it yourself for the pain in your hand. The G. L. approved this remedy, as He did the new preparation for heart illnesses.... from the same firm, Ciba. It eases breathing and increases the general tone of the heart. And I advise it for you when there is heart tiredness. It's possible to take a rest from strophanthus and take from 15 to 20 drops of Coramine.[7]

We are still sitting in Khandala, a small place two to three hours driving distance from Bombay. The temperature here is significantly lower than that of Bombay, not more than 83 to 85 degrees, with almost a constant cooling sea wind. They took me here from Delhi almost half-alive. We had to ask for a doctor and a nurse from Bombay. The nurse helped a lot because she was experienced and very sensitive. She lived with me for a whole month and only recently went back to Bombay. Although my [   ] is still strong, it was in very bad shape. Though I feel better in general and stronger, to write, even with a pencil, is still difficult; that's why I dictate to Raya, who is doing this rather well and sends you a heartfelt "Hello."[8] I think that it will be at least three weeks before there is any significant improvement.

Tell Katherine about my illness. I think of her often and send her my affection. How is her health? Send me by air mail at least six copies of the pamphlets published by the Pact Committee in Argentina, and, also, one more copy of *Foundations of Buddhism*, possibly by ship.

The copies of *Foundations of Buddhism*, which were sent by Katherine to Delhi, have not yet been delivered.

There is a misunderstanding that has occurred with N. K.'s portrait. N. K.'s portrait has to be displayed in the main room where lectures take place, but it shouldn't be displayed in the window.

A place that is wonderful today could be a disaster tomorrow, or vice versa. More than that, dear ones, the symbol of a heroic deed was always the carrying of the Cross and the drinking of the Chalice of Poison. Also, a heroic deed can't be "without result," because a heroic deed occurs due to cosmic necessity, and its results are measured by Supermundane measures.

When Christ suffered on the Cross, who understood that the old world was finished and a new dawn had already come, and a new God had risen over the Earth? Every Teaching requires heroism. Dear ones, is it possible to forget the Great Guiding? Has it changed? A hero, by drinking the Chalice of Poison, accomplishes his mission in the physical body, but will continue it in the subtle body. Others still have to carry their cross till the predestined time—and they will carry it out. So, drive away little doubts and grow wings of courage and hope, which will carry you over all abysses.

How many fears we had to listen to and how consistently groundless they all were! Let faith and trust in the Guiding Hand be aflame in your heart; let opened eyes see the logic for what happens. Of course, I wish to see you, my dear ones, very, very much, but for this I am awaiting Instructions. All thoughts are flying to the New Country, but the departure is not definite yet.[9] Patiently I wait for the affirmed date.

The chaos of thinking that we see in the whole world requires special foresight and prudence.

Every morning I look through the photographs that I have of Our Beloved Pasenka. How much light and quietness were around him! My heart is whispering an ancient hymn—Quiet Light, Lucid Light, Beautiful Light.

June 28, 1948
Khandala, India

Now about karma. Is it possible for my dear one to think that difficult karma created by people is so easy to resolve? That it's enough to break away from relationships and the karma will be settled? Recall this wise precaution "Do not make enemies," because enemies remain enemies, sometimes for many thousands of years, and their hostility can decrease, or can increase in tension until it becomes the madness of betrayal. The magnet of hatred is strong, and for its manifestation there is no need for hostility from the victim's side; it is nourished by its own rage, envy, and hatred. Jesus did not have distrust or animosity for Judas, who had even been trusted with the keeping of money, but Judas' hostility and hatred was long-lived and delivered by him from the depth of the centuries, and culminated in an unprecedented betrayal.

You wrote "What happened between us and the trio remains permanently imprinted in the Akashic Records." [1,2] You are correct, and this disturbance of the cosmic balance (betrayal is a disturbance of the cosmic balance) has to be restored by Cosmic Justice, which acts first of all goal-fittingly and unexpectedly in accordance with cosmic laws or circumstances that we can't yet grasp.

You will ask, "How can one resolve one's karma?" The answer was given by the Lord Buddha—karma is overcome by the perfection of all elements that make up the structure of our being. Karma is constructed from our thoughts, intentions, words and deeds. Thought is a major factor in the creation of karma, and that is why it is so important to work on the broadening of consciousness. Thought is the prime impetus of the universe. The Teaching of Living Ethics affirms that karma cannot burden the harmonious being.

My dear, one should not be afraid of the possibility of new meetings with the traitors, because it is precisely the traitors who help us to rise and reach the wonderful crown, the "Fiery Diadem."

It says, "Betrayal, like a shadow, follows the hero," laying for him the best steps for the shortest path.

You ask, "Is it possible to atone for one's betrayal?" Yes, even Judas could be cleansed, but this atonement requires eons of hard, selfless labor. But repeated traitors, and those branded by the fiery seal of the Higher Power, won't be able to atone for their betrayal on our Earth, during its Manvantara, and will have to go to a lower planet or even become cosmic waste.

It is necessary to overcome any fear and to have real courage of spirit, because in front of the courage of the conscious spirit, the shadows of hatred falter and fade away. I will tell you, my dear ones, without betrayal, there can be no heroic deed.

Being unwilling to meet again those who have been our enemies can slow down our way and deprive us of the best possibilities. Avoiding dealing with one's karma prolongs the way. So, in this or another life, we will again meet our betrayers, but we will be better equipped, because we wisely strengthened our auras with the broadening of consciousness.

Remember, it said in *Agni Yoga*: "He who has erected a fire of hatred will have to bend over to feed it each piece of coal."[3] Truly he will have to pay for each piece of coal. By the way, it was said to Talbot, the traitor of Joan of Arc, when karma again brought him together with his victim, and the old hatred, under whose influence he admitted his obsession, broke out in a rage from him, only to fade under the force of his victim's ray. Unfortunate man, though he dreamed about the tiara of the Uniate Episcopate and the easy luxurious life in connection with such status, he died on a beggar's deathbed as a church guard in Jerusalem, already carrying in his heart the image of her who liberated and protected him. The next path of his, of course, will be much better, and, possibly, he will be able to become a useful and selfless worker in the service of humanity.

You ask, "Can we consciously prepare new karma when in the Subtle World?" Everything is possible for the conscious spirit, but for this it is necessary to have developed a clear consciousness, not only on the physical plane but in the subtle spheres as well. Many people, if their consciousness were examined, would exhibit a very unclear understanding of the very vital Laws of Being. How would they be able to consciously prepare new karma for themselves without a clear understanding of it, and of the laws that rule it? First of all, to have a conscious existence in the Subtle World people have to realize the significance and strength of thought, not only on the physical plane, but precisely in the Subtle World, where everything is created and all is moved by thought. Thought is a prime lever of the universe. Thought is an engine of the World. The power of thought kindled with love is infinite.

The aboriginal people of India are not savages, because the Teaching was given and is given in India. But even savages sometimes know better than civilized people about the Subtle World and their existence in it. Though this knowledge is very primitive, it does exist and it helps them to adapt to new conditions. Of course, in the Subtle World people are attracted to each other and connected through sympathy, and there they avoid meeting with enemies. There people can apply all that they have accumulated on Earth. But to appear there with new accumulations of knowledge, if they haven't striven to it while in their earthly existence, is almost impossible. But on Earth it is like in a crucible—very different energies collide, are attracted to each other with refinement and transmutation as more perfected or subtle energies under the influence of the fire of the awakened spirit. From these collisions and unexpected connections of the different energies, new energies are born carrying new creativity and new possibilities. Earth is a place of testing, atonement and great creativity—the place of the last Judgment, because it is here that selection proceeds. Remember, dear one, that only on Earth can we accumulate and assimilate the new energies or renew the substance of our energies. Therefore, one should welcome every incarnation, instead of wanting to avoid it. If people only knew how the Great Spirits had labored, taking upon Themselves the most difficult, most burdensome incarnations, often not necessary for Them, but so ardently necessary for the salvation of Earth to save men from destruction, to save them from being caught in Satan's net!

The Great Pilgrim was, of course, Christ, but who is the Christ Himself? In her book *Esoteric Christianity*, Besant points to a place in the Gnostics where it says that before Jesus appeared for a sermon, the Higher Spirit moved into Him.[4] And this Spirit, after the crucifixion of the body and during the next eleven years, appeared to Mary Magdalene and taught her the secrets of the Supermundane spheres, which she wrote down. During the time of the Gnostics these writings were known as "Big and Small Questions of Mary Magdalene," but to our day are left only fragments of small questions. All this is the truth, and that great Spirit was, of course, the same One, the Avatar Vishnu.

Now about the centers. Each new inflammation indicates that the fiery process is going on repeatedly and in succession, one center after another, and sometimes two or even three (depending on the groups). After these centers were inflamed more than once, they received a sort of immunity. The inflammation of the new fires is very dangerous, because other fires can also become inflamed with them, and if all precautionary measures aren't taken, then the fiery death is almost unavoidable. I was already on the verge of fiery death three times, and just now, for the fourth time, avoided the deathly danger. The excess fire moved into the solar plexus, but that apparently wasn't enough, and I had to allow inflammation of the nerve stems along the ribs. The shingles acted like a lightning rod. My pain, of course, was not so much from the shingles as from the inflammation of the centers in my back (the center of the lungs –

vagus). It has been three months that I am ill, and the shingles are still continuing, but without the eruption of small blisters. But on the right side of the torso, on the ribs, on the inflamed skin in the form of dark spots, there is a strong burning sensation. All the skin around it is painfully sensitive, but nevertheless, there is already a new inflammation. Luckily, the fires of these centers (knees, head) are not that painful or continuous.

There are many centers and some of them have twin branching.

I am much stronger now, but it is still difficult to move my hands to write or to look through the papers. The pain in my back forces me to stop working; this pain is from my heart. Before moving to the Motherland, I was supposed to complete the entire process of fiery transmutation of the centers to gain some immunity from fiery death. Now I am going through repeated inflammations.

We are still sitting in our house in Khandala; as soon as Instructions come, we will continue our path and send you a telegram. I think that for the first half of July we are going to stay here in this wonderful quiet and coolness. The temperature stays between 70 and 76 degrees, but is most often 74 degrees.

Khandala is a charming place, and it is significant because of the ancient caves of Buddha named the "Karla caves," the replica of which are in Ajanta—and my sons are saying that the main cave with mortar is even more interesting than the one in Ajanta.[5] For us this place is significant and dear because here Blavatsky met M. M. when she and some companions took a trip from Bombay to these caves. Back then nobody knew about the existence of these caves, and there weren't any roads, so they had to walk and to climb almost vertical cliffs. But the travelers reached there and were rewarded with the Vision of M. M., Who welcomed Blavatsky at the cave's entrance and, after a short conversation with her, disappeared. After that, Blavatsky went into the cave and also disappeared. Her companions looked through the entire cave, but found nothing; then they decided to set their tents near the cave and spend the night in vigil. At sunrise, from an unexpected hidden passage, M. M. appeared again, together with Blavatsky, and addressed her companions with greetings and encouraging words. We were told about this unusual manifestation by a Hindu Theosophist, who came with Svetik and his wife to visit us. By the way, he said that it's possible to find a description of this wonderful manifestation in the second volume of *Olcott's Diary*. When I heard about this manifestation, the place became illuminated to me with a bright ray of supermundane beauty, and I understood why the G. L. directed us here.

July 25, 1948

Khandala, India

N. K.'s painting, "The Condemned City," was created before the [Bolshevik] Revolution of 1917, and since then it has been in Maxim Gorky's collection. The year 1920 is confusing to me, and also the mentioning of Finland, because in 1919 we were already in London. Besides, long before the First World War and also during it, N. K. had not been painting with oils, but only with tempera of the Vurm brand. Maybe this is a copy of a painting by N. K. There were many copies made of his paintings, and now we hear about these even in India. Only Svetik can identify its authenticity. My dear one, one must not be afraid of the biggest traitors; it is precisely they who increase heroism in us. What is worse, much worse, are the small, often unwitting traitors, of whom there are many. They aimlessly drain your strength and poison your aura. We do not have to be terrified, but must courageously realize all the dangers and all the responsibilities of earthly existence, from which there is no liberation except through the path of the development of consciousness, learning, and perfection of all our being. The path of the Arhat is difficult, but it is granted to everyone who seeks Higher Knowledge and whose Heart is kindled by the fire of selfless service to the Common Good.

I am touched very much by the love expressed by you to Our Dear Beloved N.K. I know that this feeling will not subside in your hearts. No, it will grow and crystallize into a new and deeper understanding of this wonderful One—a True Hero, because he lived by those Precepts that he so beautifully and vividly expressed and manifested in his achievements and flights of thought about the most Beautiful, about the most Sacred—about the Great Hope of the World—about Shambhala.

So often in the evening George and I discuss Our Treasured One, who bequeathed to us his path.[1] We are trying to recall all his words and expressions so loved by us, in his everyday life; and a deep but painful tenderness toward him and an amazement at his crystalline purity overflows in us. All of him shone with an inner light because of his purity of heart and thought. All of us, especially in the last years, had a feeling of inexhaustible tenderness toward him and a desire to guard him from all that is rude and ugly. But would this still be possible in the coming years of difficult confrontations? It is our quiet joy to realize that he will have the possibility to broadly apply his gifts without having to care about procuring a living, which always caused him so much suffering because our subsistence depended on the sale of his paintings. We often were pained when a beloved painting had to go, but we needed to make a living and the paintings had to be sold. I know, dear ones, that your spirit will not wither, because you are true and tested guards, and joy will return, as we are going to build what was bequeathed by him. Nothing is gone! All signs of the Great Trust given to us remain and were and will be sacredly guarded.

Think, dear ones, how much creative and constructive work awaits us! One should do all to carry on, to collect, to place the foundations of the new science, to build the City of Knowledge and to raise the Banner of Peace—the Banner of the Powers of Light. How much labor with the Sacred Books! How much is still not translated and not known! So they will be published, as will his diary, *My Life*. All his writings should be reexamined and republished. And how many problems there are to obtain a proper building for his wonderful creations! There will not be another singer of the Mountain Abode of the Himalayas. He is the first and the last one!

We will remember that the power of spiritual closeness is not like the earthly one. The time will come, a true moment, when you will be illumined by the greatness of spiritual closeness, and this moment will change your whole being because it will affirm forever the inalienable quality of this highest sensation of the Mystery of Being. Your difficult present labor has temporarily distanced you, but it will build a foundation for better closeness. I, myself, am getting stronger, but the pains haven't left me yet; I am very tired from the heart's arrhythmia. I am not frightened by them, because I know that new currents, or rays, are passing through me, and I have to assimilate them before moving from India. After several difficult nights, I feel better again. Our stay in Khandala is continuing, but we have information that the ships might come in September or possibly in August. We know the given date can't be changed; that is why we wait quietly for the first call, to embark on our new journey.

August 10, 1948

Khandala, India

Now about the possibility that you pointed out of floods in America. It should be taken into consideration, and if there is going to be a chance to move closer to the first Museum, or even higher up, you should seriously think about it. Listen carefully; maybe a better building will be found. Indeed, I was shown the city completely flooded, with only the R[oerich] Museum standing high above the water level. You see, the paintings can be destroyed.

Of course, the process of opening the centers, or more precisely, their partial opening, can take place in the city, but, of course, only when one's living conditions are relatively good, and there is proper discipline in one's life. But the fiery transmutation requires a prolonged stay in Nature, on the heights, and in some solitude. Also, the fiery experience could only have been given as it was to one who for millennia manifested closeness to the W[hite] Brotherhood and earned the Fiery right.

Gubareva is correct about her two ways of writing. The fact that her individual style, everywhere and always, remains unchanged confirms that she is writing under the Ray. The Ray awakens the "Chalice," and from there emerge those symbolic images in which projected thoughts are enveloped. Also, the tide of thoughts that one can barely manage, is characteristic of the influence of the Ray on the Chalice or on the outer centers of the brain. Simple automatic writing does not involve the higher centers; with this purely physical process, there is influence upon the center of the hand, but the higher centers are not involved. Her articles are beautiful, and her letter to me showed her in a very positive light.

During difficult days, when the spirit hesitates and the heart is anguished, it is good to recall paragraph 201 in *Community*: "Even when the consciousness is being notably deepened, there can be difficult hours. It may seem that the bond with the Teacher does not exist, and that the Teacher does not exist, but he who knows says, 'Maya, begone! I know my bond with the Teacher.' A great deal may appear in the way of personal ideas apart from the Teaching, and he who knows will say, 'Maya, begone! I know the foundations of the Teaching.' It may seem that one is deprived of all coworkers while obliged to try to take up the burden, and he who knows will say, 'Maya, begone! I know that true coworkers are scattered over the face of the Earth!'

"Maya of all ages knows when to touch the brain. From the depths of former experiences Maya evokes a fine thread of waverings, covers reality with evidence, and sweeps away the furrow of attainments. Multicolored Maya, it is time to know thee and to say with full authority: 'Maya, begone!' "

And here are the parting words that were given after our Light and Beloved One passed away:

"My Orphaned Warrior, you must hurry to accept your new Burden. Stay strong. You must carry the "Chalice" to the Motherland. You understand correctly the situation here. The Motherland will erect a monument to F[uyama]. With courage enter into the whirlwind of events. I will meet you on the crest of the waves. Manifest courage, dear ones; avoid disappointment. Your inner emptiness is like the charred steppe after a prairie fire. Lightning bolts of the spirit will be rare, and a gray gloom will envelope you. The weary heart must be healed by true understanding. Gratitude should be summoned from the heart. It will lave the wounds of the spirit."

August 19, 1948

Khandala, India

New rays are reaching and influencing our Earth. The rays work in accordance with Cosmic Goal-Fitness. They clean and heal the atmosphere of our Earth, which has become so saturated with the poisons of hatred, greed and malice that the life-giving rays of the Higher Spheres cannot enter. For the salvation of the planet it is necessary to pierce this poisoned atmosphere—the dark gray aura of our Earth, which is disfigured by spots of absolute darkness.

It is said that everything in the Akashic Records that is imprinted by fire is immutable. This same fiery immutability marks the Lord's Banner and also the future center of the Lord. The immutability must be affirmed in the hearts of all who strive toward the World of Light and Spiritual Culture. We also know how strong is the Shield of realization and truth; not only trust, not only faith are necessary, but also the understanding of being absolutely right.

India has become closer than close. With the passing away of our Dear One, we realize and are convinced that he became a part of the life of the country as one of its most powerful spiritual motivators. India is the motherland of the greatest Giants of Spirit. Of course, India strongly feels the connection of his creations with its own great heritage. India recognized him as its inalienable spiritual Guru. All the most distinguished writers, creators and critics unanimously expressed that he is the greatest artist of our time and will stay thus, because in addition to the perfection of his artistic mastership, his creations carry to humanity spiritual messages, enveloped in all the irresistibility of the new beauty. The spiritual aspect of his creative work is unforgettably imprinted in the consciousness of the best leaders and thinkers of this country.

Never, no one and nothing will be able to suppress the Divine Spark kindled by the Giants of the Spirit and, through centuries, guarded in the hearts of the best sons of India.

How miserable is the thinking of those who, with a grin, speak about the mysticism of Roerich. Madmen do not know how limited they themselves are, or what they deprive themselves of! They do not understand that this mysticism is Maya only for them; but for those who can see, it is the greatest Reality. Upon the life of the Abode of Light reposes the basis of the rightness of the entire work. Near the Great Service there should be unconquerable firmness of the consciousness of rightness. When our spirit knows about the uprightness of the basis and the unalterability of our work, wings will grow by themselves and carry us over all abysses.

Striving and effort are the keys to all achievements, and in the fiery experience it is necessary to strain all one's centers in order to make possible their fiery transmutation and achievement of the next step. The harmony and sublimation of all energies are reached only in a state of highest tension. But, of course, this tension shouldn't overly stress the physical organism. It is always necessary to remember this danger, otherwise an irreparable disruption of balance and even premature death can occur. But, of course, the fiery experience is not conceivable without the guidance of the Supermundane Teacher. But it is necessary to prepare oneself for this achievement without delay, because we never know when the long wished-for moment will come.

September 2, 1948

Khandala, India

Dear and beloved ones, I received your wonderful letters of the 16th, 20th and 25th of August. I regret so very much that I could not send you a telegram celebrating the acceptance of the Pact. The Pact is accepted and signed, but there has not yet been an official notification of it, though the local, major newspaper, the *Times of India*, twice placed a notice about the acceptance and signing of the Pact by the Indian Government and a brief history of it. We've heard that notices appeared in other Indian newspapers and magazines, but other than in the *Illustrated Weekly* and *Blitz*, we haven't seen anything yet. You see, there is not a clipping bureau in the whole of India! Svetik hasn't notified us as to whether he informed the Associated Press; he also promised to inform you by cable how things are, but apparently, did not find out anything new.

Of course, the situation here is so difficult and tense with the Kashmir war and the position taken by Hyderabad that one can't insist on exceptional attention for something that in the opinion of many is not vital and urgent right now. Many, or rather the masses, do not realize the urgency of not only the acceptance but also the raising of the Banner of Peace, so that the great significance of the guarding of the treasures of culture for the world's evolution may be instilled in the nation's consciousness for future generations. Without guarding the achievements of culture, humanity will revert to the times of the worst kind of barbarism because it will possess all the methods of destruction, and [suffer] complete numbness and paralysis of the higher centers, which are the only things that can give us higher life and eternity. People still do not believe in the existence of the living dead, but nevertheless, there are a lot of them.

I am sending you two notices from the *Times of India*. We expect Svetik and his wife tomorrow. If we learn anything new, I will send you a telegram, but I strongly doubt it because events are becoming more serious. Would it be possible to make a request to the Associated Press as to whether they have heard about the signing of the Pact? Today I sent you two copies of *India*, which shows on the cover N. K. and Nehru in our Himalayas, and also enclosed is a good, heartfelt article about our Beloved, and a third piece dedicated to Tagore with N. K.'s article about Tagore and Tolstoy. I also sent the issue of *Blitz*, a very popular newspaper here, in which there is an article about the Pact and its history, though some of the facts are distorted. It is going to be interesting for you to look through the whole issue. This newspaper correctly reflects the situation and the mood in the country. The enemy's front line is coming closer and closer, and it could easily come in close proximity to our valley. There was a new flood over there, and once again all the bridges have been swept away.

I am afraid that my letter of August 20, with the enclosed list of the members of the Pact's Committee and their addresses, did not reach you because I sent it to your old address; but I see from your letter that you are coming back on August 31. If it arrives before your return (letters by airmail arrive by the seventh day), will it be possible for you to get it? Notify me if not and I will send the copy that I have.

Your thought to move the Pact Convention from Italy to South America is very much in agreement with my heart. Of course, it is going to be quieter, because there are clouds gathering over Europe. It is helpful to establish and to secure connections with a New Country and new friends. In my previous letter, I advised my South American friends to choose a date for the Convention. Because they know the situation locally, they will know better when to arrange the wonderful expansion of this culturally significant activity.

All your considerations and plans regarding incorporation, establishment of the committees and broadening of all the Pact's activities are very vital and constructive. I understand that Dudley's worries do not hurt anyone or burden anyone, but at the same time it is important to encourage and to give the respect that goes with a degree of responsibility, which may not be large, but is connected to a particular title. That is why, with all my heart, I accept your decisions. Act according to the circumstances and preserve in your heart a consciousness of the rightness of your work. The Great Service should be accompanied by an unconquerable firmness in understanding one's rightness. When our spirit knows about the rightness of the foundation and the immutability of our mission, wings will grow by themselves and carry us over all abysses—as I wrote in my previous letter.

So, as soon as I find out something new or more definite from Svetik, I will share it with you. We already are used to waiting for the execution of the simplest action, not for months, but even for years! In our age of unheard of acceleration in transportation and communication, it emphasizes especially the paradox of the slowness in other spheres of life; the result is destructive discord.

Today news came about the death of Zhdanov.[1] What changes it will bring! Nevertheless, it has to be realized that one can't force a nightingale to chirp like a sparrow, and even less a parrot to sing like a nightingale. We will live; we will see.

Katherine sent a notification about Maurice's death, and Svetik forwarded a local newspaper that wrote warmly about him and about his musical gift. I am sending you this article. We sent Katherine a telegram asking her to present our condolences to his wife, because we do not have his address here. I did not answer his last letter, and on August 26, the day of his death, I was thinking about him and regretted that I had postponed the answer. The next morning George was asked to go down to take a phone call from Svetik, and when George left I felt a sharp sadness. I knew that my son was going to bring sad news about somebody's illness or even departure. And really the news was more than sad. I feel so bad that I didn't answer him! Our Beloved always answered him. I can't forgive myself that I did not send him a heartfelt word, and who knows, maybe he needed it very much. Every day I think of him and send kind thoughts. Of course, it is going to be easy for him there. His love for the Teaching and devotion to the work will lead him to the G. L. Much will become clear to him, and he will strive to a new and better heroic life. For the true follower of the Teaching, life without heroic deeds is deprived of its meaning and beauty.

In my last letter I wrote about your possible move closer to the previous Museum; Eightieth Street and above is very acceptable. I am not worried; when the time comes, everything is going to happen as it is supposed to. But you need to get used to the thought about such a possibility and not be frightened; carefully listen and look at all that comes your way or has been offered to you.

The collision is going to be brief and sudden; do not be afraid, and be affirmed in knowledge of the victory of Light. ARCA, of course, quieted down, so that it will be able to rise again for broader activity. ARCA established a new step for the Banner of Peace. Then came Sinochka's letter of the 26th with notification about the death of Maurice and about the consul's leaving after a most silly happening. Of course, as long as the ambassador remains in the country, nothing has to be stopped. That's why you should continue, dear ones, the program that you outlined, and stop only if the ambassador leaves the country. ARCA will be resurrected when the time is right and will manifest a broad and wonderful activity in the future.

The question about the papers that Maurice left regarding the museum and the lawsuit is, of course, important to bring up. I do not think that his wife allowed "The Blonde" to take them, because she knew her role in the betrayal.[2] I think that it would be good to contact his wife to clear up some questions.

I do not think that it is possible to have the original document of the Pact with all the signatures. It's probably in the Government's Archive. But is it needed? It is well-known to everyone that after the Pact was accepted and signed in the White House, it went through the Congress—the Senate—to be ratified.

You see, what is done cannot be undone. The acceptance of the Pact was such a respected action that the country can be proud of the President, who manifested its acceptance. Of course, I understand Dudley, and I wish so much that I could give him a clear formula for the notification of all countries. I hope that it will be possible because Svetik, if need be, will be going to Delhi to meet somebody for that and to learn about the proper form for the notification. Sometimes it seems to me that we are too careful, but on the other hand, knowing the poisonous irresponsibility of the press in America, you may be right to display special care about all that issues from our institutions. So, dear ones, let us show a little more patience and find out in what form news about the acceptance and signing of the Pact by the Government of India should be sent.

Let us build; let us fight without fear of anything, knowing about the victory of the Forces of Light. The New Country will be the best country in the World. I hug you, darlings, with all my heart. A heartfelt greeting to all our friends. Wishing you all the Light.

September 27, 1948

Of course, just because events here have slowed down, that does not yet mean that our beloved India will follow in the footsteps of America, but it's sad that so few leaders have broad-minded political views. Few are used to thinking on a broad scale or on a planetary one, but what we need now are those with a mind of planetary scope, because their influence in spreading ideas has, without a doubt, increased phenomenally. People do not want to realize that they live in a world of thought and not in a world of mechanical robots that cannot foresee or prevent. Lack of foresight leads to all kinds of disasters. The inability to take into account major factors that define a future direction is failure and defeat. So, the possibilities are given to many. Now it's up to history to judge.

Regarding "Mystic Peak": Articles appeared in our newspapers about repeatedly failed attempts to fly over the sacred mountains. Of course, the cause is not with "Mystic Peak" itself, but in the special atmospheric and magnetic conditions in this "sea" of snow summits. The brave pilots can fly as much as they wish, but the real "Shangri-La" will never be within reach for them. The one who knows the truth smiles at the naiveté of the daring ones. Only ignorance and a lack of imagination can prompt people to such a quest without proper equipment, or without the necessary preparation, which is not only physical, but, for the most part, spiritual. They would succeed more readily if they started looking for "Shangri-La" in spirit first, in their heart. Then "Shangri-La" itself, or persons connected with it, could approach and provide a new direction to their lives, if the quest was sincere and based on centuries-old spiritual accumulations. The Path is open to everyone, but rarely, very rarely, does someone find it. One should ponder what would happen if someone who was not prepared by many years of drawing nearer in spirit, suddenly happened to be in the atmosphere surrounding "Shangri-La." Could he endure the unbearable pressure of the crossing currents and the special gases and fluids? To find oneself in an unconscious condition in the middle of a sea of snow and ice—the prospects are dire.

October 10, 1948

Khandala, India

Now about the vision of our beloved Pasenka, full of Light, by one of the A[gni] Y[oga] members. My advice, Sinochka, is to listen without commenting. It's possible to tell them: "The best explanation of what you've seen is in your spirit. Only your spirit can know the meaning of what was shown to you." There aren't many discerning people, but one shouldn't dissuade or force upon anyone one's own explanation, because it may stop the awakened spark. Let them see what they can see, and let's hope that these visions contribute to their spirit's development!

Our Departed, full of Light, left in a state of yogic transformation; his double burned out while he was alive, and that's why he could rise to the higher spheres without delay in the astral layers. Now he is immersed in sacred sleep to build his strength, and that's why he cannot use his strength for manifestations. But often the Great Teachers of humanity, if They need to influence a particular person, impersonate someone close to him, and They do it in a way that the organism of that person will not be frightened or harmed. When I was young, when I didn't know anything yet about the Great Teachers, in the difficult moments when I was addressing myself to my father, who had passed away and was coming to me in a wonderful dream and always with a majestic image, sometimes his face was dimmed and he would give me decisions for the future and insist repeatedly on pointing out particular actions. Later I understood that this was not my father who was coming to me, but Himself, the G. L., taking the image of my father so as not to frighten me, and to secure my trust in Him. To many people who knew about him, visions of N. K. could have been to help lift their spirits and for the development of their consciousness. But real manifestations of N. K. can happen only after a period of time, and if it is in accordance with his work. Knowing his readiness and haste to accomplish all he had planned, I think that he is not going to waste time and will incarnate soon in a better shell more suitable for the completion of his tasks. He will come to provide the New Country with its predestined powerful and unprecedented growth.

When the spirit starts to live consciously in the three worlds, the change of sheaths for a better new life is always joyous. We have to agree that in the world's circumstances as they are now, already in old age and weakened by the betrayed heart, it would have been difficult for him, yes, almost impossible, to remain strong and to live long enough to see the blossoming of the New Country. Many cannot understand yet about rapid reincarnation and think that hundreds or thousands of years must pass between incarnations. But the world is in such a condition that great Spirits accelerate their incarnations and voluntarily carry the world's burden for the salvation of humanity, to keep our planet from exploding.

October 22, 1948

Khandala, India

I was very happy to read about the new approach to coming together for the meetings of the A[gni] Y[oga] members. It is necessary to establish a harmonious atmosphere through unity and by raising the vibrations of those present. For this goal, of course, there is nothing better than wonderful music and an environment of beautiful works of art. The paintings by our Luminous One are the best basis. Brief, but fiery, addresses to the Powers of Light before the beginning of the meeting will ignite the hearts, which need to maintain their inner fire.

Discuss more about the establishment of the link with the G. L. and constantly remember about a chosen Guide, thinking about the meaning of life and better application of one's own powers for inner refinement and the broadening of consciousness. The broadening of consciousness will open new possibilities to the understanding of true service and will bring the joy of discipleship. Remember, dear ones, that nothing attracts the hearts like an attitude of love. How many of these pearls are scattered in the books of the Teaching! Nothing compares to the Power of Love. The Bonds of Love are unbreakable. The karma of hearts that have been united in love through millenia—is Supermundane Beauty!

I was happy about the reestablishing of the Academy: Education is the most joyous field.

Now, *The Fiery World*, # 374. The entire paragraph points to the separation of people's consciousness from Cosmic Laws. That's why the statement "Everything is reflected in the consciousness in a way that is not in accord with the Laws of the Cosmos" only confirms this ruinous separation.[1] Disunity of the worlds is the result of this discord. Only in accord can the right interchange and communion be built. Completing his life on Earth, the man who has not accepted in his consciousness the Cosmic Laws remains a prisoner of his own effects in the Subtle World, and he has to expiate these effects in his new incarnation on Earth, but this time more burdened and with even larger limitations than in the previous one. The stay in the Subtle World between incarnations for a man disunited and who does not understand the laws of being is very difficult, and rarely, very rarely, is it possible to awaken the spark of a new consciousness. In that burdened condition the help of Higher spirits is needed. Only They with their charity can open slightly and rouse the deadened spark. But to save a little fire under the ashes of desires and malicious intentions, the heart must become kind and feel the warmth of love in earthly life. So, dear, with sadness it has to be repeated, "Everything is reflected in the consciousness in a way that is not in accord with the laws of the Cosmos," and if it were different, we would be much closer to paradise on Earth, as in Heaven. The world's condition is such now that it is apparent how hell's activity is transferred to Earth.

November 8, 1948

Khandala, India

You know from the books of the Teaching how some dates are kept secret. You know that knowledge of the right dates is a higher knowledge. You know how the enemies, the dark forces, are trying first of all to find out about the dates and are trying to manipulate details of various circumstances in order to alter the dates. That is why those who know the dates keep silent and reveal them only when the last of the needed circumstances is beyond the reach of the enemies. I recall that as a child, even though I did not know about sacred laws, I did not like to inform anyone about dates; for example, the date of our moving to the estate for the summer—I truly felt that if I was to mention the date, some unexpected circumstance would delay our departure. Usually it happened this way.

I'd like very much, dear ones, if you would find a building in the part of the city that was indicated. Manifest resourcefulness; let not that which is evident dim your sight. Almost always I was able to find houses and certain items in accordance with Instructions, but a quick mind and full attention had to be manifested. I do not know if you remember that when I was in London I wished to find nice, small, leather envelopes for the four of us and one for Chklaver, so that we could keep our favorite sayings in them and always have them with us.[1] My thoughts were, where can I find the best ones? The street was given, and the numbers 40 and higher were given. On my request for the shop's name, four letters were given—at first, the letter "U," and later, the word "far." I was surprised by such a name. The next morning I went to look. I imagined a leather envelope, and naturally, I was looking for leather goods shops, but there weren't any such shops on the part of the street that I had been instructed to search. Disappointed with this failure, I decided one last time to stop on the other side of the street and look at all the buildings. Wasn't there a shop somewhere on a second story? When I stood at the corner, my attention was drawn to a big store, its wide window displaying rows of umbrellas, canes, riding-crops, etc., but below the umbrellas were displayed two or three, small, dog collars. At this same moment, the huge canopy began slowly turning and lowering over the window, and

I saw a large letter "U." My heart palpitated; the following turn opened the whole word "Umbrellas." I waited to see if there was going to appear the word "far." As it opened further, a big "L" was revealed, and the remaining letters spelled "afarge." So all the signs were evident: one letter at the beginning of a word and three others at the end of the new word, "Lafarge." I went immediately into the store, but after I looked in the display case behind the glass and saw only endless rows of umbrellas, I was a little confused. When the attendant came up to me, I, feeling a little embarrassed, explained that I would like to have five leather envelopes. The answer she gave was that they do not carry leather products except for large-size collars. But I had noticed fairly nice-looking, silk evening handbags under the glass counter, and, clinging to the last possibility, I asked her, "But, maybe you can offer me something acceptable in another material?" Suddenly she recalled something and said: "O, yes. Yesterday they sent some silk things to us from Paris." And as we approached a showcase in the middle of the store, she took out a wonderful envelope of the needed size, made of a beautiful silk fabric with an Eastern pattern of Bodhisattvas holding fiery chalices, ornamented with birds and flowers: all of it wonderfully decorated with tiny gold on the brocade.

I was amazed and thought, it's not likely that they would have another one like this one, but to my surprise she took out three more for me that were absolutely alike. Then she said: "This is all I have." I paid fairly well for these wonderfully found envelopes and then said to her: "Of course the fifth envelope could be less fancy and expensive." She went to the next room for tissue paper and a box to wrap the envelopes and came back smiling: "Madam, you really are the lucky one. When I was looking for an empty box, I found, in among other stuff, the same size envelope in gray suede. "Could this fit your need?" Can you imagine my joy? I had everything I needed. This remarkable episode is unforgettably imprinted in my memory. Who knows, maybe now something unexpected will happen with the finding of the building!

I enclose for you a copy of my reply to Weed.[2] It will be interesting for you to read about the new planet. This cosmic manifestation is going to be visible soon. Remember how in the book *Illumination*, on page 73, paragraph 19, it says: "Half the sky is occupied with an unusual manifestation. Around an invisible Luminary an immeasurable circle has begun to radiate, rays rushing along its brim."[3] This manifestation will be visible only for a few moments, but will last for seven days. Crossing the Sun's rays with the rays of the invisible Luminary, there will be displayed a fantastic sight. The rays of the invisible Luminary are made visible by the power of the Sun's rays. The power of these new rays will act as a detonating fuse on the craters; tensed by the poisonous gases on the Moon and the Sun, there will be a combustion of an awful, powerful gas. Therefore, the poisonous atmosphere of the Moon will undergo a bright improvement. Under the influence of the new planet, the Moon will become a new Moon.

The Moon will be revived and will give new healing rays to the plant world. The life of the plants on the revived Moon is going to be so vivid, so magnificent that through a telescope our Moon will look not like a globe of "cheese" but like a moss-grown globe. The rays of the new planet will increase as will the development of the magnetic power of the Moon. In the beginning, the Moon will be covered with the beauties of vegetation, as it first was; but under the influence of the new planet it will become covered with new plants and new kinds of insects. The Earth will become a new garden under the rays of the new planet and the renewed Moon. The vivid Moon will become like a new hothouse for the Earth. The Moon, revived by the rays of the new planet, will become a collector of the magnetism of the rays of the heavenly bodies that are in our Solar System and the rays passing close to it: the best country will be the one with the best vegetation under the rays of the New Planet and the revived Moon.

So, the New Era will be manifested by the ardent sign, by the sign of the Mother of the World. There are many very interesting pages in the *New Cosmogony*.[4] As the G. L. says: "My Cosmogony describes our solar system in a much fuller and more interesting way than do all existing books." The New Planet will become visible soon, but at first we are only going to see its rays. Of course, its rays are already active, but there aren't many who can assimilate them. To make good use of them, time is needed—and it will come.

I approve of music before the beginning of your meetings. Live performances, if they are wonderful, are always better than mechanical ones. But the Gramophone is not bad. We used to listen with pleasure to Wagner, Rachmaninov, Scriabin, Mussorgsky, and Jewish songs sung by Nina Koshets.

November 13, 1948

Khandala, India

I hurry to send the Instructions. The matter is that there soon will be a better destiny for your activity in America. "Bolling may purchase a house on 92nd or 94th street, but I do NOT need a house, because the building of the Museum will be returned. The New Country will be manifested in victory and the Museum will be returned to you. Justice will be restored. Write to them: 'The best step will be in the new building because of the new circumstance, because of the definite new circumstance. The New Country will show an interest in the Art of its genius compatriot. The Country will have a new appreciation of all his work under the rays of the new planet. The new planet, which will appear on the horizon, is definitely connected with your moving in. Its rays will be visible in November, but the planet itself will appear on our date in December.' "

I very much request that Sinochka and Dudley keep this news to themselves and practice complete silence. The Museum is going to be returned, and the rays of the new planet will destroy the enemies of Light. A few years will pass and bring many changes. Tell Weed that winter in Florida is not dangerous, but it is better in the beginning of March to return to New York and to move uptown. November of next year is going to be very difficult, especially for Florida. Also, California will be in danger in March and April until the new April Moon. Warn Bolling by talking to him, but ask him not to panic, or he will bring damage to himself and to the work. And you, dear ones, have until March to move to the new place. The coming year will be momentous and formidable.

It's time to outgrow the one-sided understanding of symbols. At any time, symbols can have different meanings in different cultures, and the meaning of a symbol can change, depending on circumstance and location. So, a tree is a symbol of everything that is alive and grows, but there are also dried-out trees, or those without roots, and those trees have to be removed. It is the same with human deeds—some are developing for good, but others carry a poison and should be stopped. Remember how in the East (whence most of our symbols come) the disciple who turns away from his Teacher was compared to a tree that does not have roots? And he, the disciple who ascends the ladder of succession through the centuries, was called an ever-blooming Banyan. Do not be disappointed by those who read the Teaching without understanding it. The time will come when their eyes will be opened, but take into consideration that some tenets of the Teaching will not be understood by somebody, and any word will be misinterpreted by somebody.

The entire Universe is based on repetition, on repeated movement, or RHYTHM. There is nothing created without repetition; any accomplishment requires repeated accumulations. Without repetition nothing is learned. Memory itself is a repository of unending repetitions. All our life is a continuous chain of repetitions, but man does not notice them and is easily moved toward new ascents and findings, being equipped with previously learned manifestations, movements, situations, concepts, etc., and thus is it in the Teaching. Only by learning the principles of the Teaching through repetition can a Disciple easily move on to the next accomplishment. A comparison with a carpet on a staircase shows that repetition makes things much easier, just as a carpet eases the ascent on a staircase. So the comparison with a cobblestone road, which is constructed with stones that are alike and skillfully selected, facilitates the Path. The repetitions, just like cobblestones that are nicely selected in varying combinations, do not tire one, but are easily remembered, enabling the disciples to move easily and smoothly toward new achievements on the Path laid by the Great Teachers of humanity.

The apparent monotony of identical stones disappears for those who see and learn about the skillful construction of the Path. For this one should master the art of repetition—that is to say, to repeat in a new light or in new ways of co-measurement and application. Assimilation does not mean to become thoughtless and indifferent, but to be inspired, knowing the truth and direction of the cobblestone road has been established with the care and love of the Great Teachers of humanity.

Wormwood, [of the genus] Artemisia, is a grass with a strong scent, which is widely found in the mountain places of Tibet, India, Russia, and Switzerland, though I think it also grows in America. In Switzerland, a drink of wormwood tea is given for inflammation of the glands. An oil of this plant is helpful if gently rubbed into an aching spot. The way of making it and the way of using it should be researched, because every person is different. It is always suggested to start with a very small dosage. The tea of wormwood shouldn't be strong. It has a good effect on the glands, purifying them.

The dosage for musk is also relative. Some may take one grain two times daily for a cold, whereas for others one is enough. It may also be two or three grains at once, but only with experience can it be determined. I used to give N. K. one mid-sized grain of musk with a pinch of baking soda, and he took valerian tea after that. When I myself have taken it, I have not followed any specific dosages, but have taken it according to my physical condition. The worse I feel, the more musk I take. Musk is difficult to digest, but soda makes it easier.

Sinochka is right. It is a serious misprint. It should read: "When we can and do, then we achieve." Or, it could even be said: "We achieve not when we can, but when we want to." Because "can't" often is relative; we just think that we cannot.

Of course, the dimensions of the planes refers to the different qualities of the different spheres. Where the dense world requires effort (let's say when moving from one place to another), the Subtle World not only does not require effort, but offers easy mobility. This is because in the Subtle World people can move about easily; indeed they can fly.

If you will be reprinting the first part of "L. M. G." [*Leaves of Morya's Garden*], of course the first title should be preserved as it was in the second volume, only the name in the second volume should be put in full, which is also *Leaves of Morya's Garden.*

It will be possible to start sending out pages from *Illumination.* It is possible to name these pages as "the leaves from the second volume of L. M. G.," or if you wish, from the book *Illumination*—do it however you think is best.

What books to advise people to read is a very difficult question. People's consciousness and accumulations and education are so different that all straight-knowledge should be applied in order to recommend the right book. But books like those written about Ramakrishna, and all books written by Swami Vivekananda, of course are very useful.[1, 2] What are also very good are books of Yogi Ramacharaka. There are a few volumes: *The Ways of the Hindu Yogis*, *The Foundations of Hindu Ideology*, other yogas, etc. I only remember the approximate titles. I think that it is easy to find them in America because they say he was a disciple of Vivekananda, when Vivekananda was there. I advise you also to read them. Schuré and Renan, I wouldn't suggest. Schuré has a lot of mediumistic nonsense. For all developed consciousnesses, of course, all the books of Blavatsky are a well of wisdom, and also *The Mahatma Letters*, but a knowledge of the fundamentals of Eastern Philosophy is necessary. I think that it is possible to find good books at the Vedanta Society. From Besant's books, of course, the best is *Esoteric Christianity*. Let the readers pay attention to the statements of the Gnostics that Besant quotes, when Christ, in His subtle body and during the eleven years after His resurrection, was giving instructions about the secrets of the Supermundane World to Mary Magdalene. And this is how it was. The writings of Mary Magdalene have almost all disappeared, and only scraps remain; but now it is possible to find them in the Gnostic literature. In this way the Gospel of John was written down by Mary Magdalene. She was the one highly educated disciple among the followers of Christ. If it was not for Mary Magdalene, it is doubtful whether anything of the original words of Christ would have reached us. *At the Feet of the Master* is not a bad book. I also love a small book compiled by Jinarajadasa, *Episodes of an Unwritten History*.[3] I love the book by Cooper-Oakley, *The Diary of Madam D'Adhémar*.[4] There one can find very interesting pages about the life of Master Rakoczi in connection with the French Revolution. I very much love the book of Sinnett, *The Occult World*, the life and miracles surrounding Blavatsky.[5] This book was much approved by Master K. H. Two volumes of Olcott's diary give the description of his meeting and work with Blavatsky and all the miracles that took place then.[6]

February 7, 1949

We live among primitive tribes that are almost wild. Of course, the services they can provide are quite limited, and an unbelievable amount of time and effort must be spent for anything; but essentially, these darker people are much better than the city people. We will stay near the Taj Mahal for a few days, hopefully not more than a week. I will be happy to return to those mountains again, where I experienced so much joy.

There is now a speeding up of all cosmic events. In the Cosmic Plan, all possibilities are broadening and improving, and therefore there is some delay in our moving. Dear ones, pay attention to all Instructions because the coming time will be difficult, very difficult. Nothing should confuse you, because Help, as always, will be given. All who are under the Shield of Light, of course, will be protected. Let not a single change or sudden happening surprise you. Blessed grains can be sown only in a purified field, because to build in chaos is impossible. But when the Cosmic Forces are taking part in this reconstruction, there is a lot that can happen in the twinkling of an eye, and many years will not be needed to get rid of the accumulation of poisonous and destructive gases in our earthly atmosphere. The cleaning may start suddenly, where it's least expected.

The co-measurement and wisdom of the Cosmic Mind decides the destinies of many countries. The best of humanity should be helped, otherwise the waves of malice would overflow the World.

Of course, after March 15, tell your friends it would be better to stay in the northern part of the city. Tell your secretary about the Advice and about storing supplies. Thanks and a kiss from me to dear Magdalen Lehrer for the wonderful graphic. It is so fitting in its meaning to our Beloved and Illumined One. Of course, the graphic that was sent in August of 1947, did not reach us because it was a time of horrors in the country and a terrible flood in our valley. There was a lot lost then.

Her graphic stands on my small writing table. I suffer very much because of the small size of my desk. I am used to a small room, but it is difficult to get used to a small table; everything keeps falling to the floor. I am overflowing, as usual, with writings and books. I have collected all my prophetic dreams and visions—a great picture emerged, truly Apocalyptic. We are reaching the end of Armageddon, and after the coming world drama will come a period of calm and increased development in the new countries. And the star of the Mother of the World will come closer and will illuminate our cleansed Earth with Its Rays. All the little orange fires will burn out under its rays, and a world of prosperity will be established on Earth.

March 16, 1949

Let us show our trust to the Guiding Hand and, unexpectedly, much will turn out better than hoped for. We are so used to trusting in the G. L. about everything that we never think about how something may happen or what will come of our plans; but our concern is just to follow the Instructions as well as possible and to manifest the necessary mobility and resourcefulness when there is a sudden change of circumstances. We were striving to the New Country, preparing everything for our departure when, instead, we received an Order to move to Sikkim. We moved and were staying in a small, local hotel, while we began looking for a house to rent. There was nothing acceptable, or rather only the European-style houses were for sale, because their owners were in a hurry to leave this wonderful land. Still, I kept hearing, "The house is ready to accept you."

A few days later, when another possibility for a house fell through, George decided to take the advice of the local agents and in the morning went to the market. Before he had time to reach his destination, a car drove up with two natives who offered to show him the Sheriff's house. George objected, saying that the Sheriff's house was not for rent but only for sale. One of the fellows replied, "But I bought that house yesterday and would like for you to rent it." Can you imagine George's happiness? Previously he had gone to see that house, but its owner had said that he would not not rent it out, but wanted to sell it. So, we are sitting in our tower-rooms admiring the magnificent view of the Himalayan ridge and the wonderful flower garden in front of our house. All of my favorite flowers are there in unbelievable abundance.

You may ask how long we are going to stay here. I will answer: "We will move on from here when we are Instructed, in accordance with circumstances." Our plans are broad and the pattern is made according to possibilities that appear and our ability. And I have to tell you: everything is happening "wiser than wise." But one should not interrupt with a mood of pessimism, and most importantly, one should not be afraid of any new changes and challenges.

Dudley must also calmly acquire new knowledge in his given field, and everything will come when it's needed. And our other friends, after the thunder and sandstorms have passed from the world, will engage in broader and more useful work, and their resources will increase because of cooperation with new countries and friends. Mainly, nobody has to be afraid, or apprehensive, while their inner substance is keeping alive the fire of striving and devotion to the high Ideals. The Powerful Shield of the Hierarchy of Light will rise above them and protect them from misfortune. So, dear ones, I wish you good luck; act wisely and carefully, but doubt nothing; everything will come in its time. The Agni Yoga books, of course, should be unpacked and put in place after the storm has passed, which is expected by the end of this month. The new moon has a great significance in cosmic manifestations.

Gubareva caused me much sadness. She, apparently, was hurt by my letter about precautions regarding an earthquake in California and my advice about her health. She did not like the bad news and became silent. It happens with undeveloped consciousnesses. It is difficult for them to understand the simplicity of the grandeur of Truth. They like more the sugary splendor and the tinsel of rituals and the different "initiations" promised them by the enterprising organizers of such "entertainment." It is only half the trouble if it is entertainment and there is no underlying fraud or profit. I feel sorry for her, but we won't force her will and thrust the Teaching upon her. She was honestly looking for Light, but when she found It, she could not keep It. She could easily receive the first signs, but for further advancement it is necessary to have a large measure of self-discipline with accumulated striving to achieve the broadening of consciousness, discernment, and enlightenment. It is not good that she suspected that it was our desire to exploit her for our activities, when we only wished, with all our heart, to help her. More than anything, I am afraid of mistrustful people. Truly, I could not expect her to be so limited, after reading her autobiography, but apparently, autobiographies are written with some self-admiration and do not always reflect a true image. Therefore we won't disturb her; let her realize her mistake and knock again. We will say, "The Door is open, but only she can enter."

March 29, 1949

"Crookety"
Kalimpong, India

But I say: You know the consciousness of the people; you know how much time is needed for ardent people to move toward following the given Advice. Unfortunately, our friends showed much lightmindedness and did not fulfill even half of what was Indicated. It could be said to them: "Strong doubt is the doubt of the blind and the deaf." If a country collapses, the doubting ones should understand the consequences of that disaster and how their peaceful life would be disrupted.

Doubt turns into horror when new events occur, and all given Advice is shown to be quite proper. But I repeat that friends should not treat Advice light-mindedly. If something in the Indication does not come true, that means that it is postponed, to be manifested in the future. One should display complete readiness to carry out all given Advice, fulfilling it as fully and precisely as possible. The Advice remains, and is unalterable in connection with the Cosmic Plan. All that is indicated will happen as Cosmic Immutability.

You, dear ones, can find strength and calm in knowing about the coming cataclysmic events. Do not tell the newcomers, but Weed and Bolling may read about the Cosmic Plan. It is impossible to specify a precise day or hour for Supermundane Decisions so far in advance, because they may change due to new circumstances, which may postpone or hasten events that call for a Cosmic Decision. But the Decision itself remains unchanged, because it was made on the basis of the Cosmic Plan, which will happen "in the twinkling of an eye," when all circumstances for its realization will be present. Our Ray can delay its execution for a short time, but cannot change the basis of the Cosmic Plan, which is in accordance with many reasons and events. The events are in accordance with Our Decision, not vice versa. Manifest, dear ones, understanding of the complexity of reconciling cosmic and Supermundane events with our earthly calendar dates. Some events happen in four dimensions, but our Earth operates in three dimensions. Since all events are interrelated, we can see that this is where both their immutability and their deviations lie.

So, convey to your friends the Word about the Cosmic Plan and confirm that all that has been Indicated has an important basis, and all Advice is given in the right place and at the right time, and reveals the wise foresight and care of the G. L. for them and their families. Truly, we do not know either the day or the hour when suddenly something will break into our life. At first it was stated that the dangerous time would start from the 15th of March and would continue into April. When the questions poured in requesting precise dates, which can't be exactly determined because of the laws of group Karma, a great difficulty arose and interruptions occurred, caused by worry about the safety of close coworkers.

Thus the Cosmic Plan remains immutable, as are the Indications given regarding the work. Dangerous areas remain so; also during the next several weeks, the Advice is to not travel through the country because of increased radioactivity in some places; it is better to stay within the limits of Michigan and its environs. I can repeat that a cosmic manifestation will follow after the terrible event that is called "the people's madness." And only to Sinochka and Dudley can I say, "The most important has begun." A change of government in my country will cleanse it. This change will be beneficial, as a new step in the development of the people's consciousness. The country will become a beautiful country and will manifest Cosmic Justice. The words about the Beautiful Country you may keep to yourself, as they are not needed for anyone now. One must spare the consciousness of people and "not hammer a nail in the coffin" of the consciousness, which is not ready to understand the new world. Our friends are good people and they help the cultural institutions. That is why you should let them care about their own affairs and carry out the good Advice.

I am not worried either for you or for the destiny of the institutions, because I know a wonderful future, which is getting so close that even I, in my old age, will see the foundations of it. But, dear ones, do not belittle yourself with unworthy thoughts and doubts, and remember about your importance in the fulfillment of the works and plans of the G. L. All your plans will deal with completely different circumstances and possibilities. So hold out a little while more, and then swim out into the wide waters, so, dearest ones, you will not only save face but will become wise people and prophets of the cosmic course of events.

April 28, 1949

"Crookety"

Dearest ones, try to develop a deep calm in yourselves, repeating the wise saying: "And this too shall pass." Transport yourselves in consciousness into the future; and not only into the future, but try now, in the earthly life, to sense your own life in the Supermundane World, and all events, all difficult situations in life, will lose their sharpness. You are carrying out work that has been entrusted to you, and if you are sincerely trying to execute what was Instructed, nothing can shatter you or your position. But when carrying out what was Indicated, remember one helpful condition—it is always better to say less than to give too much. We all are sinners in this, wanting to tell others, to warn others, without considering the karmic load.

I ask you very, very much to behave with absolute calm, and without irritation or taking offense at different kinds of hints, or even unfair accusations coming from close friends. "Upcoming events will justify all warnings given to them." Begin at least to display some patience. Without these attacks the Path of the Teaching would not be a heroic one, but simply an easy way of passing through earthly obstacles. But any easement deprives one of new achievements. That is why strong spirits choose difficult paths, so they may reach the crown of the Arhat sooner, when the spirit finds the calmness of immutable knowledge and can act regardless of the opinions of those who are blind and deaf.

People so thoughtlessly extinguish their own fires; they do not think what it means to put out the fire of psychic energy. They do not know that putting it out means depriving themselves of eternal life in the Subtle World. You see, eternal life is not our absolute property or heritage. No, it needs to be earned by hard labor and by the purging of the ego in the fire of selfless heroic deeds. The one who puts out the fire of higher psychic energy becomes a living corpse. His subtle body begins to decompose during the earthly life, because he lives only by the fire of his passions, and he crosses over to the World of Shadows as cosmic waste, in its fullest meaning.

I think that we are going to stay here about six more months and then move farther to the north. Already I cannot go down into the valleys. Staying in Delhi exposed me to mortal danger, and as always, I was saved only by the miracle of the G. L.'s Rays, but at the price of terrible sufferings.

By the way, Inge's nausea and vomiting were caused by the influence of the G. L.'s Rays. These Rays stimulate the solar plexus, which becomes slightly irritated and, of course, results in nausea, vomiting and even fainting. I suffered many times from this solar plexus stimulation, from its rotation, and almost every day suffered the so-called dry heaves, which lasted a very long time. But this stimulation helps in the assimilation of the Rays. I think that Inge is feeling better now, as assimilation of the Rays is already taking place. Part of Dudley's nervousness comes from the same stimulation of the solar plexus. Indeed, he also is under the G. L.'s Rays.

I do not think that Sinochka's illness was something serious, because it was Said: "Let Sina take warm milk with soda during this indisposition." Of course, tiredness is often accompanied by irritation of the mucous membranes. Besides, excessive radioactivity in the atmosphere first of all harms the mucous membranes, and care is required. Most important, one should keep a strict diet, a mostly milk diet, preferably of goat's milk, because a goat's milk contains comparably more psychic energy than a cow's. Cereals and the lightest vegetables, nothing raw, only boiled. That which consists of fat and sweet things are not good. Sugar is not good; glucose is better. Also avoid bread made with yeast. Barley flour is much better than wheat, which has a lot of acidity, especially when refined. Barley strengthens the capillaries and tissues. A drink made from barley with glucose and a few lemon drops for taste is the best drink when there is an illness of the mucous membranes. Also, barley soup is good, with fried carrots for taste.

August 3, 1949

Kalimpong, India

Of course, the stage I've gone through was the difficult one. The degree of my cosmic collaboration with the G. L. is, as it is said, the most rare. The condition is difficult, not explainable in words, because the realization of it is not on the earthly plane; but even a partial realization of it causes great physical suffering. Now that this step is completed, there remain only a few consequences that have to be overcome.

It has often been repeated how important it is to save the paintings, and how necessary it was to take them from the previous building to save them in the new building chosen for them, because in these paintings, the G. L. sees the foundation of the art of the Future. All that is for the Future should be, as you know, our first concern.

August 27, 1949

"Crookety"
Kalimpong, India

Do not doubt my words; what I tell you comes from the words of the G. L. Banish any hint of doubt—this terrible boa, I do not know anything more horrible! Indeed, the ray of the enemy is sowing doubts. How can we give access to it? How can we get rid of it if it is able to assimilate our energy?

Every undertaking of Light is subject to attacks by those who extinguish the Light, but nothing can suffocate the progress of the ideas of Light and the building of the general good. The attackers should be viewed as stimuli for our energy, which could otherwise come to a standstill. Incitements are needed everywhere and in everything—this is a Cosmic Law. Battle brings the birth of new possibilities, new energies, and new combinations.

So, my dear ones, try to develop in yourselves the calmness that nothing can destroy in any event of life. This is the best protection and weapon against any enemy. Precisely, one should not worry. Only through difficulties can we learn resourcefulness, patience, and great calmness. Where the Ray of the L. is shining and is not rejected, everything is turned for the best use. With this consciousness, disciples and coworkers of the W[hite] Brotherhood go along their Path.

Among your new activities, of course, you will now pay attention to the Red Cross of Culture. It is necessary to organize lectures, concerts, and discussions about the importance of the protection of culture and to introduce the activity of the Banner of Peace. When there is vandalism and destruction during world collisions and shocks, it is appropriate to call the protection of the cultural treasures, a "crusade." Truly, it is a "crusade" in view of the world significance of cultural treasures as irreplaceable and the common property of humanity.

It's possible that somebody will be seriously interested in this "crusade" and will be able to organize a group that in time will grow into a powerful progressive movement on the cultural field of battle. Truly, culture needs protection, and it is necessary to know how to fight for culture. Only then will humanity begin to emerge from its condition of running wild. It is time to become human, in the full meaning of this great concept.

The Psychic Center is located in the Sacred Land, from which the G. L. sends psychic energy to all quarters of the world. But during the time I mentioned, magnetic currents of our Earth were in terrible discord with this Psychic Center because of the poisonous rays of the enemy planet, which was then passing close to Earth. This planet is invisible to the physical sight and is a conglomerate of poisonous gases that have poisoned the Earth's atmosphere; as a result, there are going to be new illnesses. But of course this will not be accepted now by scientists.

The spirit of Blavatsky accumulated knowledge over many centuries. That is why she could compile *The Secret Doctrine* and bring into the world confirmation of and lost knowledge about the existence of the Great Brotherhood. One should never make comparisons; who can understand or know the difference in the organisms' structures, which have been chosen for the carrying out of particular missions?

Blavatsky, in her previous lives, already revealed herself on the yogic path, but in this life she had to assume the body of a powerful medium because her task was to work among many people, amidst constant hostile attitudes toward her and surrounded by disharmonious auras, and to manifest miracles to convince the chosen ones of the existence of other laws of Nature, of the existence of higher knowledge.

September 5, 1949

Kalimpong, India

I understand that you are going through difficult times, but for whom now is it easy? But, may trust in the Guiding Wisdom and readiness to courageously face the difficulties of life never leave you. With all spiritual power, keep calm, because, truly, we do not know either the day or the hour when something will come. "There are many changes that will happen and many situations that will be changed." Every day we also wait for the solving of our problems, like birds on a branch ready to take wing with the first ... Sign. All previously mentioned road marks came close, but the final sign ...where is it? We know that silence often precedes big decisions. Truly, the "Messenger" may already be spurring his horse! It is difficult to wait. Oh, how difficult! Yet with all difficulties one should never feel fear. Wasn't it said that fear destroys the best sprouts of the spirit? Courage, unbreakable courage, is the commandment on the Path. The fully equipped Teaching given to us will meet the new stage of activity.

I cannot imagine that the treasures entrusted to us could be abandoned, left without constant protection. Is it possible that the grandeur of Thought and Heart and the broad scope of vision outlined in the New Teaching did not make clear to them the great Source that they had come close to? Is it possible that they do not realize how much their karma would improve by partaking of the Higher Wisdom? Not a single action, even a small one, to help in the Wonderful

Work remains without reward. Help to the G. L. is returned a hundredfold. It is difficult for the Arhats to write about it, but a reminder must be made.

September 30, 1949

"Crookety "

Of course, the change in the world situation will influence everything. And the discovery of the use of atomic energy for engines means the end of Our Era of the "Dark Age" [Kali Yuga]. But not yet! Yet one can dream about the transformation of the meaning of all life. Indeed, a completely different life, a new life will begin on Earth. But now, all these early discoveries help to destroy material civilization, and that is why the spreading of spiritual culture is so important, the most urgent task. It is necessary for the masses to realize, finally, that the only value is the high quality that comes through manifestations of psychic energy, and not by revealing unbridled instincts that beget the chaos of darkness and decay.

People still do not realize that the terrible Armageddon is taking place. They cannot perceive the coming cosmic changes and do not recognize the events taking shape that will bring great shocks to the world.

This past March everything was hanging by a thread, and the cosmic danger from the subterranean fire was so great that all the Forces of Light were mobilized to break the enormous tension and cause many smaller explosions. This was achieved, and many countries were saved from terrible disaster. But will it be possible to repeat it when the cosmic date comes again, or will we, inhabitants of the planet, be its destroyers? California and Florida are still in danger; also the increase of the ocean level has not been completely forestalled.

No Rays of the Great Lord can penetrate a confused consciousness. Any forcing of the confused consciousness under the Ray of great tension will cause paralysis. Truly, confusion and doubt are our most terrible enemies, for they block access to the Rays. A disciple is obligated to discipline himself and cultivate calmness based on complete trust in the wisdom of the G. L. and on love for Him Who is full of inexhaustible patience and loving forgiveness for our weaknesses. Give joy to the G. L., manifest courageous calmness strengthened by a broadening of consciousness as you strive to a better understanding of the Teaching given to us.

October 12, 1949

Kalimpong, India

You are the sowers of the seeds of friendliness. Practicing mutual understanding in ARCA will promote the development of cultural understanding, skill, knowledge, and art in the "Academy" and the raising of the Banner of Peace, the Banner of the Lords, above the cultural buildings in all countries of the world. Finally, offer the knowledge of Living Ethics, the Teaching of the Future Era. This program lays the foundation for the building of Life in all its fullness. That is why, dear ones, with all the spiritual power you have, be affirmed in the great task of becoming heralds of the coming New Era, which is based on cooperation, equal rights, respect for labor, enlightenment, and on the perception of the beauty of Spiritual Leadership in its myriad manifestations of primal, or psychic energy.

I say to dear Dudley, I understand his sense of "pride" and recall the lesson that I received from false pride when I did not want to show much friendliness to the people who visited us in quest for the Path, for fear that they would think we were in need of money. It was Indicated to me then: "Know how to curb (your self) when starting Our service" and "For My work, there is no room for weakness; one may not only ask, but even demand." Of course, I immediately curbed my "false pride" and went on to do what was requested. The result was wonderful, and the foundation was laid for great work. Without sometimes forcing oneself, many things would not happen in TIME. My consciousness has become broader since then, and I understand what priceless treasures have been and are being given through us; I understand the depth and importance of all that is being given, and how pride is incompatible with Service. And what pride could possess us when we understand the essence of being and of what is happening? Truly, the only allowable pride is loyalty to the consciousness—non-admission to the consciousness of even the smallest doubt in the wisdom of the G. L. Pride should be in our unbreakable, infinite devotion.

And how easy devotion is when flaming love lives in the heart! This love says: "Always and in everything I serve Thee, O Lord, and I won't burden Thee with doubts and complaints, because I know Thy Concerns and Burdens." I love the saying of Christ, which He so often repeated: "My yoke is easy and my burden is light." But who understood this then, and who understands it now? Truly, He was giving, and even now is giving to people His Great Benevolence. The yoke that He puts on the disciples is an easy burden, because His Ray is always over you, dearest ones, and is ready to illumine your path if you do not intrude with doubts and worries, which can set your vibrations into a state of confusion. Then, no ray can reach you without your having to exert force to control your centers. But any forcing is dangerous. It is necessary for the magnetic field of your aura to be calm, then the ray can send to you the needed and urgent thoughts and create a magnetic attraction to all needed people and circumstances. Otherwise the reverse can happen. So, do not block access to the ray, which is always vigilant and ready to indicate the right desires and to attract the needed help. Those attracted to you must feel the love that motivates your every intention and action. Nothing can live without love. How worthless is our earthly world in comparison with the Supermundane! How irrelevant are all our doubts, or rather, how destructive they are, and how all our earthly offenses are mostly repayments for our previous deeds. But it is better to pay our debts on Earth than in the Supermundane World. So, my beloved ones, be proud to be the carriers of Light to the end, to the limit. Then and only then will we be able to become coworkers of the Forces of Light.

You wished to ascertain whether, at the very least, you and I will meet in the other World. I can affirm to you with all the strength of my spirit that such a meeting will happen, because all those who work in devotion of the heart for the good of humanity on the path of Service, of course, create unbreakable bonds. But this meeting is possible on Earth also, and its time is near. Remember that the care of the G. L. for the institutions in America will never be exhausted. His Ray always will be above those who assume and continue the mission. More than that, I hope, during my remaining life, to be able to help our institutions from the New Country. What was established by the G. L. and had the name of N. K., our unforgettable, illumined Representative of Goodness and Beauty, won't ever be forgotten, but will grow and blossom. And close spirits will be needed that will continue this beautiful activity.

You ask, "Do we always have to fight with people? Can it be that they all are our enemies?" I will answer, "We always have to fight against evil in all its manifestations. As it is now on Earth, the carriers of harm are a majority, so, of course, we have many enemies. But all life as it is, in all its deep fullness, is an unending battle. But without the battle, there would be no consciousness, knowledge, progress, or achievement. In the Higher Worlds, the battle is different in quality, even stronger and more intense. Truly, the scope and the means are different there.

Who can imagine the battle in space with accumulations of the most poisonous gases, which, in their closeness to the many heavenly bodies, can poison them and deprive them of all life? But this does occur. Who can imagine the danger of the magnetic attraction of the spacious giant that goes near our solar system, and what perturbations it may cause throughout the solar system? Who can imagine the destructive influence of rays, let's say Saturn's, on humanity's consciousness? But they do act and poison healthy organisms. But also countless are the dangers hidden from the consciousness of the people, but obvious to the consciousness of supermen and godmen. Countless are the joys achieved by the ascent of the consciousness and by participation in cosmic construction. We are learning to love the fight for Goodness and Beauty.

I am already seventy, and I have undergone the Yoga of Fire. And you know, my dearest ones, from the books of the Teaching, how unbearably difficult it is to accept in the physical body, amidst ordinary conditions, the fiery energy. The fiery transmutation refined my organism. I became extremely sensitive to all disharmony and all spatial currents. It is difficult for me to be among people, and now the monsoon, and the stuffy air it brings, fatigue me very much. My Heart often skips a beat, and I have to take strophanthus; this is my saver.

But also, I do not have enough time, because so much time is given receiving communications and recording them. My sight has weakened, and it is difficult to read my jottings, which are often written down with a light pencil. All these notes must be put in order, and the flow of new messages is unending. I've just read what I wrote about my condition and think that he (Bolling) shouldn't be told. Just say that my heart has weakened and I need a little rest. By the way, at the same time I sent the telegram to you, I also sent one to him thanking him for his help to the institutions. I think that I have to write to him, but how difficult it is to write to people who do not understand the very basic elements of Service and the approach to the Forces of Light! They think that everything is possible, easy and simple! They do not know that the closer one is to the Light, the more inexorable become the Laws. I'd like to finish my letter with a discourse from *Supermundane, Book One,* #117. It supports what I have now been writing:

"Urusvati is aware of the concept of victory. When We start creative work that is protected by the battle, We affirm victory. May the tautened string of victory resound! May the signs of forward motion become visible, for there is no defeat in Infinity. May Our Call be accepted as living advice.

"Urusvati knows well the communications link with the Brotherhood; only by means of this link can one know the varied states of existence. Our Brotherhood is like a laboratory of all branches of life. The new Teaching is now being spread throughout the whole world, introducing a new knowledge of the subtle energies. Our victory too, is subject to subtle conditions. Sometimes years are required to make the right path, already outlined by Us, visible to earthly eyes. Later, people will remark on how specifically events were foreseen, and some will then appreciate Our sense of co-measurement in revealing the truth. Thus, learn from Our patience. May the adamant aspiration of the Brotherhood be an example for you in all your actions.

"Our Inner Life contains a subtle reflection of earthly ways in all their multiplicity, therefore We advise that a keen and agile mind be developed. The ancients taught the possibility of all impossibilities, and in so doing taught how to broaden the consciousness. They often repeated the parable about an inept general, who, standing on a hilltop, was so concerned about the defeat of one part of his army that he failed to turn in time to see the other part of his army win a major victory." [1]

Yes, beloved ones, the diversity of new circumstances brings complexity and difficulty, but also the beauty of creation. Therefore, let us calmly accept all that is coming our way, because we know that with the help of the G. L. all difficulties form the best steps of our ladder of ascent. In this way we will continue our creative work, saved by the battle, and will be affirmed in Victory.

I hug you, dear ones, I know how your hearts will be aflame with love for the increased activity under the Ray of the Lord. I send you all the fire of my heart, all my trust in you. How is Sophie Mikhailovna feeling? [2] Send her my heartfelt "hello," and ask her not to be worried about anything, because all will be taken care of, all will be guarded. I keep you in my heart; I send thoughts of calmness.

November 1, 1949

Kalimpong, India

About the additional paintings, I wouldn't ask Bolling right now. Give him a chance to think about it himself. Maybe you will be able to touch upon this question with Katherine, and she will agree to lend a few from her collection, of course, noting the loan. I wish to display the art of our beloved Pasenka, the Singer of the Great Shambhala, in the best way. Indeed, every painting carries with it an accumulation of such purity and lofty thought and the aura of its Creator, saturated with a special light, and special, joyous vibrations that fill the atmosphere of the rooms in which they are displayed.

I will tell only you: Armageddon has ended with the defeat of the enemy. The New Era began on the 17th of October, when the enemy was driven out of our Solar System. "The new constructive work will begin under My Rays."

November 27, 1949

Kalimpong, India

One should know about an enemy's attacks, and be able to respond when possible, but one shouldn't worry too much about it. We are on the threshold of so many changes! Great events are happening in the world; the reaping of old sowings are being cleared away and will lead to an unexpected outcome. Truly, we live in Apocalyptic times, and Cosmic Justice will reveal its verdict.

It is joyous to realize that the last battle of the Forces of Light with the Hierophant of Evil ended with his defeat and with his removal from our Solar System. Of course, there are a lot of evil minions, and they are going to continue their harmful actions, but they will weaken without a new flow of power and support from their dark lord. Existence on Earth will be much better after the coming purification. The Stronghold of Evil collapsed, together with its Dark Master.

It was possible to postpone the final catastophe and minimize its scope, but it is still inevitable. Early warnings gave the possibility to friends to save their assets and wisely follow all given Advice. Nobody was told to broaden their affairs; on the contrary, Bolling was stopped in his big plans. To give warnings only on the eve of events or disasters can only create a panic and aggravate the danger. Early Orders are wise foresight and good action. There is a saying, "Don't count your chickens before they hatch." In my opinion, this is always applicable.

Besides, the catastrophe was postponed by a great sacrifice, about which our friends maybe will learn when they pass over the line. The destiny of the entire planet was hanging by a thread! And now, though the danger has decreased (for the whole planet), it was not entirely avoided and is approaching again. So, I ask all friends and close coworkers once more to again be more careful during March, especially in the second half of the month.

I, too, sometimes do not know the precise dates and wait patiently all the time. But this not knowing is our best protection and is necessary. It is better to discipline ourselves in patience, trust, and the development of calmness. Trust is necessary and must be complete, because the G. L. sees what we cannot see. It is impossible to imagine how complicated is the pattern of circumstances, and especially of karmic interlacing. And this complexity is changing constantly and producing new opportunities or harm, and it is precisely these opportunities or harm that modify events. Here the complete trust of the disciple who follows the leadership of the Teacher is needed. Read in *Community* about the Immutability of the Plan.

Work, carrying in your heart the Image of the Beloved; create in His Name, send Him ardent Love, and at the right moment will come the unexpected Answer. Always unexpected, because it is necessary for many cosmic circumstances to coincide. Mostly, the attention is always on the condition of the heart, so take care of your heart, keep calm, and thus strengthen your nervous system. The power of the G. L. is great, and now it becomes even more magnificent and indisputable. A lot can happen during five months, but complete trust and complete absence of doubt and fear from the closest disciples is required.

This is a difficult time for me now because of my work with the G. L. on both the Cosmic Plan and the Earthly One. This cooperation does not permit me to pay attention to the little nothings of life. It requires ardent concentration for the receiving of the messages, which not only must be written, but also remembered. I am writing and memorizing, but it is difficult to keep systematized because the messages often touch upon varied topics, from themes of cosmic significance to everyday practice. But all my being is striving toward knowledge and cosmic construction. Earthly knowledge appears to be without meaning and limited, but the consciousness united with the Cosmic Consciousness of the G. L. knows the essence of things, the significance of all that happens, and sees the future.

The signpost pointing to decisive events is approaching and may coincide with our moving northward. Dear ones, be calm. The fury of events is not going to touch you. You are working for better cooperation between both countries and help will be given to you from the New Country. Give yourself a command: complete calmness and trust in the G. L. and you will be under His Ray. Nothing is going to touch you. Just have more trust and all the constructive work will proceed under the joyous sign of the realized Help, sent always at the last hour when we ourselves have strained our abilities to the limit—that's the

Law. Otherwise our talents wouldn't be developed; and our subtle body, instead of refinement in tense striving, would grow heavy with sleep; and spiritual perfection, the only thing that offers conscious supermundane existence, would be stopped. Now I can give you one more sign—the flood in England will start before the one in your country. This way you will have time to take precautionary measures. A heartfelt greeting to Sophie Mikhailovna. May she always preserve her trust. My heart sends the call for Trust, and I believe that you will be able to inspire that Trust in all our friends.

December 31, 1949

Dear and Beloved, your letter of December 19 arrived. There is a lot of worry in that letter, but, of course, it is unavoidable when the general confusion of minds fills the lower layers with trembling; but we can draw a special power by attaching ourselves to Hierarchy. We gain courage and patience when we overcome the last vestiges of the Black Age.

I am glad that the Academy opened with a concert, but a short word about the significance of Art in the spiritual, creative, and constructive life of nations and about the cultural activity of our institutions would be very appropriate. I was sending you thoughts and the power of my spirit.

Sinochka and Dudley should not worry so much about their activities. It is necessary to affirm full trust in the Guiding Hand and develop unbreakable calmness of spirit. "The Hand that gives will never be empty." But then circumstances should be created that are suitable for the accepting of the "Gift." This condition is not too difficult; one must simply maintain benevolence of spirit.

I hope that Eugene's return will bring the much needed calmness to Jeanette. Tell her also: "The Hand that gives will never be empty." When there is trust and heartfelt love, the "Gifts" will not be delayed; but trust is necessary. Doubt paralyzes our outer centers and the best messages cannot reach us. With doubt one cannot cross a ditch on a narrow board, or descend a staircase without a handrail. Many small, common actions become impossible when there is doubt, and even more when one is working with subtle energies.

Loyal coworkers who remained courageous will not be left without Help. They always can count on Help in time. But this Help sometimes comes at the last hour, otherwise people never would be able to develop within themselves the necessary willpower, patience, resourcefulness, and skill.

I ask you, dearest ones, to remember that many difficulties will be solved in the best and most unexpected way.

Also, respond with calmness to unsuitable and wrong opinions and actions of friends. They have many concerns and problems of their own; do not ask too much of them. Carefully observe their moods and do not complicate their lives by asking them to execute immediately what they do not see as urgent.

Incorporation of the Pact is needed, but where the incorporation will be does not matter as long as it is not constricted by laws imposing difficult requirements and conditions. Also the name does not matter at all—the simpler the better. Always the principle remains—to act according to circumstances.

I won't hide that Weed's opinion made me very sad. He is a Rosicrucian, and he should have had more understanding. Service for the Common Good does not always immediately bring a profit. Of great significance is the fact that the work for the Common Good is still following the Plan, where dollars have no power, but this work brings the highest Good to humanity and increases its welfare. The Banner of Peace in its embryonic state does not bring welfare to the people because of the ignorant people's consciousness. But the Banner, accepted by the consciousness of enlightened minds, brings the highest Good to humanity. It brings an end to the mad demolition and destruction of higher treasures; it brings safety to human life, which is needed not only for our planet but also for the other worlds. But who thinks on such a scale? Nevertheless, the time is coming when we will have to look not only outside the limits of our home and country but beyond the limits of our planet as well. So, be warm toward friends, and, more important, keep calm. The cosmic step is approaching and it needs to be met courageously. A lot is going to change, and new people will come at the right time; so keep the magnet of your heart clean and do not disturb its vibrations, otherwise the power of attraction will be gone.

How many consciousnesses are far from understanding the foundations of the Teaching of Life! It's sad that we do not have translations of all the books. In the first books many necessary qualities are pointed out for approaching the more difficult steps of Agni Yoga.

Notes

May 9, 1945

1. "Sinochka" is a diminutive of Sina Fosdick.
2. Literally translated means "living off the old fat."
3. S. Metalnikov was the author of biological books and a professor at the Pasteur Institute in Paris.
4. ARCA stands for the American Russian Cultural Association, which was created in the United States in 1942 and remained in existence until 1948.
5. Dudley Fosdick was the chairman of the Roerich Pact Committee in New York, vice-president of the Agni Yoga Society, and vice-president of the American Russian Cultural Association.

August 14, 1946

1. *Hierarchy,* para. 337 (New York: Agni Yoga Society, Inc., 1933)
2. Ibid., para. 377 and 379.
3. Ibid., para. 331.
4. The World League of Culture was founded in the early 1930s by American coworkers of the Roerichs.
5. Magdalen Lerer, a member of the Agni Yoga Society, of the Committee of the Roerich Pact in New York, and coworker at ARCA.
6. Katherine Campbell Stibbe, vice-president of the Agni Yoga Society and president of the Nicholas Roerich Museum in New York.

January 13, 1948

1. India had recently signed the Roerich Pact.
2. This is a discussion regarding the wait for a permit to go back to the Motherland.
3. Gisela Ingeborg Fritschi, secretary of the Board of Directors of the Agni Yoga Society in New York.

February 7, 1948

1. Boris Konstantinovich Roerich, brother of N. K. Roerich. His wife Tatiana Grigorievna Roerich lived in Moscow.
2. James Lyon Gartner, correspondent of Helena I. Roerich in the USA.
3. Barnett Conlan, Irish poet and art critic, who wrote many articles about Roerich's art.

April 16, 1948

1. "Pegleriada" is a series of articles that were written by Westbrook Pegler, a notorious journalist. The articles attacked N. K. Roerich.
2. "Svetik" refers to Svetoslav Nikolaevich Roerich.
3. Strophanthus is a cardiac stimulant that is derived from a tropical plant.
4. Igor Grabar (1871–1960), a Russian painter.
5. Devika Rani Roerich (1894–1994), an Indian actress and the wife of Svetoslav Nikolaevich Roerich.

June 8, 1948

1. Louis Horch, financial manager, member of the Committee of the Nicholas Roerich Museum in New York.
2. Henry Agard Wallace (1888-1965), United States Secretary of Agriculture in the 1930s, later vice-president of the United States.
3. Joseph Weed, chairman of the American-Russian Cultural Association and well-known Rosicrucian writer and Teacher; Baltazar Bolling, member of the Committee of the Roerich Pact in New York.
4. *Fiery World III* , para. 597 (Agni Yoga Society, Inc., second printing 1980).
5. Gubareva, author of articles about N. K. Roerich and Agni Yoga, whose work was published in American periodicals.
6. Shingles: (also called herpes zoster) a disease of the nervous system, producing clusters of blisters on the skin.
7. Coramine: a pharmacological agent that stimulates circulation and respiration.
8. Iraida Bogdanova (1914–), participant of the Central-Asian Expedition of N. K. Roerich.
9. The New Country refers to Russia.

June 28, 1948

1. The Trio referred to are Louis and Nancy Horch and Ester Lichtmann.
2. Akashic Records: The subtle spiritual essence that pervades all space, in which is recorded all that occurs in the universe, including thoughts and feelings.
3. *Agni Yoga,* Verse 114, says, "He who has erected a pyre to burn Truth will have to bend and lift out each piece of coal." (New York: Agni Yoga Society, Inc. ,1952).
4. Annie Besant (1847–1933), a leader of the Theosophical Society and associate of H.P. Blavatsky.
5. Ajanta, is a complex of Buddhist cave temples in the state of Maharashtra, dated 200 B.C.–600 A.D.

July 25, 1948

1. George Nikolaevich Roerich.

September 2, 1948

1. Andrey Aleksandrovich Zhdanov (1896–1948), Soviet State and Party leader, member of the Politbureau. Considered to be one of the greatest enemies to culture in the Soviet Union.
2. "The Blonde" was the nickname used by Helena Roerich for Esther Lichtmann—one of the traitors.

October 22, 1948

1. *Fiery World III*, para. 374 (Agni Yoga Society, Inc., second printing 1980).

November 8, 1948

1. Georges Chklaver, a lawyer, who after the October Revolution lived in Paris and composed the text for the Roerich Pact.
2. Joseph Weed, prominent Rosicrucian teacher and member of the board for the Agni Yoga Society.
3. *Leaves of Morya's Garden: Illumination*, para. 19 (Agni Yoga Society, Inc.,1979).
4. "New Cosmogony:" A last portion of the Agni Yoga teaching that Helena Roerich was receiving in the final years of her life.

November 13, 1948

1. Ramakrishna (1834–1886), Hindu philosopher, great Vedanta leader.
2. Vivekananda (Narendranath Datt) (1863–1902), Hindu philosopher, disciple of Ramakrishna, author of definitive books of Vedanta Teachings.
3. Curuppumullage Jinarajadasa (1875–1953), President of the Theosophical movement and disciple of Helena P. Blavatsky.
4. Isabel Cooper-Oakley (1854–1914), writer, activist of the Theosophical movement, and disciple of Helena P. Blavatsky.
5. Alfred Percy Sinnett (1840–1921), Anglo-Hindu journalist, activist of the Theosophical movement.
6. Henry Steel Olcott (1832–1907), President-Founder of the Theosophical Society and H. P. Blavatsky's closest associate.

October 12, 1949

1. *Supermundane, Book One*, para. #117 (Agni Yoga Society, Inc., 1994).
2. Sophie Mikhailovna Shafran, Sina Fosdick's mother.

Index

White Mountain Education Association

The White Mountain Education Association was founded in 1982 in the United States of America and is a not-for-profit, 501 (c) (3) tax-exempt organization. The purpose of the organization is to offer the Teachings of the Ageless Wisdom. The Ageless Wisdom Teachings are a collection of all those spiritual laws, rules and revelations of the ages, which have been given to humanity to help promote culture, beauty, and healthy, joyful, prosperous and creative living.

The White Mountain Education Association publishes books, booklets and a bimonthly newsletter titled *Meditation Monthly International*. *Meditation Monthly International* features a diversity of articles and viewpoints from contributing writers worldwide. Information about the White Mountain Education Association, as well as the latest issues of *Meditation Monthly International*, and individual articles on the Ageless Wisdom Teachings and Great Spiritual Teachers can be found on WMEA's Home Page. WMEA's World Wide Web address is: http://www.wmea-world.org

As a vital, working organization, WMEA offers:
- Spiritual Classes on the Ageless Wisdom
- Class by Tape Program
- Correspondence Study Courses
- Meditation Courses by Correspondence
- Leadership Training and Teacher's Certification Program
- Seminary/Ordination Program
- Lectures
- Annual Conferences
- Seminars and Workshops
- Monthly Group Meditation Meetings
- Sunday Services/Torchbearers Children's Class
- Ministerial Services
- Spiritual Counseling
- Ageless Wisdom Bookstore

Agni Yoga Series

The following is a list of books of the Agni Yoga Series, published by the Agni Yoga Society, Inc., 319 West 107th street, New York, N.Y. 10025:

Leaves of Morya's Garden I (The Call) ---------------- 1924
Leaves of Morya's Garden II (Illumination) ---------- 1925
New Era Community ------------------------------------ 1926
Agni Yoga -- 1929
Infinity I --- 1930
Infinity II -- 1930
Hierarchy -- 1931
Heart -- 1932
Fiery World I -- 1933
Fiery World II --------------------------------------- 1934
Fiery World III -------------------------------------- 1935
AUM -- 1936
Brotherhood -- 1937
Supermundane I --------------------------------------- 1938
Supermundane II -------------------------------------- 1938

Letters of Helena Roerich, Vol. I ---------------------- 1939
Letters of Helena Roerich, Vol. II --------------------- 1940